Naming the System

Naming the System

Inequality and Work in the Global Economy

MICHAEL D. YATES

MONTHLY REVIEW PRESS

New York

Library of Congress Cataloging-in-Publication Data
available from the publisher

Yates, Michael D.
    Naming the system : inequality and work in the global economy
/ Michael D. Yates.
        p. cm.
    Includes bibliographical references and index.

    ISBN 1-58367-079-3 (pbk)
    ISBN 1-58367-080-7 (cloth)

The photographs in this volume are reproduced courtesy of David Bacon
http://dbacon.igc.org

MONTHLY REVIEW PRESS
122 West 27th Street
New York, NY 10001

www.monthlyreview.org

Printed in Canada

10 9 8 7 6 5 4 3 2 1

To my late friend, BRUCE WILLIAMS, who first taught me
about life in the poor countries, and his wife, CLAIRE WILLIAMS,
who offered me kind hospitality when I needed it most.

List of Tables

Acknowledgments

Let me first thank my former academic colleagues, Monica Frolander-Ulf and Clark Strausser. Monica and I drove to work for fifteen years and during our long sojourns from Pittsburgh to Johnstown, Pennsylvania, I learned many things from her, about life in gathering and hunting societies, about the poor in Jamaica and Africa, about the equality of women, about the many good things unions had done in her native Finland. I am grateful for this knowledge. Clark taught me what I know of financial markets, and although our political perspectives are different, I would rather be in a foxhole with him than with any number of liberals! Who else would have had the patience to teach me the econometrics I should have learned in graduate school?

Several people have read all or part of the manuscript and offered valuable comments and criticisms. Thanks to Gloria Rudolf, who from her outpost in Panama, where she has been doing excellent field research among the rural poor for many years, took the time to remind me that class is not the only form of oppression and that peasants are far more than victims of capitalism. Thanks to my comrade, Louis Proyect, who fed me a steady stream of useful articles, made many useful suggestions, and reminded me that the struggles of indigenous peoples are central to the

fight for a better world. Thanks to James Craven, economics professor and Blackfoot Indian, whose own life serves as a model of principled activism and compassion for the oppressed and who gave me valuable information on the political economy of American Indians. Thanks to Canadian comrades Sam Gindin, Cy Gonick, and Herman Rosenfield for good suggestions, and especially for those of Herman on the chapter on Marxist economics. Thanks to Sabri Oncu, who not only read the manuscript but has been working to get it published in his native Turkey. Thanks to Charles Brown, Sean Sweeney, Harry Magdoff, and John Mage for helpful suggestions and encouragement.
I spent several months working at the *Monthly Review* office in Manhattan. I owe a special debt to my workmates there, not just for lots of thoughtful discussions but for lots of laughs too. So, thanks to Martin Paddio, Hyacinth Anthonysen, Claude Misukiewicz, Andrew Nash, and Renee Pendergrass. There would be no book nor any *Monthly Review* without your herculean efforts.

Finally, let me thank my life mate, Karen Korenoski. She has taught me the most valuable lesson of all, that how I conduct my life must be consistent with the principles I try to impart to my students and by which I believe the larger society should conduct its affairs.

CHAPTER ONE: Getting Our Bearings

ECONOMICS IS A CONFUSING SUBJECT

I was a college economics teacher for many years. Whenever I met someone who had attended college, I asked them if they had taken an economics course. Typically they said, sheepishly, no, they had not because it was rumored to be both boring and difficult. If they said yes, they had, they added that they had not done very well and did not remember much about the class. Of course, this ended that part of the conversation. I knew that if I asked them something about economics, their eyes would glaze over or they would stammer in embarrassment. Economics was for the experts, and they were not going to make fools of themselves in front of one.

College students and graduates do have opinions on economic subjects, and so does nearly everyone else. This is not surprising. The subject matter of economics is the production and distribution of output, and these things are significant. The production of food and its price, for instance, are matters of life and death. Almost all of us have to buy our food, and we get the money to do so by selling our ability to work. Therefore, the availability of work and the wage paid for it are also subjects of fundamental interest. Today, the working people of the world are beset by many economic difficulties. Hundreds of millions go hungry every day, drink contaminated water, suffer deadly diseases, see their children die, send their children to work before the age of ten, work unconscionably long hours for low pay, find themselves unemployed, live in shacks without running water or sewage, lose their land, breathe poisoned air, and face repression and brutality daily.

While economic concerns abound, the problem is that people have little understanding of them. Their heads are filled with erroneous notions and many misconceptions. Just listen to the talk shows on U.S. radio stations, shows in which the hosts ask listeners to call the station and discuss whatever topics have caught the host's attention. The hosts make one foolish statement after another, and so do the callers. One fellow says that the media cause economic depressions. Another says that taxes are the problem. A third blames everything on the lazy and shiftless people on welfare. A fourth says, "Buy American and keep the immigrants out." And so on. I once saw a bumper sticker on a pickup truck that read, "No Taxes: Federal, State, or Local." I wanted to stop the driver and ask him how he thought the road on which he was driving would have been built had there been no taxes.

If ordinary people are confused about economics, it is reasonable to suppose that those from whom they get their information are likewise bewildered. Most people learn about the world by watching television news, listening to the radio, or reading a newspaper. This is a pity because the newscasters, commentators, columnists, and journalists are not especially well informed. The newscasters just report things, mostly relayed to them by the government. It would be a rare anchorperson who knew how the unemployment rate is calculated or what the Gross Domestic Product includes and excludes or the meanings of fluctuations in currency exchange rates. The commentators are as bad as the radio talk show hosts. They simply babble or preside over shouting matches. When they confront someone who really does know something, they either erupt in anger or change the subject. The talking heads on the television financial channels exude economic authority, but if you watch them regularly, you see that today they tell us one thing and tomorrow exactly the opposite, both with equal sincerity. There are a few columnists and journalists, some of them professional economists, who try hard to comprehend economics and convey it to their readers. It is worth reading them, but unfortunately most people do not, if only because they do not have access to them in their local media, or, for many people in the world, because they cannot read.

MANY ECONOMISTS ARE CONFUSED TOO: A "NEW ECONOMY"?

Unlike the majority of ordinary working people, the newscasters, television commentators, and talking heads probably did take an economics course in college, maybe more than one. So if they are passing along misinformation to their viewers, it is a safe bet that either they misunderstood their instructors, or the teachers themselves were not particularly knowledgeable.

It might sound sacrilegious for an economist to castigate his brother and sister economists for their lack of enlightenment. But there is much evidence for this. Let us take a particularly striking example. Economists have for a long time embraced various kinds of "economic miracles." This has most often been the case for so-called developing countries. (In this book I will call them "poor countries.") A particular country, formerly mired in economic stagnation and backwardness, suddenly begins to show signs of rapid economic growth, usually defined as steady and large increases in the Gross Domestic Product, or GDP. (The GDP is a measure of a country's total production, and, as we shall see, hides as much as it shows.) Once this happens, the economists who specialize in economic development begin to write scholarly articles analyzing the new "economic miracle" and extolling its growth policies as examples for other poor nations to follow. Invariably and almost without exception, the miracle proves to be short- lived (and on closer inspection failed to improve the lives of the mass of working persons), but it is very rare that the economists learn from their mistaken analysis. Instead, they move on to the next "economic miracle," and the whole process starts anew. One day it is Brazil, the next day it is Thailand or Argentina. For some time now, it has been China.[1] But the process is always the same—a burst of enthusiasm for the new model of development from the economists, the collapse of the "miracle," the refusal to learn anything from the collapse, and the search for a new miracle.

The same sort of embrace of miracles occurs in the rich economies as well. But here it ordinarily involves the economists declaring that the economy is no longer subject to the cycles of prosperity and recession that have characterized all capitalist economies from their beginning. The U.S. economy, for example, entered a ten-year period of GDP growth in 1991, the longest such period in the history of the country. As the expansion picked up steam and as the stock markets rocketed upwards, economists began to suggest that the economy had finally overcome its tendency toward recurring crises. Reflecting such sentiments, the editors of *Business Week* stated, "Revolutionary technology and rapid globalization . . . will send productivity soaring, allowing faster growth with low inflation and modest unemployment. This dynamic could last for decades, bringing unimagined prosperity worldwide."[2] The stock boom, in turn, would create millions of new, and much richer, stakeholders in the economy, either by way of stock holdings or pensions. Alan Greenspan, chairman of the Federal Reserve System's Board of Governors, believed that the technological change fostered by the electronics revolution could allow for steady, unending growth if the monetary authorities kept the money supply and interest rates at just the right levels.

As the long boom continued and GDP growth accelerated, we began to hear about the "new" economy, one so unlike anything previously seen that it required new ways of thinking about economics. This "new" economy meant different things to different people, but some common threads were woven into most accounts. A common notion among financial analysts was that traditional methods of valuing stocks traded on the stock exchanges no longer applied. Ordinarily, a corporation's stock commands a price because the business owns various real and tangible assets, like machines and factory buildings, and has utilized these assets and the labor it employs to make profits. A corporation without assets and profits would not be one attractive to stock buyers. However, as the twentieth century came to a close, the high-tech "dotcom" companies were issuing stock that buyers could not get enough of. Companies like Priceline.com and Amazon.com saw their share prices rise meteorically, despite the fact that they had never shown a profit and had, by traditional standards, almost no assets. But instead of warning the public that such price increases could not be sustained, and were, in fact, the product of a great stock market "bubble," Wall Street gurus said that these were the companies of the glorious high- tech future, and that their certain future profits justified even higher prices. Two such financial soothsayers wrote a book with the title *Dow 36,000* in which they predicted that the Dow Jones index of blue chip stocks would rise inexorably and without pause to 36,000, more than three times its already unprecedented level.[3]

Many other features of the new economy were also discerned by the economists.[4] For example, consumers were supposedly concerned, as never before, with high-quality goods and services tailored specifically to their individual needs. Since rapidly changing technology was continually creating new, high-quality products, consumer needs were perpetually changing as well. This rapid change placed new demands on businesses. They had to be maximally flexible, capable of changing product lines quickly and able at all times to meet discerning and highly individualistic consumer needs. The tremendous range of choices available to consumers meant that customers would not be loyal to any company that could not offer speedy gratification.

What made possible the new discernment of consumers was the new electronic technology. Programmable machines, robots, and high-speed computers made it possible for companies to profitably produce relatively small quantities of output and to speedily change this output, as well as more efficiently coordinate purchases, production, and sales. Firms stuck with the mass-production technology of old, with its enormous fixed capital and rigid assembly lines, were doomed to lose the competitive struggle. Firms had to be free, therefore, to rapidly introduce the best technology, so that they could rapidly introduce new products to satisfy swiftly changing consumer demands. As former Secretary of Labor Robert Reich envisioned it, cutting edge firms would consist of a small core of highly skilled managers and very limited production facilities. They would maintain numerous, flexible relationships with the subcontractors who would actually supply and hire the workers. These subcontractors would, in turn, contract out part of their work, and at the bottom of the chain of subcontracting would be millions of hyper- mobile and super-skilled independent contractors.[5]

In this new economy, unskilled workers did not need to apply. Flexible production using advanced electronic technology required flexible, highly trained workers. Such workers would not only have a lot of education, but they would also constantly retrain themselves to learn the nuances of ever-changing technology. Management guru Tom Peters said on a radio talk show a couple of years ago that even in such heavy industries as steel, in which the product was once produced in hot, dirty, and noisy mills by workers with strong backs and weak minds, work was now done in clean, technologically advanced workplaces by highly skilled "brain" workers. Needless to say, what was now true for heavy industry was true for the service-producing industries now absorbing about four-fifths of the U.S. labor force. Here there was, according to one writer, "a return to a contemporary version of a craft economy, where the most valued contribution is the skill of the worker. The new crafts workers are business managers, consultants, and marketing and financial experts as well as scientific and technical researchers and computer specialists."[6]

The new skilled workers were to be treated with respect by the employer and made full participants in running the enterprise. Modern management now focused, it was said, on the team nature of modern production, and workers, often called "associates," were no longer treated as hands to be manipulated but as members of the corporate team. Indeed, employers now routinely concerned themselves with the development of the whole person and urged workers to think of the company as a place where their social life and their work life merged into a creative whole. Stock options and profit sharing further fused the interests of associates and firm.

The new economy was a global economy. Capital now moved around the globe in search of profits more rapidly than ever before. Both finance capital, which traversed the globe at warp speed, and physical capital, which moved more slowly but still fast enough, were no longer bound within the confines of any nation. Modern technology allowed business to move from high-cost to low-cost places and to integrate production into a worldwide input-output chain. An insurance company headquartered in the United States could have its clerical work done by home workers in western Ireland. Computer programmers in India could design programs for use anywhere in the world. Globalization also meant that nation-states were no longer capable of regulating businesses. Just as soon as one nation tried to do so, businesses left that nation, forcing it to back down and eliminate the controls. Capital, in other words, was steadily transcending the nation-state. And according to the proponents of the new economy miracle, capital mobility and government helplessness were good things. Rapid "globalization" would prove extremely advantageous to people everywhere in the world; it would make the poor countries rich and the rich countries richer still. What was once available only to a minority of persons would now be available to everyone. Governments could only get in the way. The conclusion was not only that governments could not stop globalization but should not since the benefits were so obvious.

Today, it would be difficult to find an unabashed champion of the new economy. The notions that the stock market could climb and that the economy could grow indefinitely were shattered in 2001. First the NASDAQ stock index of technology company stocks, the darling securities of the long boom, collapsed, losing 60 percent of its value in a few short months. High fliers like Amazon.com and Priceline.com, companies with on-paper worth in the billions of dollars in the Spring of 2000, sank like stones as stock buyers finally realized that companies that own nothing and make no profits aren't worth much either. Tens of thousands of formerly valued "associates" found that their stock options were worthless, at about the same time they got their pink slips.

The collapse of the technology stocks soon spread to other stock markets, and by early 2001 all of the major markets were in free fall. The stock market deflation was both a sign of and a contributor to the economic downturn that soon followed. Had the mainstream economists and commentators bothered to look, they would have noticed that corporations had gone on an investment frenzy during the boom, purchasing all sorts of capital goods, especially computers and computer-related equipment. This investment (readers should note that when economists speak of investment, they are talking not about individuals buying stocks and bonds, but about businesses buying newly produced machines, buildings, and equipment) meant that companies could now produce much more output than they previously could. This would not be a problem if the demand for the output kept pace with the rising supply. But large corporations, competing in global markets, make investments not just to meet demand but to keep up with their competitors. If one business invests in a machine that embodies the most modern technology, its rivals must do the same or risk losing some of their share of the market. So as the boom proceeded, investment increased the capacity to produce to a greater extent than the consumers' capacity to buy. For example, *Business Week* reported that in 2000, "semiconductor makers, computer companies, and communications equipment boosted factory capacity by a breathtaking rate of nearly 50%." However, the rate of utilization of all this new capital did not grow nearly as fast. In one extreme case, the utilization rate of the thousands of miles of underground fiber optic cables laid by communications companies in the 1990s was a mere 2.5 percent in early 2001.[7] The result was worldwide overcapacity, an ability to produce more than could be bought. Faced with this overcapacity, firms inevitably stopped making investments, and the economy slowed down.

The economic downturn was compounded by the faltering stock markets. When share prices were rising, the paper wealth of the stock owners grew and, feeling richer, these owners spent more money, adding fuel to the boom. But when stock prices went into reverse, the opposite occurred: people were now poorer and not so inclined to spend money. This "negative wealth effect," as it is called by economists, began to take hold just as consumers and corporations were saddled with record amounts of debt. The debt and the depressed stock market further dampened people's desire to spend money, and this made the overcapacity problem all the worse. Banks, themselves profligate spenders and borrowers during the boom, now tightened up credit, making it more difficult for consumers and businesses to borrow their way out of the slump.[8]

The point of this extended discussion of the great expansion and the subsequent recession is not so much to explain it as to note the mistaken ideas of so many economists who seemed to believe that what had always been true of capitalist economies—that they exhibit cycles of expansion and contraction—was no longer true.

Contrary to the pronouncements of numerous Wall Street analysts and operators, stock markets always come back to earth. As we shall see, even Alan Greenspan, who the media and hero-worshiping biographers made into a sort of cult figure during the boom, was powerless to prevent the capitalist economy from being true to its nature. He could not stop the largest bankruptcy in history, that of the Houston-based Enron Corporation, in November 2001. A prototypical "new economy" company, with few tangible assets but numerous subcontracting arrangements—through which it created a host of new and supposedly more efficient markets, largely on the

---

THE LONG RUN

Mainstream economists are always talking about the long run. They tell us that we have to be patient and look to the long run when, presumably, everything will run smoothly and all problems will be solved. If stock prices are falling precipitously, don't worry, they will rise in the long run. This wisdom is always given by the economists at brokerage firms, who every day on the U.S. financial channel, CNBC, tell us not to sell our stocks no matter how low their prices have fallen. When the Federal Reserve pushes interest rates to very low levels and this does not cause a quick economic recovery, don't be alarmed. Recovery will occur in the long run. If it is now true that a majority of the earth's residents have not benefitted from globalization, it won't be so in the long run. If a nation has to implement austerity programs that hurt the workers today, all will win in the long run.

Unfortunately this belief in the efficacy of the long run is typically used by those with power as a tactic to keep those without power in line, much as the religious promise of a better life in heaven was used to convince the poor that their suffering on earth, a suffering that usually benefited the rich, was not something they should worry about. At my college, we were told year after year that we had to make sacrifices so that things would get better in the long run. The trouble is, however, that life is always lived in the here and now, in the short run. When I retired, what mattered was how my pension funds were performing at the moment. It was no consolation to me that poor performance today would be reversed in the long run. Similarly, years of austerity and retrenchment at the workplace or in an entire country add up ultimately to lives of misery. And as the great economist John Maynard Keynes famously put it, "In the long run, we are all dead." [10]

Internet—Enron was the epitome of Robert Reich's "agile" firm. But like
many corporations before it, its reach was greater than its grasp. It engaged
in dubious accounting practices, and when the economic crisis prevented it
from continuing to buy things with other people's money, it failed. And
like its predecessors, it provided generous "golden parachutes" for its top
officers and hung its formerly much valued "associates" out to dry. Many of
its employees even lost their pensions. Enron's pension funds were held in
the form of Enron stock. With the bankruptcy, these stocks, and the pensions they were supposed to fund, were now worthless.[9]

Had the economists cared to look, they would also have noticed that
what was happening in the United States had already occurred, and with
greater force, in Japan. Japan's economy has been stagnating since 1990,
and in 2003 is in its fourth recession in thirteen years. Japan missed the
last capitalist boom, but its economy had grown with remarkable rapidity
for at least three decades prior to the 1990s. In fact, Japan's economic performance was the greatest of all economic "miracles," and millions of pages
were written extolling the virtues of all things Japanese. Scholars and business consultants and executives flocked to Japan and then wrote about
what they had witnessed and put into effect Japanese practices in their own
companies. It was said that the Japanese government actively and brilliant-
ly engineered the country's economic growth and that Japanese corporations pioneered human-centered labor relations that made Japanese
workers the world's most productive. Most of this Japan worship was based
upon less than accurate observation and faulty analysis.[11] Japan's "miracle"
was bound to end, and end it did, with a bang and with terrible repercus-
sions for the masses of Japanese workers. Unemployment is at record levels;
fewer and fewer workers have the lifetime jobs for which Japanese corporations were so famous; more and more workers are laboring at dead-end,
part-time jobs; and Japanese corporations and banks are awash in bad
debts. These days it is hard to find anyone who openly admires Japan's economy. Quite the contrary, today the economists are busy bashing the very
things they extolled at the height of the Japanese miracle.

As we shall see later in the book, the much vaunted benefits of globalization have been slow to materialize for any but the already well-off. It is
almost an article of faith among mainstream economists that "free" trade
is a benefit to all. But even if we accept the idea that the long economic
boom was the result, in part, of the increased and more open trade among
nations, then we would also be forced to accept the notion that more inte-

grated economies are more susceptible to economic slumps. That is, if all nations can grow together, they can also tumble down together. If the U.S. economy falters, U.S. consumers may buy fewer goods made abroad. If this happens, foreign consumers will very likely buy fewer U.S.-made goods, and this reduction in demand will reverberate back onto the U.S. economy, and so forth. However, the data on worldwide poverty and unemployment make it difficult to maintain that a more global economy has done anything to benefit the majority of the world's people. Instead, it has made them less able to care for themselves and more dependent on economic forces over which they have no control. Neither in the poor nor in the rich nations has globalization, and the new economy of which it was a critical element, created a large class of skilled workers who could anticipate years of high pay and intense employer competition for their services.

THE METHOD OF ECONOMICS

How is it that economists are so wrong, so often? Why do they continue to hype economic miracles? Is there something wrong with the method of economists, that is, the devices that they use to try to uncover the truth?

Economists ordinarily employ a scientific method. This method can be described as a three-step process. The first step in economic analysis is for the economist to make some simplifying assumptions. That is, the economist says, "Suppose that certain things are true to start with. What follows from them?" The idea of starting with statements we assume to be true may strike readers as odd, but it is not. We cannot know the truth directly. It is not usually obvious. And we have to have some starting points in our investigation, to avoid an endless chain of "whys." When a father gets tired of answering his child's interminable "whys," he says, "Because I say so." This statement can be likened to the starting points or assumptions of economists. They say, for example, "Let us assume that all people act entirely out of self-interest." Now, of course, all people do not act entirely out of self interest. But the economist supposes that they do and asks, "If all people do act solely out of self interest, what do we expect will happen?"

To find out what we would expect to happen if everyone acted selfishly, we trace out the logic of the assumption. To do this, we employ the techniques of logic and mathematics. Once we do this, we have a set of hypotheses or predictions. For example, mainstream economists take the assumption of self-interested behavior and narrow it down to have meaning in an economic context. In capitalist economies, the production and distribution of output (or "goods and services" as outputs are normally called in such an economy) take place in markets. Markets are where buyers and sellers meet (not necessarily literally) and make exchanges. So the economists take the assumption that everyone acts out of self-interest to mean that the buyers and sellers in markets act only in their own interests. To make this assumption amenable to the tools of logic and mathematics, they further refine it and assume that each participant in the market is a "maximizer," trying to get the most of something. For the sellers of automobiles, for example, the substance maximized is profits.

If we assume that each market participant is a maximizer, we can trace out the logic of this assumption in such a way that we end up with a large number of predictions or hypotheses. For instance, one such prediction is that, in a world of "maximizers," if a government raises the minimum wage, employers will cut employment. That is, the economist predicts that the minimum wage and employment are related in an opposite or inverse way; an increase in the one (minimum wage) is associated with a decrease in the other (employment). There are thousands of other examples of predictions that derive from the maximizing assumption.

The first two steps—making assumptions and deriving hypotheses from them—are sometimes called "building a model" of the economy or some part of it. However, we cannot get at the truth at this point. All we have is an hypothesis (or lots of them) derived from the initial assumptions. We need a further and crucial step. The predictions must somehow be tested against the evidence. When the government does, in fact, raise the minimum wage, does employment, in fact, fall? The test is the absolutely critical part of the scientific method. Without it, we have nothing except an exercise in logic.

Testing predictions against the evidence is a difficult undertaking. Problems abound. In the natural sciences, researchers can conduct "controlled" experiments. They can set up their experiment in such a way that they can hold fixed any number of variables that might affect the outcome. With these variables fixed, they can then allow one other variable to change. Any change in the outcome, then, is likely to be due to the change in this one variable. It cannot be due to the other variables, because these have not been allowed to change. In the world of human interactions, however, it is not always or even normally possible to conduct controlled experiments. Therefore, there is always a certain element of uncertainty inherent in social science research. We can never be sure that the change in the result (employment in the minimum wage example) is the consequence of the change in the variable we are interested in (the minimum wage). It may be due to a variable we could not control. Economists have devised a large number of ingenious tests of predictions, using methods that operate as if we had conducted a true controlled experiment. Unfortunately, these seldom have the same power as tests in the natural sciences.

There are many other testing problems. Measuring economic variables is often difficult or subject to differences of opinion. Economists have defined such commonplace entities as profits and incomes in entirely different ways. What this means is that a test of a prediction may give different results depending on how the variables are defined. An economist may predict that an increase in corporate profits will increase corporate investment, but the test results may hinge on exactly how profits are defined. Even if there is agreement on definitions and it is possible to precisely measure the variables, the results of any test may be due to chance. It may appear as though a higher minimum wage is correlated with lower employment, but this may just be the result of the particular sample of workers the economist chose to investigate. If we took a sample of 5,000 persons drawn randomly from a much larger population (random means that each person in the population has the same chance of getting chosen in the sample) and calculated the average height, we would almost always get an average very close to that of the entire population. But not always. By chance, we may have picked only the tallest persons for our sample. The same problem occurs in every test of an economic prediction.

All of this is not to say that we can never discover the truth in economics. If numerous studies are done by independent researchers and all of the results are pretty much the same, we can be fairly certain that the hypothesis is true. If very large numbers of the predictions derived from tracing out the logic of a particular set of assumptions are supported in repeated research by different researchers using different sets of data, we may also conclude that the assumptions themselves are true, or at least very useful in our search for the truth.

THE PROBLEM OF IDEOLOGICAL BLINDERS

If it is possible, albeit difficult, to seek and find some truths in economics, why is it that economists have such a bad track record, consistently showing an unscientific faith in economic miracles and failing to grasp fundamental aspects of a three-hundred-year-old economic system? Perhaps the best way to answer this question is with some examples.

Throughout this book, we are going to contrast two general ways of understanding our economic system. The first, and by far the dominant, theory of capitalism is called the *neoclassical* theory; the economists who profess this view we will call mainstream (or neoclassical) economists. These are the economists who begin with the overarching assumption that people always single-mindedly pursue their own self-interest, or, as we said above, act as "maximizers." The second theory of capitalism we will call the *radical* theory, and, as we shall see, this theory has very little in common with the neoclassical model.

Our first example takes up the neoclassical prediction that an increase in the minimum wage will cause a loss of employment. This is a prediction almost universally believed to be true by neoclassical economists, and one that they claim is supported by hundreds of tests. But in 1995, two prominent economists at Princeton University, David Card and Alan Krueger, published a book, *Myth and Measurement: The New Economics of the Minimum Wage*.[12] In this book, they subjected the neoclassical minimum wage prediction to the most rigorous testing ever done. They were helped in their tests by several "natural" experiments. The minimum wage in the United States is set by Congress in accord with the terms of the 1937 Fair Labor Standards Act. However, the individual states are free to establish a state minimum wage higher than the federal minimum. In 1992, New Jersey increased its minimum wage above the national wage, while neighboring Pennsylvania did not. This meant that, for minimum wage employers, such as fast food restaurants along the states' common border, conditions would be pretty much the same except for the higher New Jersey minimum wage. That is, this situation could serve as a controlled experiment. The neoclassical theory predicts that fast food employment should be lower in New Jersey relative to Pennsylvania, as New Jersey employers laid off workers in response to the higher wage costs imposed by the new minimum wage. Put another way, employment growth should be slower in New Jersey fast food establishments than in those in Pennsylvania.

Using the most sophisticated statistical techniques available, Card and Kreuger found the opposite to be true; employment growth was higher in New Jersey, other things equal. Using other states and different data sets, they tested the neoclassical hypothesis repeatedly, never finding the neoclassical prediction to be correct. They reexamined previous minimum wage studies and found most of them gave similar results when done with better statistical devices. Most remarkably, Card and Kreuger found that professional journals in economics had practiced "selection bias," tending to accept only articles that claimed to demonstrate that the neoclassical prediction was true.

Card and Kreuger, themselves trained as neoclassical economists, were shocked at the hostile responses to their book from mainstream economists. Within a few months, the *Wall Street Journal* reported that other economists had found Card and Kreuger's conclusions unwarranted because their methodology was faulty. No one seemed to notice that the new study was funded by the fast foods lobbying group, a fact that should have immediately raised skeptical eyebrows.[13] A perusal of current textbooks in labor economics shows that the neoclassical minimum wage doctrine is still presented as obviously correct, although Card and Kreuger's book might receive some mention.

The difficulty in ascertaining the truth in economics is compounded by the power of what we might call the "monied interests," the fast food industry in this case. Often the truth cannot overcome this power. Consider another example. Since at least the years of the Reagan administration, powerful politicians, conservative commentators, and corporate leaders have been trying to convince us that the U.S. social security system should be radically changed. Its more fervent opponents want the system abolished, while more "realistic" enemies prefer a gradual privatization. Social security is a very popular program, and many recipients of funds from the various social security trust funds (in addition to retirement income, social security provides health care for the elderly, disability benefits, and child survivor's insurance) would be financially devastated without them. This has led social security's antagonists to resort to a host of false arguments. They have ignored critical data and made unfounded assumptions about the growth of the economy and the stock market to try to persuade people that the trust funds would soon be bankrupt and that today's young people would not get any money when they reached retirement age. We would be better off to eliminate the payroll taxes that fund the system and buy our own stocks and bonds.

Renowned neoclassical economists have lent intellectual support to the privatizers, none more prominent than Harvard professor Martin Feldstein. Feldstein has issued a barrage of articles, books, and op-ed pieces urging the abolition of social security. It is interesting to have a look at Professor Feldstein's past. He became prominent in the 1970s for research he had done appearing to show that the social security program led the citizenry to save less money than they would have saved in the absence of social security. Feldstein argued that since a society's ability to make investments (the production of capital goods) depends on its willingness to forgo consuming goods and services (i.e., save money), his research implied that more investment and economic growth would have taken place had there not been a social security system. His findings matched his antipathy to social security (and all types of social welfare programs) and both no doubt attracted Reagan to him, since Reagan had been railing against social security for many years.

The new president made Feldstein the chairman of his Council of Economic Advisers. The Council of Economic Advisers was established by the Employment Act of 1946. Its function is to give economic advice to the president and to prepare the annual *Economic Report to the President*. Naturally a stint on the council helps an economist's career, and often his or her pocketbook, immensely.

Two scholars at the Social Security Administration, the federal agency that oversees the system, asked Feldstein for his data. He sent it to them three years after they first requested it, and they went to work trying to replicate his results. They could not do this, and after a careful examination, discovered a computer program error in Feldstein's original work. When they fixed this, they found that not only did social security not reduce savings, it actually increased them, something which others had also found but, lacking Feldstein's political cachet, were not able to place clearly before the general public. Now, in a world in which the search for the truth is paramount, Feldstein would have been in some trouble, at least in the court of scientific opinion. However, his reputation escaped this scientific fraud (albeit inadvertent) unsullied. He returned to Harvard and has made lots of money as a consultant while remaining a virulent foe of social security. Not long after the barrenness of his research was revealed, he claimed to have reworked his data and achieved his original result.[14]

The reason why false arguments and bogus research have survived in this case is not hard to find. The social security trust funds contain hundreds of billions of dollars. Wall Street wants this money, the largest pool of untapped reserves in the nation. Wall Street is home to the richest and most powerful business persons around, and they are using this power to promote a gigantic disinformation campaign to get their hands on the money. Economists like Feldstein are just willing, and well-paid, pawns in this enterprise.

Both of these examples illustrate a vexing problem for students who want to understand the economy. Not only are there technical difficulties. It takes skill to make useful assumptions and to trace out the logic of these assumptions to generate predictions. It is not easy to devise adequate tests of predictions. The definition of variables and the conversion of definitions into data present their own problems. But in addition to these formidable difficulties, the student also has to contend with the reality that in a capitalist economy, those who have the gold may make the rules. They may obstruct the pursuit of the truth, refusing to allow research that contradicts their interests to see the light of day or giving wide publicity to research that coincides with their needs. Economists, in turn, may either pander directly to the desires of the wealthy or they may become so enamored with the elegance of their theory that they stop seeing the need to test hypotheses. Instead, they may come to accept the predictions themselves as the truth, acting in essentially the same way as a religious zealot. In either case, their careers are unlikely to suffer.

Readers then are advised to study economics with care. Be aware that not all research is what it claims to be. Be mindful that in economics the truth does not always win out. Understand that in matters economic, powerful private interests come into play. Above all, be skeptical. Your own beliefs, the predictions of economists, and every statement in this book must be put to the test.

AIMS AND STRUCTURE OF THIS BOOK

The aims of this book are threefold. The first goal is to give readers a good understanding of the capitalist world economy and the position of workers within it. Today, capitalism dominates the world as never before. There is hardly a spot on the globe that is not firmly embedded in a capitalist economy, and there is no part of daily life that is not similarly enmeshed in the sale and purchase of goods and services. I state right at the beginning that I think that these developments, the spread of capitalism into every corner of the earth and its invasion of every nook and cranny of life, do not bode well for humanity. In this belief, I also state at the outset, I am in a minority. Most economists maintain the opposite; they claim that capitalism, in as unfettered a form as possible, offers humanity its best hope for liberation from economic want. I do not believe that this "neoclassical" analysis is correct; it is, in fact, the source of much of the misunderstanding of economics discussed in the first part of this chapter. Therefore, a part of my attempt to provide readers with a clear grasp of the capitalist world economy will involve a critique of the neoclassical positions on the main themes of this book.

The book's second goal is to stimulate readers to find out more about the global economy, especially about the billions of workers whose labor makes it function. The capitalist world economy is extremely complex, and, while certainly not beyond the grasp of those untrained in economics, requires much effort to grasp it (of course, if what the economists have been taught is full of errors, readers might be better off not having been trained). A short book like this can only scratch the surface of things. To help readers learn more, I have included some suggested resources at the end of the book.

The third, and perhaps the most important, objective of the book is to encourage people to take action to change the nature of the economic system. The epitaph on the tombstone of Karl Marx in England's Highgate Cemetery is a quote from one of his books. It says, "The philosophers of the world have only interpreted the world in various ways; the point is to change it." I hope that after having read this book, people in the rich countries, normally so complacent, become angry enough to want to do something about the deplorable conditions in which most people live. And I hope that people in the poor countries, already angry, become clearer in their understanding about what are the causes of these deplorable conditions. I hope as well that readers begin to see that their own lot in life is terribly constricted by the economic forces unleashed by those with power over them. In other words, what I hope for is an informed anger, one based on an understanding of what is going on.

Over the past few years, just as it appeared that capitalism was transcendent and would reign supreme forever, just when a prominent historian infamously proclaimed the "end of history," large, raucous, and radical movements opposed to capitalism have arisen.[15] These movements have protested against the North American Free Trade Agreement, the International Monetary Fund, the World Bank, the World Trade Organization, Third World debt, sweatshops, military dictatorships, wars, the treatment of indigenous peoples, the denial of medication for AIDS and other diseases, the privatization of public services, the new trade in slaves, racism, sexism, homophobia, and a host of other modern-day evils.

These new movements give us hope for a better day. However, to continue to grow and to be effective, they need to have a clear understanding of economics. There has been a tendency for large segments of these movements to oppose just the surface manifestations of the capitalist economic system and not to see that it is the system itself that is the source of the trouble. A good knowledge of capitalism, what it is and what it does, will be essential for all future struggles for human liberation.

There are seven more chapters in the book. Chapter Two takes up the nature of the world capitalist economy. It emphasizes one of the essential features of capitalism—a deep and enduring inequality in the distribution of income and wealth. It is important to know this and to find out the causes of it, because inequality in distribution is seldom examined by neoclassical economists, who are ordinarily content to tell us either that inequality is a good thing or that its worst manifestations will disappear in the "long run." Chapters Three and Four examine the world of the workers. Capitalist economies always display a fundamental division between those who work and those who control this work. Nearly everyone in the world must labor for someone else in order to live, so if we want to comprehend the world economy, we must know about the workers— who they are and how they live. We will see that, for the most part, workers labor at meaningless jobs for low pay and are subjected daily to sickness and danger. We will also see that workers invariably find their jobs insecure and themselves frequently unemployed. Chapters Five and Six are devoted to a search for the truth about the world capitalist economy. Chapter Five further explains the neoclassical theory and puts it to the test, so to speak. Tests of the theory against the evidence find this theory wanting. The modern-day political program that derives from neoclassical economics is called neoliberalism, and Chapter Five also attempts to expose the unscientific and class-biased nature of the neoliberal project. Chapter Six provides an alternative explanation of economic reality, one deriving from the works of Karl Marx. We shall see that this theory provides a much more fruitful way of understanding global capitalism. The seventh chapter explores what are called the "contradictions" of capitalism, those features of the system that open up space for people to challenge it. We will see that, although capitalist economies are extremely resilient and tend to give an appearance of invulnerability to change, in fact, they contain the seeds of their transcendence. This chapter lays the groundwork for the eighth and final chapter which examines the actual struggles for social change that have existed since the beginning of capitalism, from workers' movements to the new movements against globalization. This last chapter argues that we must "name the system"—capitalism—if we want to build a better world.

CHAPTER TWO: Capitalism and Inequality

Our economic system is seldom called by its proper name. We hear of the market economy or the free enterprise system, neither of which tells us what we need to know. It is true that in all modern economies, markets are critical and ubiquitous institutions; nearly all aspects of production and distribution involve buying and selling, the activities that define markets. But markets predate modern systems of production and distribution by many centuries. The phrase "free enterprise" is still less informative. Certainly not everyone is free to begin an economic enterprise, except in a completely abstract sense.

The economic system, or mode of production, that dominates the contemporary world is capitalism. It is not a very old mode of production, although debate rages over just how old it is and where it began. Most historians believe that capitalism originated in what is today Western Europe. The economic system it supplanted in Europe is known as feudalism, which was a land- based mode of production centered around large agricultural estates called manors. These manors were controlled, though not owned in a modern capitalist sense, by a group of nobles, and the work of growing food and producing everything else was done by serfs. While the word "serf" derives from the Latin *servus* or slave, the serf was not actually a slave. Serfs had certain, usually informal, rights to use plots of land and take some of the food from them. Their children then had similar rights. In return, the serfs had to pay a part of the output to the lord and also labor a certain number of days per year on land set aside specifically as the lord's property. The relationship between the lord and the serf was extremely unequal: serfs could not leave the manor without the lord's permission; a serf had to get his lord's permission to marry; and in general there was absolutely no chance that serfs could move out of their class. Most production in the

33

feudal economy was for immediate use; there was not much market activity. Significantly, there were no markets in land or labor. The manors could
not be sold, and the workers did not sell their ability to labor.[1]

The manner in which feudalism collapsed and capitalism arose is complex and a matter of considerable disagreement among scholars.[2] However,
we can make four general comments on what is called the transition from
feudalism to capitalism, which occurred roughly from the fifteenth to the
nineteenth century. First, as capitalism developed the feudal manors gradually became private property, in the modern sense that the property could
be sold and no social obligations went along with its ownership. Second, as
land was transformed into private property a new class of persons with no
access to property was created. This landless class was the working class, and
its members were able to live only by selling their ability to work, their labor
power, to those who did own the property. Third, the creation of both private property and the working class was everywhere accompanied, indeed
made possible, by massive force and violence. Serfs had to be compelled to
give up their long-standing right to use the land. The more powerful class of
property owners either used direct violence against serfs or secured the
power of newly created central governments to do their dirty work. Often-
times, governments enacted laws that amounted to legal coercion. Before
capitalism, serfs had the right to use the manor's "common land," those
parts of the manor not planted with crops and often used to gather fire
wood and water or to hunt and trap animals. In the interest of the property
owners, governments enacted laws that converted common land into private property and made the use of the land by nonowners a crime, sometimes punishable by death. A peasant who formerly had trapped animals for
food on the common land might now be hanged for doing so.

Fourth and of great importance, capitalist economies were, from the
beginning, expansionary. From England, Holland, France, and the other
early capitalist nations, capitalism began to spread around the globe. And
just as serfs were expropriated of their land, so too were the native peoples
of Africa, Asia, and the Americas removed by force from theirs and often
enslaved by the Europeans in the process. Capitalism was born in theft and
would not have been possible without it. The first capitalist countries had
decisive advantages, especially in the production of superior armaments,
and used these to conquer and colonize much of the rest of the world.
These nations stole the wealth of the conquered peoples, and this wealth
fueled, and some would say made possible, the economic dominance that a

handful of capitalist nations enjoy today. Although mainstream economists deny or ignore it, capitalism has been *imperialist* (some nations enjoy-
ing political and economic control over others) from the beginning.[3] As we
shall see, the destruction visited upon large parts of Africa, Asia, and the
Americas from the fifteenth century onward has made it impossible for
many nations to develop, even to the extent of feeding themselves.

Whether they be rich or poor, capitalist economies always have three
defining features. First, the nonhuman "means of production" (the land,
the raw materials, the tools, equipment, and machinery necessary for production) are, for the most part, private property and owned by a small fraction of the total population. This means that those things to which we
must have access in order to live do not belong to most of us but to a minority of persons in the country. Food is grown on land. We must have access
to the food, and therefore to land, if we are to eat. But we do not own the
land and must obtain an indirect admittance to it. Second, the vast majority of people get their admittance to the land and the other means of production by selling their ability to work to the owners of land, raw
materials, tools, equipment, and machinery. Capitalist economies are in
part defined by the existence of widespread labor markets. As we shall
again see, these labor markets do not always function smoothly, and sometimes people find that there are no buyers for their labor power. In a word,
they become unemployed, something it was impossible for a serf or an
ancient gatherer and hunter, or even a slave, to be. Unemployment is a
uniquely capitalist phenomenon. Although there was widespread misery
in feudal and slave societies and people were often forced to work, selling
one's labor power was not a necessity of life as it is in capitalism.

The third feature of capitalist economies is that the owners of the
means of production take it upon themselves to organize the production
of goods and services, and they do so with the single-minded goal of making a profit. They are free, by virtue of the legal protection that governments in capitalist societies always grant them, to organize their private
property in whatever ways that minimize their costs of production. And
they are also free to charge whatever price a market will bear and to stop
production altogether if the profits available in a market are not to their
liking. This means that the owners' drive to make profits is not necessarily
in the interests of the majority of people. It regularly happens that the
pursuit of profits actually does damage to people, and it is not at all
uncommon that it sometimes kills them.

Production in markets also creates a disconnection between people's consumption and their work. In pre-capitalist societies, work and consumption were directly connected, that is, production was for immediate use or consumption. What people made and what they consumed were the same for the most part. In capitalism there is a great impersonality to consumption; we do not know who made the things we use or the conditions under which they were made. Goods and services appear as if by magic in the marketplace; they do not wear the markings of their makers. This feature of capitalism allows us to consume without thinking, and this is probably one of the reasons why it has been possible for people to associate consumption with well-being. (In the last chapter, we shall have occasion to see what happens when relatively well-off consumers in the rich countries begin to think about the social circumstances in which their consumer goods are produced.)

Although all capitalist countries share these essential features, it is important to realize that each country has a unique history, one that shaped how it came into the capitalist fold, how capitalism developed, and how opposition to it has developed. It is also important to note something else. In this book I argue that the fundamental dividing line in capitalist societies is that between those who own the nonhuman means of production and the workers these owners employ as wage laborers. The relationship between these two groups is the critical one in terms of understanding the capitalist economy's dynamics. However, this relationship is inextricably intermingled with other relationships, most importantly, the relationships between men and women and between persons of different races and ethnicities. It is one thing to be a white worker in the United States, for example. But it is quite another thing to be a woman or a Black or Hispanic worker. A Black woman is likely to face not only exploitation because she is a worker but also exploitation because she is a woman and black. In addition, she may face various kinds of harassment from working-class men and working-class whites. The world is full of multiple and complex oppressions. And, as will become clear, multiple forms of resistance as well.

CAPITALISM IN PRACTICE: INEQUALITY AMONG NATIONS

Today, almost every economy in the world exhibits these three features and, hence, is capitalist. If you take a dart and throw it at a map of the world, it is almost certain that if the dart does not hit water, it will land on a capitalist country. Just twenty years ago, this would not have been so like-

ly. Then there were two great modes of production: capitalism and socialism. The socialist economies had abolished most private ownership of the
nonhuman means of production and had organized production not for
profit but for direct social use. Their labor markets did not work as they do
in capitalist countries; one of the most important features of socialist labor
markets was the absence of unemployment. Among the socialist nations
were the Union of Soviet Socialist Republics, China, East Germany, Poland,
Czechoslovakia, Hungary, Bulgaria, Rumania, Albania, North Korea, Vietnam, Laos, and Cuba. The economies of these nations had achieved certain
socially desirable results, mainly in terms of the provision of decent
health, education, and various social services to the majority of people,
and mainly because they had utilized national economic planning instead
of relying on the market.[4] However, for reasons we will touch on later, the
socialist economies embraced many practices, some deeply anti-social,
which, along with relentless opposition from the most powerful capitalist
nations, led to their demise in the late 1980s and early 1990s. China still
exists as a nominally socialist economy, but its leaders have pushed it force-
fully along a capitalist path. In all of the world today, only Cuba and North
Korea have predominantly socialist features.

If the world is capitalist, what kind of a world is it? What do capitalist
economies look like in practice? While it is true that there are many vari-
ants of modern capitalism, the capitalist world, taken as a whole, has certain features. In the remainder of this chapter, we will look at one of these
features: pervasive and enduring inequality in the distribution of output
and a consequent inequality in nearly all social outcomes, from infant
mortality to life expectancy to access to schooling.

We said in Chapter One that economics is the study of production and
distribution of output. The neoclassical economists tend to focus their
attention on production and to ignore distribution. There is a reason for
this. If we concentrate on production, we cannot help but notice that capitalist economies, especially the largest ones such as the United States,
Japan, and Germany, produce stupendously large amounts of output. The
Gross Domestic Product, or GDP, is a measure of the output produced in an
economy. The nominal (see box below) GDP of the United States in 2000
was more than nine trillion dollars, while those of Japan and Germany
were $2.8 trillion and $1.8 trillion respectively. These numbers represent
amounts of output unimaginable in pre-capitalist economies. Neoclassical
economists believe that only capitalism, with its built-in drive to make pro-

duction grow, is capable of producing such large outputs. They also believe that only large outputs can make people happy.

The GDPs of capitalist economies vary enormously. The GDP of the island of Tuvalu is only $10 million. Of course, it is unfair to compare nations in terms of their GDPs. One obvious reason for differences is that nations have unequal populations. So a better measure of output is GDP per person, or per capita. However, once we divide countries' GDPs by their populations, we see immediately that there are very great disparities among national GDPs per capita. The world is divided into rich nations and poor nations. In this book, I define the following countries as rich: the United States, Canada, Japan, Australia, New Zealand, Ireland, Great Britain, Iceland, Norway, Sweden, Finland, Denmark, France, Belgium, Luxembourg, Germany, Austria, the Netherlands, Switzerland, Spain, Portugal, Italy, and Greece. The remaining countries I call poor countries.

SOME DEFINITIONS

It is useful to know what the common terms of economic discourse mean (and do not mean). Here are definitions for some important terms used in this book:

1. GROSS DOMESTIC PRODUCT (GDP): The GDP is the money (market) value of all final goods and services produced in a country in one year. Outputs that do not go through the market, such as food grown in home gardens or fields for household consumption and the services provided for a family by an unpaid homemaker, are not included in GDP despite the fact that they are economically useful products. GDP includes only "final" outputs. For example, a newly produced automobile with a selling price of $20,000 would count in the GDP of the nation in which it is produced as $20,000. But the market price of the glass used in the car's windows would not be counted separately, since its price is already included in the $20,000. GDP measures output produced in a country, hence the word "domestic." The cars produced by Volkswagen in Brazil count in Brazil's GDP.

2. INCOME: Income is what economists call a "flow" concept; it "flows" to people over some period of time. We distinguish among labor incomes such as wages, salaries, and income from self-employment (note that we would always include a time dimension when we say what our wages are; we earn so many dollars per hour, per week, per year); property incomes such as rent, interest, and dividends; government transfer incomes such as social security, unemployment compensation, and

I realize that there are countries outside of the ones I have called rich that have characteristics somewhat like those in the rich countries. Examples might be Israel, Taiwan, Singapore, Malaysia, and South Korea. However, these countries are either quite small in terms of the world economy or enjoy unique circumstances which make them special cases. Nothing is lost by using the simple nomenclature of rich and poor. Most of the world is poor in any normal meaning of the word; only a small fraction of the world is rich. This is true whether we are talking about nations or individuals.

I believe that the differences in per capita incomes and many other differences between the rich and the poor nations are critically important to understand if we want to comprehend capitalism. As we shall see, neoclassical economists play down all economic differences, their view being that those nations at the top of the heap in terms of GDP per capita are simply more advanced along the capitalist path. Those nations further down the >

---

public assistance; and other incomes such as alimony payments and pensions. Incomes do not have to be in a money form. They can also be "in kind," as when a worker is paid in room and board or a poor person receives food stamps. However, most data on income only count money incomes.

3. NOMINAL VERSUS REAL GDP OR INCOME: The GDP can increase if production stays constant but prices rise; in fact, production could fall and GDP rise if the increase in prices is relatively greater than the fall in production. Similarly, workers' wage rates might rise but their ability to buy goods fall, if the prices of the things they purchase rise relatively more than their wage rates. Economists attempt to factor out the effect of price changes and calculate real GDP and real income. The real (as opposed to the nominal or money) GDP or income attempts to measure the actual output produced or the goods and services that can be purchased with money income.

4. PRICE INDEX: Calculating real values is complicated. First a measure of the change in prices must be invented. Such a measure is called a price index. A commonly used price index in the United States is the Consumer Price Index, or CPI. The CPI measures the percentage change in the price of a collection, or "basket," of commonly consumed goods and services. Then the change in the price of this basket is compared to the nominal wage or GDP to see the extent to which the change in the nominal GDP or wage is due to an actual increase in production and purchasing power or simply to a change in prices.

ladder will become like those at the top eventually. The same argument is used for poor persons within any country; they too will be better off eventually. In this chapter and in Chapter Six, I will argue against this position.

GDPs per capita vary from less than $500 in Sierra Leone (in Africa) to more than $20,000 in a few rich capitalist countries, mainly in Europe and North America. Many of the nations in sub-Saharan Africa have per capita GDPs of less than $1,000. Generally speaking, those nations that were once colonies of the European powers and then economically dependent on the Europeans and the United States have the lowest GDPs per capita, while the colonizing and imperialist states have the highest. The highest ranking Latin American country (Chile) ranks 40th in the list of the world's 191 nations. The highest ranking African nation (Libya) ranks 58th. Of the poorest fifty countries in terms of per capita GDP, twenty-seven are in Africa. Thirty-one of the top fifty are either in Europe or North America.[5]

GDP and GDP per capita are limited tools for assessing the well-being of a nation's people, although it is in general true that people do not live well in countries with very low GDPs per capita. The GDP measure itself fails to measure all of a nation's production. It excludes, for example, food produced directly for consumption, something common in the poorest countries. Therefore, the per capita GDP understates the true production of output wherever there is significant production of nonmarket goods and services. It is difficult to imagine the average resident of Sierra Leone surviving on $464 annually; it is reasonable to assume that many people there consume goods not produced for sale and therefore not counted in the per capita GDP. Furthermore, all market production is part of GDP, but by no means is all market production useful. That is, GDP makes no distinction between obviously useful products like cooking oil and destructive ones like nerve gas and cluster bombs. If people get sicker and have to purchase more medical services, the GDP per capita rises (assuming that the population does not change), while if medical care improves to the point at which people do not have to go to see a doctor much, the GDP per capita falls.

One way to get around these difficulties is to use a measure of economic performance other than GDP. Various social indicators can serve as proxies for the effectiveness of an economy. Good choices for such indicators might be life expectancy, infant mortality, literacy rates, and school enrollments. In Table 2.1, the ten richest and the ten poorest nations in terms of per capita GDP are compared with some of these social indicators. We can see the general correlation between social indicators and per capita GDP, and we can also see the gulf that separates the rich and the poor countries. Even these rather gross indicators tell us that the quality of life of the average person is not at all similar in the United States and Eritrea.

TABLE 2.1 Rich and Poor Countries in the 1990s: Ten Richest and Ten Poorest by GDP per Capita

RICH COUNTRIES:	GDP/PERSON	LIFE EXPECTANCY at birth for women/men	INFANT MORTALITY rate per 1,000 births	SCHOOL ENROLLMENT per 100 in age group: women/men
Luxembourg	$34,134	80/73	4.83	99
United States	34,096	80/73	6.82	99/100
Monaco	26,608	83/75	5.92	N.A.
Switzerland	26,270	82/75	4.53	97/100
Singapore	24,288	79/75	3.65	81/84
Norway	23,763	81/75	3.98	108/110
Belgium	23,125	81/74	4.76	127/123
Denmark	23,068	78/73	5.11	112/111
Austria	22,651	80/74	4.50	101/103
Canada	22,635	82/76	5.08	103/104
POOR COUNTRIES:				
Yemen	$724	58/57	70.28	35/90
Afghanistan	704	46/45	149.28	22/49
Comoros	682	60/57	86.33	44/54
Cambodia	654	55/52	66.82	67/85
Burundi	650	44/41	71.50	34/44
Tanzania	649	49/47	80.97	41/42
Congo, Dem.	612	52/49	101.71	41/62
Eritrea	598	52/49	76.66	33/41
Ethiopia	509	44/42	101.29	22/37
Sierra Leone	464	39/36	148.66	29/43

SOURCES: For GDP per capita, see the convenient chart at http://www.cnn.com/WORLD/global.rankings/; for the other columns, see United Nations Department of Economic and Social Affairs, World Statistics Pocketbook (New York: United Nations, 2001).

We have, then, an economic hierarchy of nations. No matter what measures of economic development we use, we see this. What is more, even the nature of production differs considerably among nations. At capitalism's dawn, the soon-to-be wealthy nations of Europe forced the soon-to-be poor nations of Africa, Latin America, and Asia, by military conquest and war, to supply them with minerals and agricultural products (and slaves). The conquered countries were characterized, long after they won political independence, by a heavy reliance upon production of one or a few minerals and crops. As late as 1950, a typical Latin American country devoted an inordinate amount of its resources to the production of tin (Bolivia), copper (Chile), sugar (Cuba), bananas (Honduras), coffee (El Salvador), or meat (Argentina). These products were then exported, mainly to Europe and the United States. Much of the land and the mines were owned by foreign businesses and local elites, neither of which had an interest in diversifying these economies so that they resembled those in Europe and the United States. This meant that the Latin American economies were dependent on imports for everything from basic food products to machinery and equipment. Roads would be built from ports to mines and plantations but nowhere else. The physical capital needed to operate the mines and farms would be imported, along with the luxury consumption goods bought by the local aristocracy.[6]

While much has changed since 1950 and a few poor countries have managed to become richer, the fate of most of the nations that were poor then has been to remain poor. Poor nations don't necessarily specialize in agricultural or mineral production (though a fair number still do), but the manufactured goods they now produce are seldom for local consumption. And they still must import most of their capital goods.

Consider the example of Mexico.[7] Mexico was colonized by Spain in the 1500s. The brutality of the conquest and the diseases brought by the Europeans caused the indigenous population to diminish by as much as 90 percent in one hundred years. The Spaniards used semi-slave Indian labor to make Mexico into a supplier of both precious metals and agricultural commodities, and Mexico took on the form of a classic colony, with a few rich owning most of the land (in the form of large haciendas), a heavy reliance on exports, large masses of marginalized peasants, limited industrialization, and the absence of widespread transportation and communications networks. Formal political independence in the early 1800s did little to change the colonial patterns, except that after independence the United States began to dominate the Mexican economy and to annex Mexican land.

A long internal revolution commenced in Mexico in 1910 against both the dictatorship of Porfirio Diaz and the naked imperialism of the United States and its corporations. The revolution ended in defeat for the more radical forces of Pancho Villa and Emiliano Zapata. (Zapata was murdered by his enemies. Today, he is the namesake of the famous guerillas, the Zapatistas, who have been fighting valiantly to liberate the peasants of southern Mexico.) However, Mexico's new leaders did take steps to mollify the masses of peasants and workers, enacting land reforms and some social welfare legislation. In the 1930s, under Lázaro Cárdenas, Mexico began a process of "import substitution" development. Key industries such as oil were nationalized, that is, taken over by the government, which would then receive the revenues from the sale of the oil. Taxes (called "tariffs") were placed on imported products to allow room for the development of domestic production of goods formerly imported. The domestic production of goods generated a market for the inputs necessary to produce these goods, and, again with tariff protection, some of these intermediate goods could now be produced in Mexico. By the 1950s, Mexico had begun to industrialize. And workers and peasants saw some improvements in their standards of living.

The Great Depression of the 1930s, along with the Second World War, protected Mexico and many other poor countries from the retaliation they normally would have encountered from the rich nations for having the audacity to do things that would give them more economic independence. The rich countries had too many of their own economic problems to concern themselves as overtly as they once had with the affairs of the poor nations. However, the great powers regained their interest in the 1950s and began to attack the economic independence achieved by countries like Mexico. And since the economic reforms of import substitution were not accompanied by real changes in the structure of power in Mexico and elsewhere, the elites in the poor countries did not have the will to resist. From the early 1970s onward, under strong pressure from the United States government and U.S. corporations, Mexico began to dismantle its import substitution program and embrace policies that made its economy more open to foreign (mainly U.S.) investment and control. It also borrowed huge sums of money from foreign banks and governments to pay for public expenditures, began to privatize state-owned enterprises (including the state oil company), lowered taxes on businesses, and cut social welfare spending, all to make Mexico more attractive to foreign capital.

Foreign capital has moved into Mexico, and Mexico's economy is much more industrialized than it was twenty years ago. For a time in the 1980s, Mexico was another economic "miracle." In 1994, Mexico signed the North American Free Trade Agreement (NAFTA), which allowed for even freer movement of foreign capital into the country. The number of manufacturing establishments along the Mexican-U.S. border swelled, and foreign companies also moved into the interior. Today, Mexico is a major manufacturer of sophisticated goods, including automobile engines and electronic equipment. In some ways, the country now resembles a well-developed capitalist

THE INTERNATIONAL TRADE ORGANIZATIONS[8]

A fundamental theme of this book is that the poor countries are poor because they have been exploited by the rich nations. This exploitation has taken place in many ways. Initially, the rich nations directly controlled the poor ones through colonization. Later, when the poor countries won political independence, they were still controlled through the economic power of the rich countries and the collaboration of their own local elites, the latter having now become an independent source of growing inequality and poverty. At the end of the Second World War, the rich countries, led by the United States and to a lesser degree by Great Britain, established international organizations to help them manage the world economy in such a way as to insure their dominance. A set of institutions were set up for this purpose—the World Bank, the International Monetary Fund (IMF), and the General Agreement on Tariffs and Trade (GATT).

The World Bank employs more than 11,000 people and dispenses many billions of dollars in loans to member countries, of which there are 181. The bank is financed by the member nations and by the sale of World Bank bonds on international capital markets. The United States, as the largest economy and contributor, dominates the bank's decisions. The bank makes "development" loans to poor countries. These loans have invariably financed large projects such as dams and power plants, as well as export agriculture. One of the bank's goals is to promote foreign investment, and this has meant that the projects its loans finance have been a bonanza for corporations in the rich nations. These corporations supply the equipment and expertise for the projects and take home the lion's share of any profits the projects generate. It has been estimated that for every one dollar the bank loans, U.S. corporations get $1.30 in procurement contracts. These projects have had almost no positive impact on the economy. Life expectancies for women and men, respectively, are 76 and 70 years. Seventy-four percent of the population lives in urban areas. Nearly 90 percent of school-age children are in primary or secondary schools. Metal manufacturing comprises 67 percent of all exports.[9]

Yet, more than five hundred years after Columbus's infamous voyages, 75 percent of the population lives in poverty, and one-third of these exist in extreme poverty (the poverty cutoff is extraordinarily low). In the "maquiladora" plants along the U.S.-Mexico border, the foreign transnational corporations pay below subsistence wages to workers who live in shacks >

lives of poor people, but they have lined the pockets of local politicians and business persons. They have also destroyed much land and many neighborhoods and filled the air and water with pollutants.

The World Bank now also makes loans to countries facing trade problems. The International Monetary Fund has long specialized in such loans. There is nothing objectionable in principle about an international lending institution helping poor countries when they face declining export or rising import prices. However, over the past twenty-five years, both the IMF and the World Bank have attached stringent conditions, known as "Structural Adjustment Policies or SAPs," to these loans. These SAPS always bear down heavily upon workers and the poor, despite the fact that it is always the wealthy, acting through the governments of poor countries, who cause the economic crises that necessitate the loans in the first place. For example, SAPs typically call for cuts in government spending, policies that encourage exports (and always take land and other resources out of production for domestic consumption), currency devaluations (which lower prices for a country's exports but increase the prices of badly needed imports), the elimination of all price supports (such as low prices for food necessities), and the encouragement of foreign investment, stock, and bond purchases. SAPs always cause cuts in social services for workers, unemployment, and lower real wages.

The post–Second World War program of the rich nations also envisioned the elimination of barriers to foreign trade, such as tariffs and quotas on imported goods and services. The GATT was established to accomplish this goal and resulted in a gradual reduction in trade barriers among nations. However, GATT's enforcement powers were not strong enough for the rich nations. So, in 1995, the World Trade Organization, or WTO, was formed to "eliminate any perceived barrier to trade and investment." Nations can file charges against another nation through the WTO, and

and in degraded environments of polluted water, waste dumps, and poisonous air. In the impoverished south of Mexico, home of the Zapatistas, "only
half of . . . households have electricity or running water." NAFTA has allowed
cheap U.S. corn to flood the market and deny peasants the ability to live on
their farms. "According to the Mexican government's own official estimates,
15 million peasants will be forced to leave agriculture in the next one to two
decades."[10] These farmers will migrate to Mexico City, a gigantic mega-city
of noxious air, massive underemployment, violence, and corruption, or to
the cities of the north, where they will provide a pool of cheap labor.

WTO "trade experts," appointed by the WTO without any democratic process and
meeting in secrecy in Geneva, Switzerland, determine whether a country has violated WTO rules.

The WTO wields enormous power. If the WTO rules against some practice of a
country that it says restricts trade, the aggrieved nation can impose stiff penalties on
the violating nation. For example, the United States filed charges against several
European countries for favoring banana imports from their former colonies in the
Caribbean. Although the United States is not a banana producer, a powerful U.S.
company, Chiquita, owns banana plantations in the region, and this company put
strong political pressure, backed by campaign contributions, on the U.S. government
to file the WTO complaints. Similarly, Mexico filed WTO charges against a U.S. rule
that prohibited the purchase of tuna caught in nets that were not built to protect dol-
phins from inadvertent capture.

The WTO has enabled corporations to resist any rule or law passed by a country
that in any way denies the free entry of foreign capital into a domestic economy.
Businesses are trying to extend the WTO's power to deny a country the power to regulate capital in any way, whether it be through shorter patent periods (to allow, for
example, the earlier production of cheaper generic drugs), any and all environmental
regulations, even national health care and minimum wage laws.

In Chapter Eight we will examine the growing movements against these institutions of global dominance. In response to them, the World Bank, the IMF, and the
WTO have been forced to address issues of inequality and poverty. While their studies are not likely to get to the roots of the problems, they do provide us with some
excellent data and perhaps give the various protest movements some space to push
their agenda forward, provided that they do not get co-opted by facile rhetoric about
concern for the poor.

In a word, the masses of Mexicans are nowhere near achieving decent lives and there are few signs that this will change within the framework of capitalism. Mexican society is marked by a grotesque inequality and a dependence on the rich capitalist countries, different in kind than it once was but not different in degree of dependence. If anything, Mexico's dependence has risen in the past three decades.

What is true of Mexico, which is by no means the poorest or least developed of nations, is true of most of the nations of the world. Neoclassical economists have developed elaborate models suggesting that over time (the famous "long run" again) there will be a convergence between rich and poor nations in terms of per capita GDP. However, there is no evidence of this. Former World Bank economist Lant Pritchett found that the gap between the poorest and the richest countries grew between 1870 and 1960.[11] For example, the ratio of per capita income in the richest nation (the United States) to the average per capita incomes of the poorest countries grew from about nine in 1870 to over fifty in 1960. Pritchett took into account the lower prices for certain consumables in the poorer countries in making his calculations, that is, he conceded that a given income might buy more goods in poorer countries. This makes his calculations that much more astonishing. He also found that per capita GDPs continued to diverge after 1960. The rich countries' economies grew more rapidly during these years than did those of the poor nations, further increasing the gap between them. A few poor countries did grow more rapidly than the rich countries for some years, and Pritchett asks how long it would take for per capita GDP to be equal if this continued. Here is what he says about India:

> . . . a few developing countries were actually "converging," that is, they were growing faster than the United States. When are these lucky "convergers" going to overtake the United States? India, for example, registered an annual average growth rate of 3 percent between 1980 and 1993. If India could sustain this pace for another 100 years, its income would reach the level of high-income countries today. And, if India can sustain this growth differential for 377 years, my great- great-great-great-great-great-great-great-great-great-great-grandchildren will be alive to see India's income level "converge."[12]

In another study, several economists at the Center for Economic and Policy Research (CEPR) looked at the differences between poor and rich countries from 1980 to 2000.[13] They chose this period because it roughly coincides

with the triumph of "neoliberalism," the political program of most neoclassical economists. Neoliberals tell us that the poor countries will be most
likely to converge with the rich countries if they let their economies be
totally dominated by private markets. In fact, under strong pressure from
the rich countries and international lending organizations like the World
Bank and the International Monetary Fund, poor nations opened their
economies to foreign capital, privatized most public enterprises, cut their
budgets to the bone, and eliminated all sorts of regulations of markets.

The CEPR economists tried to put the neoliberal hypothesis to the test.
They divided the countries of the world into five groups, from the poorest
to the richest. Then they compared how the five groups fared between
1960 and 1980 (a period before neoliberal policies were embraced) and
1980 to 2000. Their results are instructive. Consider the poorest countries.
The poorest countries in the period 1960 to 1980 showed varying rates
of economic growth and various levels of life expectancy, infant and
child mortality, and education and literacy. If we take the poorest countries in the 1980 to 2000 period (those which in 1980 were at the same
level of development as the poorest countries in 1960), we find that the
economic and social performance of the poorest countries got considerably worse. Relative to the richest countries, poor countries fared better in
the earlier period. Hence from 1980 to 2000 the poor countries fell further behind the rich ones.

CAPITALISM IN PRACTICE: INEQUALITY
WITHIN COUNTRIES

When we speak of a nation, we are making use of a single abstraction that
covers many realities. To say that there are great inequalities among nations,
that these inequalities are of long standing, that they are rooted in a history
of colonialism and imperialism, even that life expectancies in Sierra Leone
are about half of those in the United States, is to speak in an impersonal
manner. What we need to ask next is how these disparities are reflected in
differences among the life circumstances of people within nations. And
what exactly do these inequalities mean? Do the inequalities, as such, affect
the way in which a society functions and people live their lives?

It would be difficult to imagine that, in a world of tremendous inequality among nations, there would be equality within nations. If a country is
capitalist, the nonhuman means of production are owned by a small minor-

ity of persons. Therefore, by the very nature of capitalism, wealth (all of a person's belongings that can be converted into money) must be unevenly divided. The wealth owned as means of production, in turn, generates income in the form of rent, interest, dividends, and capital gains (which arise when an asset, or form of wealth, is sold at a price higher than the one at which it was bought). Inequality in wealth means that incomes will be unequal too. In addition, while most people get their income from labor, different people receive different wages for their labor power. So in addition to wealth-generated inequality in incomes, there is the income inequality due to unequal wages. Since most of the world's countries are dependent on a few richer ones, the workers in the poor countries will be, in general, much poorer than those in the rich countries and that much poorer relative to the owners in their own countries and in the rest of the world. In other words, there are many and deep layers of inequality in the capitalist world.

As a general rule, the poorer the country, the sparser are data on inequality in wealth and income. The data are improving, however, and we can state certain things with some confidence. The main facts are that there is enormous inequality in wealth and income in nearly every country in the world; there is great inequality among all of the people of the world; inequality both within countries and among the world's people is growing; and inequality, in itself, does great damage to a nation's health and welfare.

There are various ways to measure inequality. The first step is to choose the unit of analysis. This can be the individual, the household, or the family. (A household is a physical space in which people live, ordinarily identified by a national census. The people living in a household do not have to be related to one another. In a family, the persons must be related by blood or marriage.) The amount of inequality in a nation or worldwide will depend on which unit of analysis is used, although the trend in inequality, whether it is rising or falling, will very likely be similar no matter which unit is employed.

Once the unit of analysis is chosen, a representative sample is selected from all of the households, individuals, or families. It is too expensive and time-consuming to analyze every unit, but if the sample is constructed properly, the results from the sample will mirror those of the entire population, although there will always be some small margin of error in our results.

Suppose we use families as our unit of analysis. Surveyors go out into the field and contact the families chosen in the sample. The surveyors ask questions about the families' yearly income—how much has the family received and from what sources (wages, interest, etc.). Then the family incomes are arrayed from the lowest to the highest. The array of incomes is next divided into a certain number of parts, typically five for family incomes. Each of the parts has the same number of families in it, so that if the division is into quintiles (five parts), each quintile contains one-fifth of

AN ANOMALY

While a nation's economic and social indicators are normally highly correlated—that is, richer countries enjoy a better standard of living—this is not always the case. Cuba is a good example of how they can diverge. Cuba was once a classic example of a former colony that gained (formal) political but not economic independence. Cuba won independence after the Spanish American War (the Cubans remember this war as their war for independence), but the United States used its military might to deny Cuba real independence.[14] As every Cuban, but almost no person in the United States, knows, the United States forced Cuba to accept the notorious Platt Amendment to its own constitution. The amendment gave the United States the legal right to intervene in Cuba's internal affairs, something which the U.S. did on numerous occasions, in the process converting Cuba into a de facto colony. U.S. companies owned Cuba's sugar plantations, refineries, hotels, and casinos. Cuban politics were a sinkhole of corruption and violence. Extreme poverty was widespread. In 1953, less than 10 percent of all rural households had electricity, indoor plumbing, or refrigeration. Basic health care and education were either unavailable or of poor quality. There were some rich Cubans and a small middle class, but even these were usually dependent on U.S. business interests for survival.

Cuban workers and peasants had a long history of rebellion, and under the leadership of Fidel Castro and Che Guevara, they succeeded in 1959 in toppling the corrupt government of U.S. puppet Fulgencio Batista. Soon isolated by the United States, the new government quickly became more radical, expropriating some U.S. businesses and embarking upon a project of revolutionary change. Chief among the government's goals was to improve the lives of the poor majority by providing quality education and health care. In these goals, the government has been successful. Despite a savage U.S. embargo that makes it extremely difficult for Cuba to obtain through trade many necessary goods and services and in the face of massive U.S. military power, the Cubans have managed to change their country from a corrupt

the families in the sample. The first quintile will contain the poorest one-fifth of the families, the second, the next poorest fifth, and so on up to the fifth quintile containing the richest fifth of all families. There will be a cut-off income separating each quintile from the one next to it; we can say that the poorest fifth are those families with incomes less than a certain amount. It is important to note that the cutoff point separating the fourth >

playground for the rich to a model of what can be done when a nation dedicates itself to liberating all of the people.

Today, and despite a decade-long economic catastrophe (food production fell by 40 percent between 1990 and 2000) caused by the collapse of Cuba's former ally and benefactor, the Soviet Union, Cuba has social indicators much above the average for Latin America and compares favorably in many cases to rich countries like the United States and Canada. Cuba's GDP per capita is only about one-fourteenth that of the U.S. and one- ninth that of Canada. But Cuban life expectancies are nearly equal to those of its northern neighbors. Cuba has 58.2 doctors per 10,000 persons, while the U.S. has 26.5 and Canada 22.9. Literacy rates are as high in Cuba as anywhere in Latin America and just a couple of percentage points lower than in the U.S. and Canada.[15] However, Cuba's income and wealth are very much more evenly divided than in almost any other country in the world, so Cuban averages do not hide much disparity. The same cannot be said of the United States, where the range of incomes and wealth dwarfs anything in Cuba. What this means is that a poor person in Cuba is relatively much better off than a poor person in the United States. Homelessness, for example, is virtually unknown.

Cuba is by no means perfect. The government has practiced an often violent discrimination against gay men and women, and the practice of religion has not always been tolerated. Improvements have been made in these areas, but more could be made. At the highest political levels, there is an absence of traditional liberal electoral democracy, although there is a great deal of participatory democracy at more local levels. Cuba has been promoting tourism as a way to get foreign exchange, and it has also allowed some private foreign investment. Both of these have generated new forms of privilege and inequality and undermined somewhat the nation's commitment to equality. But, all in all, for a poor country, so long a colony and an economically dependent nation and still the victim of extraordinary U.S. antagonism, to have survived and accomplished so much is a testament to the Cuban people and their revolutionary leaders.[16]

and fifth quintiles will be a number much smaller than the highest income in the fifth quintile. In other words, the range of incomes in the last quintile is extremely large. For example, the cutoff household income in the United States for 2000 was $81,960— one-fifth of all households had incomes above this amount. However, some households in the fifth quintile had incomes in the hundreds of millions of dollars. Therefore, to get a better fix on inequality, it is useful to break down the highest quintile into parts. Sometimes data are presented for the share of income going to the richest five or even one percent; this amount is the share going to the richest people in the fifth quintile.[17]

The next step is to add up the incomes of each family in a particular quintile and divide this amount by the total income of all of the families in all of the quintiles. This fraction tells us what share of the total income (or wealth, if it is wealth we are examining) is received by a particular quintile. Comparing the shares of the quintiles shows us how unequally incomes are divided. Here are some data on income distribution in the United States:

TABLE 2.2   Household Income Distribution in the United States, 1967-2000

	YEAR	2000	1995	1990	1985	1980	1970	1967
% Share of Household Income by Quintile	Lowest Quintile	3.6	3.7	3.9	4.0	4.3	4.1	4.0
	Second Quintile	8.9	9.1	9.6	9.7	10.3	10.8	10.8
	Third Quintile	14.9	15.2	15.9	16.3	16.9	17.4	17.3
	Fourth Quintile	23.0	23.3	24.0	24.6	24.9	24.5	24.2
	Highest Quintile	49.7	48.7	46.6	45.3	43.7	43.3	43.8
	Richest 5 percent	21.9	21.0	18.6	17.0	15.8	16.6	17.5
	Gini Index of Income Inequality	.460	.45	.428	.419	.403	.394	.399

SOURCE: U.S. Census Bureau, Table A-2, at http://www.census.gov

The data from the United States are instructive. The United States is the dominant capitalist economy, and it possesses overwhelming military might. For the past three decades it has been using both its economic and military power to pressure other nations to model their economies after its own and to allow its corporations freer rein wherever they choose to operate. But if the United States represents the future toward which other countries are supposed to head, then this will be a future of great and growing inequality. In absolute terms, the inequality of incomes in the United States is considerable. In 2000 the richest 5 percent of all households had a share of the total income pie more than 6 times greater than that of the poorest 20 percent and 1.75 times greater than the share of the poorest 40 percent. Inequality in 2000 is greater than it was at any time since the Second World War. After falling from the end of the war until the mid- 1970s, inequality has been rising ever since. The income share of the richest 5 percent of households rose by nearly 40 percent between 1980 and 2000. A study by economist Paul Krugman estimated that perhaps as much as 70 percent of all of the income growth in the United States during the 1980s went to the richest 1 percent of all families.[18]

The last row in Table 2.2 shows a statistic called the "gini index of income inequality." The Gini index is a summary measure of inequality that shows how far away from perfect equality (each quintile of households receiving 20 percent of the income pie) the actual distribution of income is. Its values can range from zero to one. A value of "zero" represents perfect equality, and a value of "one" shows perfect inequality (one household gets all of the nation's income!). As shown in the table, the Gini index for the United States has been steadily rising since 1980; it is now more than 17 percent higher than it was the year Ronald Reagan was elected president.[19]

The United States is not exceptional in showing an increase in inequality. Between 1980 and 2000, very few countries exhibited growing income *equality*. The United States is something of a world leader (among the rich countries at least) in inequality and growing inequality, but inequality is significant in all capitalist economies and has grown in many of them, including Great Britain, New Zealand, Australia, Denmark, and Sweden. The collapse of socialism in the formerly socialist economies of the Soviet Union and Eastern Europe has generated enormous increases in inequality. The growth of inequality in China is one of the major contributors to widening income inequality in family incomes worldwide.

A concept connected to inequality is poverty. When we look at the distribution of income, we want to know how those at the bottom compare to those at the top. When we study poverty, we want to know how many persons have incomes less than the level of income that can be described as poverty. The "poverty level of income" is set by government, and in nearly every country in the world the amount set is a bare bones minimum, enough money to sustain life but no more.

In the United States, for example, a poverty level of income was established in the early 1960s, in response to several influential studies showing many U.S. households living in misery despite robust economic growth, as well as to a swelling civil rights movement centered in the poorest parts of the country. Mollie Orshansky, an analyst at the Social Security Administration, was given the task of establishing the poverty level of income. She did this by using the subsistence food budget calculated by the Department of Agriculture. This food budget was an amount of money that would presumably keep a family of four in an urban area fed well enough to allow them to continue to live but not well enough to maintain their physical well-being over the long run. Orshansky then used research done by economists in the 1950s that showed that the median family spent one-third of family income on food. She assumed that poor families also spent one-third of their incomes on food. She arrived at the poverty level of income by taking the subsistence food budget and multiplying it by three (If the food budget equals one-third of the poverty level of income, the poverty level of income equals three times the poverty food budget.) This is still the way the poverty level of income is calculated.[20] In 2000, the poverty income for an urban family of four was $17,603.[21] Anyone at all familiar with the United States will know that this is an absolutely inadequate amount of money to support a family of four. The same can be said, and sometimes more so, for the poverty level of income in other countries. The safest assumption to make is that, whatever the official poverty rate, many more people in a country face extreme economic hardship.

Poverty is widespread in capitalist countries, although, like income inequality, it varies considerably. The data have to be interpreted with care, because definitions of poverty and programs available to alleviate poverty without transferring money income to people vary widely among nations. The World Bank, stung by criticism from the anti-globalization movement, has begun to take a greater interest in measuring the extent of poverty. Table 2.3 provides some recent World Bank data. The table is self-explanatory, but two points must be made. First, poverty in the United States is greater than in any other advanced capitalist nation (as is income inequality). Second, the extensive poverty in poor nations is made all the more remarkable by the extremely low thresholds used in most of these countries. To complement the poverty rates using the definition set by each country, the table also shows the fraction of persons living on less than two dollars per day. This allows us to make a more objective comparison among the nations listed in the chart. The World Bank estimates that some 2.8 billion people, about one-half of the world's population, survive on less than two dollars per day, and 1.2 billion on less than one dollar per day. Even supposing that some of these people get some goods and services outside of the money economy and that prices for some foodstuffs and other necessities are very low, these are appalling numbers.

TABLE 2.3 Poverty in Selected Countries

POOR COUNTRIES	Year(s)	Percentage of population below the poverty line set by government	Percentage of population below $2 per day
Bangladesh	1995–96	35.6	77.8
Cambodia	1997	36.1	N.A.
Chile	1994	20.5	20.3
Honduras	1993 (1996)	53.0	68.8
India	1994 (1997)	35.0	86.2
Indonesia	1998 (1999)	20.3	66.1
Nigeria	1992–93 (1997)	34.1	90.8
Peru	1997 (1996)	49.0	41.4

RICH COUNTRIES	Year(s)	Population below 50% of median disposable income
United States	1994	19.1
Canada	1991	11.7
Denmark	1992	7.5
Sweden	1992	6.7
Germany (Western)	1989	7.6
Japan	1992	11.8

SOURCE: Taken from the World Bank, "World Development Report 2000/2001," which can be found at http://www.rrojasdatabank.org/wdr2000.htm. These data are in Table 4 in the chapter on "Poverty."

We have been describing inequality in income, and we have seen that there is a lot of this and that it is of long duration, as long as there has been capitalism. However, income inequality is partly rooted in a more fundamental inequality, that of wealth, especially of wealth in the form of the means of production. Unlike income, wealth is a "stock" concept, one that is measured at a single point in time rather than over a period of time. It consists of all of the possessions owned by a person, household, or family. In measuring wealth, we ask: What is this person or this household or this family worth today? How much money could it get if it sold all of its belongings?

Wealth inequality is very much greater than inequality of income. If we exclude wealth in the form of personal possessions such as clothing, furniture, cars, and the like, types of wealth that are useful but that do not generate income or confer power on the holder, we find that a tiny minority of households own most of the "wealth of nations." Good data on the distribution of wealth are devilishly difficult to find. However, a look at the wealth distribution of the United States will serve as an adequate proxy for other nations. Sweden, for example, has a wealth inequality roughly the same as the United States, although its income inequality is less, it has a much lower incidence of poverty, and it has excellent social health indicators. It is not possible to imagine that poor countries, with tens of millions of persons living on less than two dollars a day, could have anything other than grotesquely unequal distributions of wealth. Most people in poor countries have no net wealth (assets minus liabilities) at all; in fact, like their counterparts at the bottom of the U.S. distribution, their net wealth is negative.

In the United States, the richest 1 percent of households owned, in 1995, 42.2 percent of all stocks, 55.7 percent of all bonds, 44.2 percent of all trusts, 71.4 percent of all noncorporate businesses, and 36.9 percent of non-home real estate. As with income, the trend has been toward greater inequality; the share going to the wealthiest 1 percent rose by 5 percentage points between 1990 and 1995.[22]

CAPITALISM IN PRACTICE: INEQUALITY WORLDWIDE

The combination of inequality within countries and between them means that there must be inequality among all of the world's people. Let us consider the world as a whole and construct an income distribution chart for all households. Recently, Branko Milanovic, a World Bank economist, oversaw a massive empirical investigation of the world's income distribution. He was interested not only in income inequality at one point in time but in whether inequality was increasing or decreasing. The World Bank gathered data in 1988 and 1993 from household surveys in ninety-one countries, the largest survey ever conducted. As we shall see later on when we discuss the phenomenon of "globalization," critics of the unregulated spread of capitalism throughout the globe were arguing that this was increasing inequality *within* nations. While globalization's supporters sometimes admitted this, they argued that it was reducing inequality *among* nations. Milanovic's study allowed him to see if this was true. He concluded that it is not.

Milanovic found that the richest 1 percent of people in the world get as much income as the poorest 57 percent. The richest 5 percent had in 1993 an average income 114 times greater than that of the poorest 5 percent, rising from 78 times in 1988. The poorest 5 percent grew poorer, losing 25 percent of their real income, while the richest 20 percent saw their real incomes grow by 12 percent, more than twice as high as average world income. World inequality grew because inequality grew between and within countries. The rich nations grew richer and the poor nations grew poorer; the rich within each country grew richer at the expense of the poor. Milanovic calculated that the world income Gini coefficient was between >

SOME ASTONISHING FACTS[23]

Here are some facts from a 1998 study by the United Nations:

1 The richest fifth of the world's people consume 86 percent of all products, while the poorest fifth purchases 1.3 percent—everything from meat to paper and automobiles.

2 The three richest persons in the world have assets greater than the combined GDPs of the 48 poorest nations (note that this is a comparison of wealth to income). So, if the three richest persons sold their assets, they could buy the total output of these 48 countries.

3 If the poorest 47 percent of the world's people (about 2.5 billion persons) pooled their yearly incomes, they could just purchase the assets of the world's wealthiest 225 individuals.

4 A tax of 4 percent levied on the wealth of these same 225 wealthy people would pay for basic and adequate health care, food, clean water, and safe sewers for every person on earth.

.66 and a staggering .80, depending on the way you converted one currency into another. By comparison, the Gini coefficient was .628 in 1988.[24]

Mainstream, neoclassical economists like to talk about equality of opportunity. They say that, even if there is inequality in wealth and income, people can still have the same economic opportunities, especially if the society provides some essential public services. The data presented in this chapter must surely call this notion into question. How can a poor person in any country have the same opportunity as a rich one? How can a poor country become a rich country?

Consider a thought experiment. In Pittsburgh, Pennsylvania, where I lived for many years, there is an extraordinarily wealthy family, the Hillmans, with a net worth of several billion dollars. One of their homes, along once fashionable Fifth Avenue, is a gorgeous mansion on a magnificent piece of property. About three miles east of this residence is the Homewood section of the city, whose mean streets have been made famous by the writer John Edgar Wideman. On North Lang Street there is a row of three connected apartments. One of the end apartments has been abandoned to the elements—to the rodents and the drug users. Poverty, deep and grinding, is rampant on this street and in this neighborhood, which has one of the nation's highest infant mortality rates.

Consider two children, one born in the Hillman house and another born in the North Lang Street apartment. In the former, there are two rich and influential parents, and in the latter there is a single mother working nights with three small children. Let us ask some basic questions. Which mother will have the best health care, with regular visits to the doctor, medicine if needed, and a healthy diet? Which child is more likely to have a normal birth weight? Which child is more likely to get adequate nutrition and have good health care in early childhood? If the poor child does not have these things, who will return to this child the brain cells lost as a consequence? Which child is more likely to suffer the ill effects of lead poisoning? Which child is more likely to have an older sibling, just 12 years old, be responsible for him or her when the mother is working at night? Which will be fed cookies for supper and entertained by an old television set? If the two children get ill in the middle of the night, which one will be more likely to make it to the emergency room in time? Which child will start school speaking standard English, wearing new clothes, and having someone at home to make sure the homework gets done? Which child will travel, and which will barely make it out of the neighborhood?

As the two children grow up, what sort of people will they meet? Which will be more likely to meet persons who will be useful to them when they are seeking admission to college or looking for a job or trying to find funding for a business venture? Which will be more likely to be hit by a stray bullet fired in a war over drug turf? Which will go to the better school? Which will have access to books, magazines, newspapers, and computers in the home? Which one will wear worn-out clothes? Which one will be embarrassed because his or her clothes smell? Which one will be more likely to have caring teachers who work in well-equipped and safe schools? Which one will be afraid to tell the teacher that he does not have crayons and colored paper at home? Which child will learn the grammar and syntax of the rich? Which child will join a gang? Abuse drugs? Commit a crime? Be harassed by the police because he is black? When these two children face the labor market, which one will be more productive?

These questions need only be asked for the answers to be clear. And when we consider that this poor child in the United States is better off than two-thirds of the world's population, we must conclude that most of the world's people live in a state of deprivation so extreme that they must be considered to have almost no opportunities at all. They are condemned almost as certainly as the person on death row in a Texas prison. The difference, as we shall see later in this book, is that those condemned by poverty have never just been passive victims. They are remarkably resilient and resourceful and constantly do things that amaze us. Some youngsters from the poor Pittsburgh neighborhood make it to college; some become writers like John Wideman. Sometimes poor people rise up and rebel en masse against their circumstances. And sometimes they win.

THE BURDEN OF INEQUALITY

Capitalist economies are marked by deep and abiding inequalities. At the top, there are a few very rich countries and people wealthy beyond belief. At the bottom, there are scores of poor countries and billions of people living in the most appalling conditions. These facts cry out for explanation; these conditions cry out for redress. Before we try to answer this cry, we must make two final points.

First, recent research for the United States appears to show that inequality, in and of itself, has harmful social consequences. It is obvious that poor people will be more likely to get sick and die young than people with lots of money. But now scientists have shown that poor people become more likely to get sick and die as the gap between the rich and the poor grows larger. That is, poor people in the United States will be more likely to get sick and die, other things equal (with the same incomes, for example), than poor people in Sweden. In a study done comparing states within the United States, it was discovered that, all else equal, the greater the inequality of income in a state (as measured by the share of income going to the poorest 50 percent of households in each state), the higher the mortality rate. In a summary of this research, Peter Montague writes,

> This measure of inequality was also tested against other social conditions besides health. States with greater inequality in the distribution of income also had higher rates of unemployment, higher rates of incarceration, a higher percentage of people receiving income assistance and food stamps, and a greater percentage of people without medical insurance. Again, the gap between rich and poor was the best predictor, not the average income in the state.
>
> Interestingly, states with greater inequality of income distribution also spent less per person on education, had fewer books per person in the schools, and had poorer educational performance, including worse reading skills, worse math skills and lower rates of completion of high school.
>
> States with greater inequality of income also had a greater proportion of babies born with low birth weight; higher rates of homicide; higher rates of violent crime; a greater proportion of the population unable to work because of disabilities; a higher proportion of the population using tobacco; and a higher proportion of the population being sedentary (inactive).[25]

It appears that the psychological damage done to poor people as the contemplate the gap between themselves and those at the top of the income distribution has an independent effect on a wide variety of individual and social health outcomes.

Second, the discussion of inequality in this chapter has been general in the sense that it has made no mention of certain important types of inequality. Most notable are inequalities by gender, race, and ethnicity. In nearly every capitalist country, women are poorer than men, earn lower wages, and have higher unemployment rates (see Chapters Three and Four), are more likely to be denied certain types of employment, and are more likely to live below the poverty threshold. Women are less likely in most countries to be in school than men. Needless to say, women face a much greater likelihood of being sexually abused and even murdered because of their gender. It is rare in most parts of the world to find a woman running a large business or filling an important political post.

Women are also overwhelmingly responsible for child care. When a woman does this without the support of another person, typically a husband, she is much more likely to be poor. In the United States, for example, 11.3 percent of the population was poor in 2000. However, the incidence of poverty for persons in households headed by single women was 24.7 percent.[26] The United States does not have available to women nearly as great an array of social services as are available to women in some countries in Western Europe, so the problem is greater here. But it is a general phenomenon, and there are many parts of the world in which no services whatever are available and where, therefore, the economic plight of single women rearing children is worse than it is in the United States.

People around the world are also sharply divided by race and ethnicity. The violent ethnic conflicts of the past decade and the racism so common in many countries are good evidence of this. As capitalism has uprooted peasants and workers, millions of people migrate to other countries. In their new homes, they face tremendous economic insecurity, often fueled by racism. Whether they be Pakistanis laboring in the Gulf states, Turks working in Germany, Nigerians selling goods on the sidewalks of Manhattan, Eastern Europeans removing asbestos from buildings in U.S. cities, or people from the Caribbean trying to make new lives in Great Britain, all are concentrated toward the bottom of their country's economic ladder.

Again using the United States as an example, Black and Hispanic persons face enormous discrimination, and this is reflected in their greater concentration in the lowest quintile of the income distribution, their absence from the ranks of the wealthy, their greater incidence of poverty, their higher rates of illiteracy, their greater presence in prisons, their poorer health, and their lower life expectancies.

The ranks of the working class and of the poor are disproportionately filled by women and ethnic and racial minorities. Any strategy for ending inequality, poverty, and underemployment must consider the many and complex ways in which the problems of class intersect with the problems of gender and race and ethnicity.

CHAPTER THREE: Unemployment and Underemployment

BY THE SWEAT OF OUR BROWS

Neoclassical economists build their analysis of capitalism on the assumption that every person in a capitalist society has fundamental freedom to make economic choices (see Chapter Five for a more extended discussion). We can choose to buy this or that automobile or choose to take a vacation to the beach or to the mountains. Similarly, they say, we can work for one employer or another; we are not bound to an employer in the way that a serf was bound to a lord. In the dealings workers have with their employers, workers are presumed to make a free choice, and, therefore, the employers are presumed to have no power over them. They deal with one another at "arm's length," as equals.

If it is true that workers make free choices, as neoclassical theory supposes, then if the worker is not working or is working for a very low wage or is laboring for extremely long hours, it must be because this is what the worker has chosen. For example, if I have a low-paying job, it is no doubt because I failed to make the right choice in terms of where I live or how long I stayed in school or what course of training I pursued. If I work fourteen hours a day, it must be because I have chosen to do so, because I have a low "leisure preference." If I am unemployed, it must be because I have a very strong leisure preference.

A close look at the world's workers makes it difficult to accept the neoclassical assumptions about the choices working men and women make. In Pakistan, there are several hundred thousand children employed making rugs.[1] Their average age is seven, and they typically begin work at age five. A rug manufacturer goes to the rural villages and strikes a deal with the half-starved and desperate parents. The manufacturer will pay the parents a sum of money, part now and part after the child has begun to work, and the child will be handed over, sold in effect, to the manufacturer. The manufacturer will take the child to the city and house him or her in rude and unsanitary quarters. Children labor twelve or more hours a day in a stifling and unventilated workshop, wearing out their as yet unformed bodies making rugs. Should they talk back to the employer or otherwise rebel, they are harshly and physically punished.

Child labor is ubiquitous in Pakistan and many other places in the world. Here is how one journalist described child labor in a Pakistani plant in which soccer balls are made:

> Soon after I arrived in Pakistan, I arranged a trip to a town whose major factories were rumored to enslave very young children. I found myself hoping during the journey there that the children I saw working in fields, on the roads, at the marketplaces, would prepare me for the worst. They did not. No amount of preparation could have lessened the shock and revulsion I felt on entering a sporting-goods factory in the town of Sialkot, seventy miles from Lahore, where scores of children, most of them aged five to ten, produce soccer balls by hand for forty rupees, or about $1.20, a day. The children work eighty hours a week in near-total darkness and total silence. According to the foreman, the darkness is both an economy and a precautionary measure; child-rights activists have difficulty taking photographs and gathering evidence of wrongdoing if the lighting is poor. The silence is to ensure product quality: "If the children speak, they are not giving their complete attention to the product and are liable to make errors." The children are permitted one thirty-minute meal break each day; they are punished if they take longer. They are also punished if they fall asleep, if their workbenches are sloppy, if they waste material or miscut a pattern, if they complain of mistreatment to their parents or speak to strangers outside the factory. A partial list of "infractions" for which they may be punished is tacked to a wall near the entrance. It's a document of dubious utility: the children are illiterate. Punishments are doled out in a storage closet at the rear of the factory. There, amid bales of wadding and leather, children are hung upside down by their knees, starved, caned, or lashed. (In the interests of economy the foreman uses a lash made from scrap soccer-ball leather.) The punishment room is a standard feature of a Pakistani factory, as common as a lunchroom at a Detroit assembly plant.[2]

What free choices might these children be making? In the last chapter, we learned that there were 2.8 billion people subsisting on less than $2 per day.

The overwhelming majority of these people are working for the money. Can we imagine that they have chosen their work, the wages for which guarantee that they will live in misery? Right here in the United States, there are thousands of workers laboring in the garment sweatshops and restaurants of Manhattan's Chinatown. In 1999, their average wage was $2 an hour, and they toiled for 100 hours per week. Most of them were in the country illegally and were deeply in debt to the sharks who loaned them the money to get here from their homeland. It was not uncommon for these workers to be living fifteen people to a one-bedroom apartment. I was informed about these conditions by Wing Lam, the director of the Chinese Staff and Workers' Association, a group which serves as a militant advocate for New York City's oppressed Asian workers. My wife and I visited his office two weeks after it had been firebombed, no doubt by hostile employers.

If conditions are extremely difficult for several billion of the world's employed workers, what must they be like for the tens of millions who are unemployed? From their beginning, capitalist economies have proven unable to generate enough jobs to go around. In this context, unemployment is inherent in a capitalist economy. Capitalism is unique in this respect. For most of our time on earth, for tens of thousands of years, we lived in small communal bands of gatherers and hunters. Production involved groups of human beings gathering roots, fruits, berries, nuts, and the like, and hunting animals. When food became scarce, the band moved to another place. Food was shared out in a roughly equal manner; in fact, everything of use in a gathering and hunting society was more or less available to all in the group. In such a society, the relations of production, that is, the ways in which people related to one another as they engaged in production, were, certainly by contemporary standards, extraordinarily egalitarian. Gatherers and hunters practiced a division of labor, as do all human societies, but division of labor did not imply inequality as it so often does today. Labor was mainly divided by gender, with women typically performing certain work tasks and men others, but unlike modern work, the labor of men was not valued any differently than that of women.

In a gathering and hunting society, there is no notion of private property in the means of production. No one owns the land from which the food is gathered and on which the animals are hunted. Because no one owns the nonhuman means of production, no one works for anyone else. In such circumstances, a moment's reflection tells us that it is impossible for a person to be unemployed. To be unemployed means that a person desires to work, but there is no work available. In a gathering and hunting society in which everyone is fundamentally "attached" to the land (has the right, so to speak, to use it), why would you not be able to work if you wanted to do so? To say that a gatherer and hunter was unemployed would be to say that, in a situation in which the gatherers and hunters were hungry, they simply said, "Oh, to hell with it. Let's just starve."[3] Of course, this is not to say that gatherers and hunters might not go hungry. There may be little food to gather and few animals to hunt. But being hungry is not the same as being unemployed (though the converse is often enough true).

Actually, serfs in feudal society cannot be unemployed either. They are attached to the lord's land and have a customary right to farm it. The lord does not have the right to evict them from the land and deny them their right to labor. So while serfs are terribly exploited and while they may not get enough to eat, they cannot pass into a state of unemployment. Much the same is true even in a slave society. Slaves can perhaps be sold, but they will always be put to work.

With capitalism, we have something different. Just like the gatherers and hunters, we must have access to the land and other nonhuman means of production if we want to survive. But unlike our tribal ancestors, the land we must have use of belongs to another, is private property. We have to be hired by the owner to get access to it. If the owner refuses to hire us, for whatever reason, we enter the unenviable status of unemployed. Unlike the lord, the capitalist who decides whether or not to employ us has no social obligation to give us access to his property. What makes property private is the right to do with it what one pleases. Denying some of us access to it is just such a right.

If capitalism opens up the possibility of unemployment, it is legitimate to ask how prevalent unemployment is. As we shall soon see, unemployment is a ubiquitous fact of life throughout the capitalist world. At any point in time, there are millions of unemployed persons in the world, people who would gladly work if they could locate a job. There are hundreds of millions yet again who are marginally employed, working very short hours or for such low pay that they cannot make ends meet. Such persons we shall call underemployed.

At any point in time there are large numbers of unemployed and underemployed people in capitalist economies. But at particular points in time, the numbers swell to catastrophic levels. Capitalist economies are crisis-prone. For the last two centuries, they have periodically sunk into what economists call depressions or recessions. (The difference between depression and recession is ambiguous. "Depression" conveys the notion of a serious economic downturn, as in the Great Depression of the 1930s, while "recession" refers to a milder downturn, such as has occurred in the United States at least eight times since the Second World War. One wag put it this way: "A recession takes place when you are unemployed; a depression occurs when I am unemployed.")

In periods of economic crisis, unemployment can reach 20 or even 30 percent of the labor force, and the number of underemployed can reach still higher levels. While major depressions plagued the advanced capitalist countries before the Second World War, none have occurred since then (although certain regions of the advanced capitalist nations have faced depressions since 1945). However, the poorer capitalist countries have experienced full-blown depressions in recent times. This happened in most of the formerly socialist countries of the Soviet Union and Eastern Europe when they began their "transition" back to capitalism. Among the world's poorest nations, there are those of which it can safely be said have been in a state of permanent depression for many decades. It must be remembered as well that even when capitalist economies are growing rapidly, those at the bottom of the economic pile will typically suffer circumstances similar to those experienced by larger masses of people in a general depression.

UNEMPLOYMENT AND UNDEREMPLOYMENT

The Social Costs of Unemployment

For most people it is a mixed blessing to be employed. As we shall see, for most people wages are unconscionably low, hours are either inadequate or gruelingly long, working conditions are conducive to injury, illness, and fatal disease, the work itself is tedious and boring, and treatment by employers is harsh and degrading. But it is worse still *not* to have a job. Without work, it is not possible to live, unless some other person or a government lends a helping hand.

Before we discuss the extent of unemployment in capitalist economies, we must emphasize the severe consequences of unemployment, not only for the individual but for society as a whole. In his book *Securing the Right to Employment*, Philip Harvey examines three social costs of unemployment.[4] First, when workers are unemployed, the society does not produce as much output as possible. In other words, the society's actual output is less than its potential output; unemployment wastes output. During the Great Depression, for example, millions of unemployed workers existed along with unutilized land, raw materials, plant, equipment, and machinery.

In the steel industry in 1932, firms were operating at 10 percent of their maximum (or capacity) output. In the steel towns of Western Pennsylvania, thousands of steelworkers were unemployed and going hungry. This amounted to a tremendous waste of output. The steelworkers had not forgotten how to make steel. The machinery was as productive as ever. The country still had plenty of uses for steel. Yet no steel got produced. One can imagine a gatherer and hunter coming to a town like Johnstown, Pennsylvania, where the massive Bethlehem steel mill stood idle and where able-bodied men roamed the streets. It is difficult to imagine that our gatherer and hunter could be made to understand what was happening. How could there be tools and men and unfed bellies all together? From society's point of view, such waste is utterly irrational. Yet it is all too common in capitalist economies.

Philip Harvey made an estimate of the lost output caused by the unemployment that occurred in the United States between the years 1977 and 1986. He estimated that the economy lost more than one trillion dollars of output (in real terms) during this ten-year period. If this output had been divided equally, each person in the United States would have had $1,600

SECRETARY REICH AND THE MAN FROM OKLAHOMA CITY

In 1994, not long after the publication of my book Longer Hours, Fewer Jobs, I appeared on a television show with then Secretary of Labor Robert Reich and a middle- aged man from Oklahoma City who had lost his well-paying job at a public utility company some months before. Secretary Reich is a decent man, but back then he was promoting some dubious ideas. He seemed to believe that bad jobs could be made into good jobs if only employers would "empower" their employees through various types of labor- management cooperation programs. This was a typical "new economy" idea, and, as we saw in Chapter One, without much substance. I argued during our debate that most of the jobs created in the 1990s were unskilled and poorly paid. He demurred and said that there were many good jobs out there. One of them, he said, was cashiering. I

more output in each of the ten years. So one way to think of the wasted output caused by unemployment is to imagine money you might have had and what you might have done with it, had there been no unemployment. In a way, unemployment is a form of theft, theft of output and the income that the production of that output would have generated.

A second social cost of unemployment is what we can call wasted people. Work is an essential human function. It is through our work that we transform the world around us; it is through our labor that we have developed the ability to make tools and machines and thereby increase our output by amounts unimaginable for any other species. It is also through our work that we socialize with other human beings. Labor is a fundamental social activity; it binds us together and makes us what we are. And, in a capitalist society, it is only through our labor that we get access to the non-human means of production necessary for life.

Unfortunately, as we have seen, it is possible that we will not be able to work. If no one will hire us, we are unemployed. Not only will we not be able to do something that helps to define us as human beings. Not only will we not be able to socialize through labor. We won't even be able to purchase the things necessary for survival. A moment's reflection will tell us that unemployment must surely have harmful consequences for those who experience it. Unemployment must be a profoundly anti-social experience. If we are unemployed and cannot help to support our families, if we cannot   >

---

blurted out in astonishment, "Cashiering!" I suggested that the secretary go into the grocery stores and ask the cashiers what they thought of their jobs and to notice the splints many of them wore to alleviate the pain of repetitive stress syndrome.

What brought us to our discussion of jobs was the plight of the man from Oklahoma City. After he lost his job, he thought that he would find another comparable job without much difficulty. He had skills and good references. But companies were downsizing and cutting out middle managers all over the country. He sent out 500 resumés and received no responses. His life began to fall apart. In desperation, he took two part-time jobs, one at a 7-11 convenience store. His annual income fell from the mid-$50,000s to $17,000. Most distressing to me, he had to get permission from his (undoubtedly much younger) supervisor at the 7-11 store to be on the show, because the program aired during his shift.

do something that helps make us human, how does that make us feel? Research tell us the answer—not very well.

The most important research done on the effects of unemployment on the well-being of workers has been done by Professor M. Harvey Brenner of Johns Hopkins University in Baltimore, Maryland.[5] Using research methods similar to those that have proven cigarette smoking to be harmful to health, Brenner found a causal relationship between an increase in unemployment and a wide variety of health and social problems. (He found similar results when he studied the effects of plant closings.) What Brenner did was to use sophisticated statistical techniques to create two groups of persons, alike in as many respects as possible, but differing in that one group is made up of persons who have experienced unemployment for a certain period of time (this group is called the "treatment group") while the other group consists of people who have not experienced unemployment (this group is called the "control group").

When Brenner compared the two groups, he found some remarkable results, results confirmed in many subsequent studies, not just in the United States but in other countries as well. Brenner's research during the 1980s and early 1990s found that an increase in unemployment was positively correlated with overall mortality, deaths from cardiovascular disease, deaths from cirrhosis of the liver, arrests, prison admissions, suicides, homicides, and admissions to mental hospitals. Researchers in Canada,

---

The narrator of the show asked Secretary Reich what advice he had for the man. I was glad she did not ask me. I felt that the man's life as a successful middle manager was over. He was in his mid-50s, and no company would hire him, just as no university would have hired me in similar circumstances. Employers would hire younger and cheaper labor. They then have lower health and pension costs and more years to recover whatever hiring and training costs they incurred. He would have been much luckier if we had been on the Oprah Winfrey show rather than on the then obscure FX network. Maybe Oprah or a well-heeled listener could have given him a job. By the way, Reich told the man that he should get as much training as he could. It was necessary, Reich said, for workers to be continually upgrading their skills, to make themselves continuously employable in the fast- paced and ever-changing new economy. As we shall see when we look at jobs, the secretary might just as well have told him to rob a bank.

Great Britain, Finland, Denmark, and Italy have found similar results. In Brenner's 1984 study, for example, he found that a 10 percent increase in the rate of unemployment (say an increase from 5 to 5.5 percent) leads to a 1.2 percent increase in overall mortality and a 10 percent rise in the suicide rate.[6] Studies have also shown positive correlations between an increase in the unemployment rate and family stress, divorce rates, and negative self- perceptions. It appears to be literally true that unemployment makes us depressed, sick, and more likely to be arrested, imprisoned, admitted to a mental hospital, to die.

Some researchers have tried to put a monetary value on this second cost of unemployment. In a review of such studies, Canadian economist Marcel Bédard summarizes Brenner's findings: "Brenner . . . estimated that three events in 1973–74—a 0.7 percentage point rise in the unemployment rate, the 3 percent drop in per capita income and the 200 percent rise in the annual American business bankruptcy rate—had increased overall cost to the U.S. health and justice systems by a cumulative total of over $24 billion by 1980."[7]

We shall have occasion in Chapter Five to examine neoclassical economics and the politics of neoliberalism of which it is the intellectual foundation. Neoliberalism, supported by the power of the United States and the international lending agencies it dominates (the World Bank and the International Monetary Fund), has dictated that many poor countries do things, such as drastically reducing government social welfare spending and sharply increasing interest rates, that cause the unemployment rate to rise. Brenner's studies tell us that the consequences of such policies are sickness and death. Those who engineer them are criminals and murderers. Even in rich nations, governments have enacted policies that precipitate economic recessions. They have done this intentionally to break the power of organized workers. And they have killed some of these very same workers by so doing.

A third social cost of unemployment is the cost of revenues lost to governments resulting from the wasted output plus the direct costs of the public expenditures aimed at alleviating the impact of unemployment. Unemployment forces governments to cut spending it might otherwise have done and to pay extra unemployment benefits and other social welfare benefits. Philip Harvey estimated the costs of helping the unemployed during the 1977–1986 period in the United States at $1,000 per person per year.

Defining Unemployment

To find out how many people are unemployed or underemployed, we need a definition of the terms—unemployment and underemployment. Unfortunately, countries do not define these statistics in the same way. This means that great care must be taken when comparing unemployment rates across countries. As we shall see, official unemployment rates often exclude millions of persons who are, in fact, unemployed, but are not counted as such.

Since I am most familiar with definitions and procedures in the United States, I will use these to give readers the general idea.[8] Public officials in the United States began to think seriously about counting the number of unemployed during the Great Depression of the 1930s. This was done partly in response to the widespread revolt of the unemployed themselves who were organizing, demonstrating, and militantly confronting welfare officials, police, and landlords throughout the nation. Private organizations had attempted to count the unemployed, but their estimates differed wildly; business groups estimated unemployment to be much lower than did labor-friendly organizations. The U.S. government experimented with various definitions of unemployment throughout the 1930s, and it began in the 1940s to use what is still its basic method.

Each month the Bureau of Labor Statistics and the Census Bureau take a sample of more than 60,000 households (a household is a physical space in which people live; the people in the household need not be related). Those who do not live in households, such as the homeless and those living in institutions like prisons and long-term health care facilities, are excluded from the monthly surveys. Once the households are chosen, surveyors are sent out to ask questions of the members of the households. Since the minimum age for inclusion in the labor force in the United States is sixteen (in Mexico, by way of comparison, it is twelve), the questioners are only interested in those who are at least this age. Questions are asked of the household members concerning their work activity in certain prior time periods. Various demographic questions are also asked: age, gender, race, occupation, etc. On the basis of the answers given to the questions, respondents are placed into one of three mutually exclusive categories:

EMPLOYED: To be counted as employed, a person must have worked at least one hour for pay in the week prior to the survey work. Certain persons in family enterprises who have not worked for pay but did work for fifteen unpaid hours are also counted as employed, as are those with jobs but not working due to illness, temporary leave, bad weather, strike, or employer lockout. Notice that people are counted as employed irrespective of the number of hours they worked.

UNEMPLOYED: A person who is not employed but has *actively* searched for work in the four weeks prior to the survey week is counted as unemployed. A person who registers at an employment office (public or private), goes to a job interview, sends in a job application, registers at a union hiring hall, or takes other such actions is actively seeking work. Simply preparing a resumé does not count as active search. Notice that if people stop looking for work because it has become fruitless for them to do so, as might be the case in a depression or for racial minorities unable to move from their economically ravaged neighborhoods, they are no longer counted as unemployed.

NOT IN THE LABOR FORCE: The sum of the employed and the unemployed is defined to be the *labor force*. All those who are neither employed nor unemployed go into the category, not in the labor force. A full-time homemaker who has not worked for pay nor looked for work goes here, as does a fully retired person. It does not matter if the homemaker would have sought work if day care had been available, just as it does not matter that the retired person was compelled to take early retirement but would have preferred to keep working.

Once the survey is completed, the unemployment rate is calculated very simply: it is the number of unemployed persons identified in the survey divided by the labor force. In the United States in January 2002, for example, this division yielded 5.6 percent. Because the result is based on a sample and not a survey of the entire population, there is a small margin of error associated with the unemployment rate, so that it would be more accurate to say that the unemployment rate for January 2002 was 5.6 percent plus and minus a small error (the actual error is about one-tenth of a percentage point).[9]

In interpreting unemployment numbers, it is important to keep several things in mind. First, it is most common, especially when countries are compared, to use annual unemployment rates. In countries where rates are calculated monthly or at some interval less than one year, the annual unemployment rate is simply the average of the monthly (or quarterly) rates. However, workers move among the three categories from month to month. That is, workers unemployed one month might not be unemployed the next; they may be replaced by newly unemployed workers. Therefore, the fraction of the labor force that experiences unemployment in an entire year will be considerably higher than the yearly unemployment rate. If, for example, in each of ten months, 10 percent of the labor force is unemployed but each month's 10 percent represents entirely different persons, then the average unemployment rate for the ten months is 10 percent. However, 100 percent of the labor force experiences unemployment at some point during the year.

Second, official unemployment rates, and this is true without exception, hide a great deal of labor market distress. Some people who are not counted as unemployed should be. Two such groups are involuntary part-time workers and discouraged workers. Some people labor short hours against their wishes; they may either have had their work hours cut by their employer due to lack of business or they may want full-time work but are able to find only part-time jobs. It is reasonable to count such people as partially unemployed and add them to the officially unemployed. This is especially important to do in periods of economic recession when the number of involuntary part-time workers swells. Also in economic crises, the number of people who give up looking for work because there is no work available increases. Economists call such people "discouraged workers." However, the official unemployment rate does not reflect the increase in their numbers; in fact, other things equal, the unemployment rate falls the more discouraged workers there are.

Involuntary part-time workers and discouraged workers comprise what we can call the hidden unemployed. To count them, economists add them to the officially unemployed and divide this number by the official labor force plus the discouraged workers (since discouraged workers are in the numerator of the fraction, they must also be in the denominator). Multiplied by one hundred, this new statistic is the underemployment rate. The difference between it and the official unemployment rate depends primarily on how well the overall economy is performing. Remember that in January 2002 the official unemployment rate in the United States was 5.6 percent. The underemployment rate was, however, 8.1 percent, a difference of 2.5 percentage points, or approximately 3.5 million persons.[10]

A third caveat, especially significant in poor nations, is the marginal employment of many people. Consider Mexico as a case in point. In 1994,

Canada, the United States, and Mexico signed the North American Free Trade Agreement (NAFTA). This agreement was made largely at the behest of the large transnational corporations that dominate all three economies. The owners and top managers of these companies wanted to be able to move their capital, both in money and in physical form, with complete freedom among the countries. Although many workers' organizations and environmentalists opposed NAFTA, they were not strong enough politically to defeat it. Its proponents painted a rosy picture of all-round gain from the increasing trade that would result from NAFTA. But while trade did increase, workers saw precious little of the benefits from such trade.

In rural Mexico, most people survived, prior to NAFTA, by planting, consuming, and selling corn. The selling of their corn was especially important because the money that they got from the sales bought them necessities they did not themselves produce and also paid their rents if they leased their lands. NAFTA committed Mexico to eliminating its tariffs on imported corn. The Mexican tariff had offered Mexico's peasants some protection from the cheaper, mass-produced corn of its northern neighbors. NAFTA ended Mexico's corn tariffs; they were just the kind of barriers to trade that the agreement committed the governments of Mexico, Canada, and the United States to end.

The termination of the corn tariff has been catastrophic for Mexican peasants. Mexico's three million corn farmers and their twelve million dependents cannot compete against the cheaper U.S. corn. "Corn growing has basically collapsed in Mexico," Carlos Heredia Zubieta, an economist and a member of Mexico's Congress, said in a recent speech to an American audience. "The flood of imports of basic grains has ravaged the countryside, so the corn growers are here [in the United States] instead of working in the fields."[11] The Mexican farmers are not just in the United States. They flee the countryside and move into Mexico's large cities. There they eke out a living in what economists curiously call the "informal sector." This means that they are self-employed, doing such work as selling lottery tickets, peddling trinkets on urban sidewalks, vending cheap food, and selling themselves as prostitutes.

In Mexico's official statistics, they are counted as employed. The reality, however, is that they are living hand-to-mouth. It is not possible to live for long and in good health doing such work. They are disguised unemployed and should be counted as such. They are no different than the panhandlers on the streets of cities in the United States. They are as much a sign of labor market distress as those who are officially unemployed. In countries like Mexico, there are so many people in the "informal" sector that the official unemployment statistics have become meaningless as guides to the health of the economy.

The fourth and final thing that must be kept in mind when looking at unemployment rates is the variability of these rates among different groups within the economy. The 5.6 percent rate cited above for the United States in January 2002 is for the economy as a whole. It does not tell us anything about the labor market experience of subgroups of workers. For example, workers throughout the world are divided by gender, race, ethnicity, and religion. While we will argue in Chapter Six that all workers are exploited by their employers, some are more exploited than others. This differential exploitation might be reflected in higher unemployment rates (and also in lower wages and more onerous working conditions). In much of the world, women face more labor market distress than men, and in many countries, the same can be said of racial and ethnic minorities. In Israel, Palestinians are much more likely to be unemployed and poor than are Jews; in early 2002, the unemployment rate in Israel was 9 percent, but that in the West Bank and Gaza was 40 percent.[12] In the United States, black workers have double the unemployment rates of white workers and Hispanic workers nearly double the white rate. Given the political significance of such division among workers, it is necessary for us to know how these divisions are reflected in the data on unemployment, wages, and jobs.

HOW MANY ARE UNEMPLOYED?: THE RICH NATIONS

The most accurate unemployment data are found in the rich capitalist nations. Governments have more money to hire people to collect the data and to establish bureaucracies to oversee this collection as well as its analysis and dissemination. Data for poor countries cannot be collected as effectively, so the resulting data are not as reliable. This is not to say that the data from the rich countries are unproblematic. In the United States, for example, census data are used to locate households. The problem here is that poor persons, disproportionately black and other racial minorities, move frequently and are therefore more likely not to be at the census address. They are also more likely to refuse to answer the door when the surveyor knocks. This means that these groups will be underrepresented in the sample and their official unemployment rate lower than their actual unemployment.[13] Furthermore, and again in the United States, racial and ethnic minorities are far more likely to be in prison than are whites, due primarily to the racist criminal justice system. People who are incarcerated are not included in the pool of people whose household can be chosen in the sample in the first place. If we accept the notion that black people are disproportionately in prison because they are black, and are therefore more likely to be poor and unable to find decent jobs, something difficult to deny without resorting to genetic falsehoods, then again the official unemployment rate for blacks is lower than the true one. Most black prisoners, in other words, are disguised unemployed.[14]

What do the unemployment numbers tell us? The first and primary revelation is that capitalist economies seldom attain full employment over extended periods of time. There are some exceptions, mainly the Scandinavian countries during parts of the long economic boom after the Second World War and Japan from the 1950s until about 1990. We will have occasion to look at the Scandinavian economies further in Chapter Seven, but Japan's official unemployment numbers are distorted by the facts that many women are pressured by employers and social mores to leave the labor force when they marry and the same thing is true for older workers, often forced to retire in their mid-fifties.

Since the United States is the world's premier capitalist power and is always presented as an example of the strength of capitalism, it is instructive to look at its unemployment data. Unemployment data are available back to 1890, although the data before 1940 represent the best guesses economists can make from what data they have later recovered. The median rate for the 112 years since 1890 is about 5.5 percent. (The median rate is the rate such that 50 percent of the 112 yearly rates are above and 50 percent below it.) In only thirteen years was the rate at or below 3 percent and half of these were war years. Four percent or less was achieved in just twenty-nine years, and again nearly half were in wartime.[15]

While fairly low rates of unemployment characterized the period between 1946 and the mid-1970s in the United States, and some capitalist economies exhibited rates much below the U.S. rates, it has been unusual for any capitalist economy to achieve low rates of unemployment since the mid-1970s. Table 3.1 provides some basic data. Just remember when reading it that the official rates do not count certain types of surplus labor (involuntary part-time and discouraged workers, for example) as unemployed. Therefore, a truer set of unemployment rates would be several percentage points

higher for each nation. For example, the Netherlands has shown remarkably low unemployment rates in comparison to most of the rest of Europe,
where rates stayed high in most countries even in the final years of the
strong economic upturn of the late 1990s. However, there is much disguised
unemployment in the Netherlands. There has been a sharp increase in the
number of involuntary part-time workers. And there is an incredibly large
number of persons receiving publicly funded disability benefits, more than
in almost any other European country. Critics of the Netherlands' official
unemployment statistics believe that many of those collecting disability
benefits are disguised unemployed, persons fully capable of working but
not needed by employers who have focused on making their workforce
more productive through work intensification and new technology.[16]

TABLE 3.1 Unemployment Rates, Selected Rich Countries, 1979–1998

COUNTRY	1979	1989	1998
United States	5.8%	5.3%	4.2%
Japan	2.1	2.3	4.7
Western Germany	2.7	5.6	7.2
France	5.3	9.3	11.3
United Kingdom	4.7	7.3	6.1
Canada	7.5	7.5	7.6
Australia	6.1	6.2	7.2
Finland	6.5	3.3	10.3
Netherlands	5.8	6.9	3.3
Spain	7.7	17.2	15.9
Sweden	2.1	1.6	7.2

SOURCE: Lawrence Mishel, Jared Bernstein, and John Schmitt, The State of Working America 2000/2001
(Ithaca, NY: Cornell University Press), 404.

Data for 1999 through 2002 show some decreases in unemployment rates
for 1999 and 2000 and then increases after that as the rich capitalist
countries faced their first synchronous recession since the early 1970s.
Germany is now suffering double-digit unemployment rates, with many
persons unemployed for long periods of time. Japan is experiencing its
highest unemployment rates of the entire post–Second World War

period.[17] Everywhere unemployment is appearing as an intractable problem, and even in those few countries with relatively low rates, such as the
United States (which used to routinely have the highest rate) and the
Netherlands, there are either reasons to suspect the data or other severe
labor market problems. And nowhere in the rich economies is there the
prospect of pushing unemployment rates down to the levels—below 2 percent—of Japan and some of the European countries in years past.

Before looking at unemployment data for the poor capitalist countries,
we need to examine unemployment among important groups within the
economies of the advanced capitalist nations. There are differences in
unemployment (and underemployment) rates between men and women. In
the United States, the unemployment rates of men and women are roughly
equal, although this is a recent phenomenon. In Canada, Europe, Japan,
Australia, and New Zealand, gender differences vary. In 2000, men and
women had approximately similar unemployment rates in Ireland and
Sweden, and the female rate was lower in Great Britain. Unemployment >

FULL EMPLOYMENT

It is not possible for any modern economy to have a zero unemployment rate. Even if
an economy is growing rapidly and jobs are plentiful, some persons will be looking for
their first jobs and some will be voluntarily changing jobs. Since it takes some time to
find a job, such persons will be unemployed while they are searching, even though
there are jobs available for them. Such unemployment, the result of temporary mis-
matches between available jobs and job seekers, is called "frictional unemployment."
The question is: how much frictional unemployment is there? An answer to this question tells us how well a capitalist economy can do in terms of unemployment; that is, it
will tell us what the unemployment rate is in periods of full employment.

Neoclassical economists have given a variety of answers to this question. In the
early 1960s, when capitalist economies were still in the great post–Second World War
boom, U.S. economists said that 3 percent unemployment was the best we could
expect and what we should try to achieve. As we have seen, such a low rate has seldom been achieved outside of wartime in the United States, although several other
countries have done better than this for extended periods of time. As capitalist
economies entered a prolonged period of slow growth in the early 1970s, mainstream economists raised their estimate of the lowest achievable unemployment

rates for women were substantially higher than for men in Spain, Greece, Italy, France, and Belgium, with the female rate in Spain more than double the male rate. The female rate was slightly lower than the male rate in Japan. However, in nearly all countries, women were less likely to participate in the paid labor force in the first place. For example, their employment rates (the fraction of the female population over a certain age that is employed) are lower than those of men. This means that there is very likely some disguised female unemployment. For example, some women would look for work if there was adequate day care available or if social mores opposed to women working were absent.[18]

A second critical difference in unemployment rates is that between dominant groups and racial and ethnic minorities. In Australia, for example, the unemployment rate for aborigines may be as high as 40 percent, many times higher than the rate for white or Asian Australians.[19] High unemployment rates and other forms of economic and social distress are the lot of indigenous people around the world. American Indians in the

rate to 4 percent. In the 1980s, when unemployment hit its highest levels since the Great Depression, President Ronald Reagan's economic advisors baldly stated that 5.5 percent was the best we could do. Neoclassical economists built elaborate models of the economy to "prove" that once the unemployment rate fell below this level, inflation would accelerate. Therefore, given the obvious harmful effects of inflation, it would be bad policy for the government to even try to get the unemployment rate below its "natural" level. (The economists implied that inflation is an unalloyed evil. What was really on their minds was the harmful effect inflation has on creditors, those who loan out money, who hate inflation because borrowers pay them back money worth less than the money loaned out.)

All of this is to say that unemployment is not just a fact of life in capitalist economies but an ideological construct as well. As we shall see later in this book, the truth is that it is possible to eliminate unemployment and its attendant social costs, but powerful economic forces prevent this from happening. The economists serve as ideologues for these forces by claiming that objective economic analysis demonstrates the social undesirability of full employment. Their "science" begs the question of what it is about capitalist economies that makes it impossible for them to attain full employment except in exceptional circumstances or why low unemployment rates make inflation more likely.

United States have been penned into reservations, where unemployment has been at Depression-era levels for decades.

In the United Kingdom, the unemployment rate in 1999 for ethnic minorities (Black Caribbean, Black African, Other Black, Indian, Pakistani, Bangladeshi, and Chinese) was 13.0 percent for men and 12.3 percent for women. The corresponding white unemployment rates were 5.9 percent for men and 4.7 percent for women.[20] In the United States, there has consistently been a large differential between white and black and between white and Hispanic unemployment rates. Table 3.2 tells the story. The unemployment rates in the table are multiyear averages since 1973.

TABLE 3.2 U.S. Unemployment Rates by Race and Ethnicity, 1973–1999

ANNUAL AVERAGES	WHITE	BLACK	HISPANIC
1973–1979	5.8%	12.5%	9.5%
1979–1989	6.2	14.7	10.3
1992–1999	4.9	10.9	9.0
1989–1999	4.9	11.1	8.9

SOURCE: Lawrence Mishel, Jared Bernstein, and John Schmitt, The State of Working America 2000/2001 (Ithaca, NY: Cornell University Press, 2001), 221.

Over this entire period, Black workers suffered what some might reasonably call depression-level rates of unemployment. Compounding the problems faced by racial and ethnic minorities are the facts that they are the first let go in an economic downturn and they are more likely to be discouraged workers. In the United States, the labor force participation rate of black men has shown a downward trend for many years. While the rate for white men has fallen also, it has not fallen by nearly as much (the labor force participation rate is the ratio of the labor force to the population over sixteen years of age). The only thing that can account for a sharp drop in the black labor force participation rate is a greater degree of discouragement among Blacks about their labor market prospects. The unemployment rate for black male teenagers in many of the United States's inner cities is as high as 50 percent. Housing discrimination and inadequate transportation make it difficult for these youth to leave the central cities. The result is that they stop looking for work or engage in activities that enmesh them in the criminal justice system. A hugely disproportionate share of black male teenagers end up in prison. Either way, whether they drop out of the labor force and live as best they can or get arrested and go to prison, they are disguised unemployed.

HOW MANY ARE UNEMPLOYED?: THE POOR NATIONS

Since so much of the unemployment in poor capitalist countries is disguised, official unemployment rates greatly understate the true amount of surplus labor. Here, we will present some official unemployment data for a selection of poorer capitalist countries and then use a case study of Mexico to see the extent of the difference between the official unemployment rate and the amount of underemployment. The major difference between poor and rich countries in terms of underemployment is that, in the former, underemployment most often takes the form of various forms of marginal employment, in what economists have come to call the "informal sector."

TABLE 3.3 Unemployment Rates in 25 Poor Capitalist Economies (1999, unless noted)

COUNTRY	unemployment rate (year)	rate for women (year)
Algeria	28.7%	24.0
Bangladesh	2.5 (1996)	2.3 (1996)
Belarus	2.0	3.3 (1995)
Bolivia	4.2 (1996)	4.5 (1996)
Brazil	9.6	11.6 (1998)
Bulgaria	14.1	14.1 (1997)
Chile	9.9	7.6 (1998)
China	3.1	1.1 (1994)
Colombia	20.1	23.3
Croatia	13.5	14.5
Ecuador	11.5	16.0 (1998)
Honduras	3.7	3.8
Hungary	7.0	6.3
Jamaica	15.7	22.5

Table 3.3 contains official unemployment rates for a geographically diverse set of poor countries. Note that there is a fairly large range of rates, from a low of 2.0 percent in Mexico and Belarus to a high of 28.7 percent in civil war-ravaged Algeria. Also, note that many of the rates are for 1999, the peak year of the economic expansion in the United States.

Since the Mexican rate is the lowest in the chart, let us look more carefully at the Mexican labor market. A visit to Mexico City would make it difficult to believe the official rate. To the casual eye, this vast and sprawling city, home to some twenty million people, is a vast reservoir of surplus labor. Everywhere you look there are people who obviously do not have regular employment. They are selling shares of lottery tickets or setting up shop on a blanket in the middle of the sidewalk hawking trinkets or snacks. They are begging and hustling and stealing. Scores of workers labor inefficiently over the hedges and shrubs and lawns of the many large churches that attract tourists to their dark and pious interiors. These are the former peasants >

SOURCE: International Labour Organization, *Key Indicators of the Labour Market* (Geneva, Switzerland, 2002), 262–283.

COUNTRY	unemployment rate (year)	rate for women (year)
Kazakhstan	13.7 (1998)	N.A.
Mexico	2.0	2.2
Morocco	22.0	27.6
Nicaragua	13.3	14.5
Pakistan	5.9	14.9
Paraguay	8.2	8.6
Peru	8.0	8.6
Puerto Rico	11.8	9.6
Russia	13.4	13.1
Singapore	4.6	4.6
South Africa	23.3	27.8
Uruguay	11.3	14.6
Venezuela	14.9	14.2 (1997)

thrown from their rural plots into the hand-to-mouth life of the cold-hearted cities. Only by a big stretch of the imagination can they be considered fully employed. If full-time jobs were available, they would take them. But such jobs are not available, so they eke out a living as best they can.

In a report published in the *Monthly Labor Review* (a journal of the U.S. Department of Labor), economist Gary Martin studied unemployment in Mexico.[22] He pointed out that in an economic downturn, workers in a rich country like the United States experience higher unemployment and this shows up in the official unemployment rate. Some unemployed will stop looking for work and therefore not be counted as unemployed, but the government keeps

---

WHEN THEY CAN'T FIND WORK, THE GOVERNMENT LOCKS THEM UP[21]

We are led to believe by the politicians and the media that criminals are somehow defective human beings. Either there is something wrong with their internal moral compass or, in a land of unequaled opportunity, they made remarkably bad choices. They are in prison because that is where they deserve to be. And while they are in prison, they certainly do not deserve to be pampered with color televisions, fancy gymnasiums, and free college educations. Prison time should be hard time, just punishment for heinous crimes.

The trouble with this perspective is that it bears no relationship to reality. Most people are in prison not because they are bad human beings but because they live in a bad system, the relentless dog-eat-dog system of capitalism, American-style. The aggressive accumulation of capital by U.S. corporations, unimpeded in recent decades by strong working-class movements, has systematically created an extraordinarily unequal and unjust society and condemned millions of working people to the social scrap heap.

The long post–Second World War economic boom ended in the United States in the early 1970s. The corporate elite responded ruthlessly to this crisis. Corporations went on the offensive against labor unions, both through gross violations of the labor laws and a combination of mega-mergers, downsizing, outsourcing, plant closings, and mechanization that left workers reeling and unions decimated. With a frightening unity of purpose, corporate capital created political action committees, beefed up lobbying bodies, formed new corporate front groups, and funded right-wing think tanks to pressure the government to cut social welfare spending, eliminate public assistance, priva-

track of them. The same is true for involuntary part-time workers. We can, therefore, calculate an adjusted unemployment rate, what I have been calling an underemployment rate. If data were available, it would be possible to do such a calculation for any country including, in this case, Mexico.

Martin's first step in estimating Mexican unemployment was to put Mexico's official unemployment rate on a par with the definitions used in the United States. For 1998, this yielded an increase in the rate from 3.1 percent (official rate) to 4.8 percent. Adding discouraged workers and those working very short hours (a proxy for involuntary part-time workers) gave a rate of 8.2 percent. This is considerably higher than the official >

tize government services, and spread the word that all of this was in the public interest.

These corporate efforts were extraordinarily successful. Labor unions were unable to defend hard-won worker wages, benefits, and rights; the government did capital's bidding; and the ideological terrain shifted markedly to the right. And most importantly, the bottom line began to move in the appropriate direction. However, capital's gains were workers' losses. Unemployment rose, along with underemployment in the form of part- time labor, contract work, independent contracting, and work at home. Job insecurity became a fact of everyday life for tens of millions of employees. Real wages declined, and to make ends meet, families had to supply more labor to the market. Ironically, as some workers could not find full-time jobs, other workers were moonlighting and taking as much overtime as they could get. The unluckiest workers slipped into poverty or became homeless, joining the victims of the shrinking social safety net. As expected, the unluckiest included a greatly disproportionate share of Black, Hispanic, and Indian Americans, the very people who had been at the back of the line even when times were good.

When people's lives are ripped apart, they are naturally resentful and they can be socially disruptive. Unemployment and job insecurity, as much research shows, lead to family problems, drug and alcohol abuse, and crime. In some circumstances, the economic "underclass" may organize and demonstrate; in other cases it may burn and loot. In either case, the powers that be have a "social problem" on their hands.

The strategy worked out by the state to deal with this social problem has taken two interconnected forms. First politicians, aided by bogus "research" by "scholars" at the reactionary think tanks, began to suggest and then state more openly that those condemned to misery by the corporate onslaught were themselves to blame for their desperate circumstances. This immediately took on a racist tone when it was argued

rate, but it is not that much different than a comparable rate for the United States. Given the economic distress that is visible to the eye in Mexico, it seems unlikely that rates of underemployment could be roughly the same in the United States as in Mexico. As Martin put it, "these adjustments fail to account for the large number of people in Mexico who are counted as employed, but who still live around the economy's margins. These people have only a small counterpart in the United States."[23] In other words, when people are without jobs in Mexico, they find makeshift work in the informal economy, becoming self-employed in extremely precarious and poorly remunerated labor or working for an employer who

that nonwhites were less civil than whites and perhaps even genetically inferior to them. Not only did these claims provide a justification for the harsh treatment the poor were about to receive at the hands of the state, but the latter helped the white majority of poor and unemployed to distance themselves from their nonwhite brethren, splitting the ranks of the dispossessed.

Second, the state began an astounding expansion of its police function. Over the past twenty-five years, new and more punitive criminal laws have been enacted (often racist in their effect; for example, the greater punishment for possession and use of crack cocaine than for equal amounts of powder cocaine); billions of dollars have been allocated to police departments around the country; prisons have been erected as fast as office buildings in a real estate boom; and capital executions have skyrocketed. A phony "war on drugs" has provided cover for much of this (and provided, as well, a justification for naked imperialism in places like Colombia and Peru).

Caught in this nefarious web of economic stagnation and political repression, the poor have found themselves force marched into the criminal justice system. The results have been nothing less than a police state for the poor and a de facto "ethnic cleansing" for people of color. In 1998, nearly six million persons were either in prison, on probation, on parole, or under house arrest or electronic surveillance. By contrast only 380,000 persons were so situated in 1975. Over two million people are actually behind bars, more than half of whom are black. In 1995, 6,926 blacks per 100,000 adults were in prison, compared to 919 whites. An incredible thirty million people have been profiled in computer data banks maintained by the police, and these are accessible not only to law enforcement agencies but to private employers. Public monies devoted to prisons have spiraled upward at a rate far in excess of the rate of increase in military spending, and they have dwarfed increases in spending

hires few workers and pays them below the minimum wage.

Depending on the definition used, the informal sector in urban Mexico ranges from 20 to 54 percent. The United Nations defines informal enterprises as "household operations with household finances and business finances virtually indistinguishable from one another. . . . [There must also be] some sort type of nonregistration with proper governing bodies, of either the enterprise or its employees [and] . . . a maximum size."[24] By these criteria, the informal sector made up 29.5 percent of all nonfarm employment in Mexico. To give his readers a more specific notion of what is meant by informal work, Martin says,

on education and other forms of social welfare, many of which have actually declined. Since 1992 four states (California, Florida, New York, and Texas) have allocated more than one billion dollars to prisons; since 1993 more than 200 new prisons have been built, excluding private facilities.

The burgeoning prison-industrial complex is racist to the core— 9.4 percent of black adults compared to 1.9 percent of white adults are in prison, on probation, or on parole. The ratio for blacks rises to nearly one-third for black men aged 20 to 29 and to an amazing 80 percent for black men in the heart of the black ghettoes. Black persons comprise about 13 percent of all drug users, but one-third of blacks arrested are charged with drug offenses, and three-quarters of blacks jailed are imprisoned for drug convictions. Police SWAT teams are swooping down on black and immigrant communities with increasing regularity, sowing terror in what can best be described as Vietnam-like "search and destroy" missions. Big-city mayors like former New York City mayor Rudolph Giuliani have literally made it a crime to be poor or homeless or worst of all, poor and black. Police now routinely shoot unarmed and sometimes mentally ill persons and ask questions later. Prison guards have forced prisoners to engage in gladiator fights and kill the loser.

The criminalization of the poverty wrought by unregulated capital accumulation is a step in the direction of establishing a police state. Those in prison are simply the most exploited members of the working class. Through the prison classes I recently taught, I have come to see the truth of Eugene Debs's prison creed:

While there is a lower class I am in it;
While there is a criminal element I am of it;
While there's a soul in prison I am not free.

Surveys in Mexico have found that 60 percent of informal businesses have no fixed address outside the home, and more than 80 percent borrowed no money to finance their operations. The life of the business tends to be quite short, particularly for the smallest firms, and business incomes are low. Wages also are low and fringe benefits are minimal or nonexistent. To the extent that they evade required labor laws, registration requirements, and often taxes as well, informal enterprises can be considered illegal. The main safety net against failure in an informal enterprise is that low legal, technical, and financial barriers make it relatively easy for a new one to be started.[25]

To make Mexico's unemployment rate more connected to the nation's labor market reality, Martin added to the officially unemployed those who earn less than the minimum wage. (Mexico's minimum wage is pathetically low and absolutely insufficient to sustain life. In addition, it has been sharply eroded by inflation.) Most of these workers are in the informal sector and would be considered as unemployed in the United States. This calculation adds 11.4 percentage points to the unemployment rate. Adding the very short hour workers and the discouraged workers yields an underemployment rate (expanded to include the very low wage workers) in excess of 16 percent. While none of these calculations are without flaws, they certainly give us a more realistic picture of wasted labor. We also should remember that millions of Mexico's disguised unemployed now live in the cities of its northern neighbor, forced to leave their homeland out of economic necessity. When an economic crisis strikes the United States, we do not see people fleeing across the border into Mexico, but the reverse is a commonplace occurrence.

Mexico's hidden unemployed are not unique. Much the same could be said about any poor capitalist economy. In fast-growing China, there are millions of hidden unemployed. There, the number of underemployed may be as high as 20 percent of the urban workforce. As China has become more capitalist, it has begun to suffer from the capitalist disease— unemployment. Millions of peasants have lost meaningful access to the land and have moved into the cities, where, like their Mexican counterparts, they try to stay one step ahead of starvation. Yet China's official unemployment rate in the period 1996 to 1998 averaged 3.1 percent.[26] And to say that tens of millions of persons worldwide are underemployed because they are working in marginal employment in the informal sector is not to say that they are not working hard. Quite the opposite.

We have seen that all capitalist economies experience unemployment, in both good and bad times. We have also seen that official unemployment rates understate the amount of wasted labor, in both rich and poor capitalist countries, although the problem is more severe in the poor nations. The implication of these facts is that there is a great deal of surplus labor in the world as a whole. In fact, reports from the United Nations' International Labour Organization (ILO) tell us that the world is literally awash in surplus labor, and by extension, awash in the human misery that is unemployment's inevitable by-product. In recent reports, the ILO estimates that in 2000 there were 160 million people in the world who were openly unemployed, that is, without work but searching for a job. This is approximately 6 percent of a labor force of about 2.7 billion. However, the openly unemployed are just the tip of the iceberg. The ILO also estimates that there are another 750 to 900 million persons who are underemployed, "which means that their work schedule is substantially shorter than a full shift despite their willingness to increase it or that they get paid less than what is necessary for living."[27]

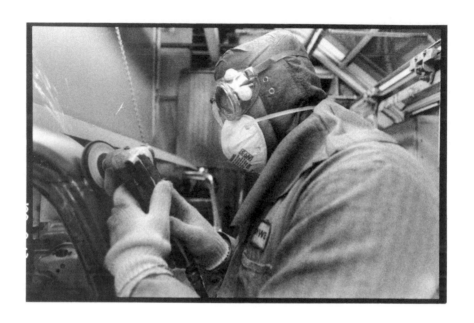

CHAPTER FOUR: **Bad Jobs, Low Pay and Overwork**

HOW JOBS ARE DESIGNED TO STAY LOW-PAID

To hear mainstream economists tell the story, the world's economies face perennial shortages of skilled laborers. The electronics revolution has meant that the skill content of contemporary jobs has steadily risen, requiring workers to be not just literate but computer literate. The future will be one of most work becoming relatively skilled, and so societies must see to it that their workers are up to the task by being adequately schooled and trained.

With as much as a third of the world's labor force consisting of persons unemployed or underemployed, it is impossible to give credence to what are essentially fantasies about work. To understand the world of work, we need to grasp a basic and important point. All economists agree that the goal of private businesses is to maximize profits. Whenever possible, therefore, businesses will try to cut their costs of production, including the cost of labor power. The cost of labor power is measured not just by the money outlays for wages and benefits but indirectly by the ability of workers to interfere with managerial control of the workplace. That is, managers do not want workers to be able to interfere with the smooth flow of production.

If we look at workers in terms of skill levels, it is clear that skilled workers are more expensive than unskilled workers and that they also have the capability of interfering with the process of production to a greater extent than do unskilled workers (at least unorganized unskilled workers). They are more expensive because they are, by definition, in shorter supply. They are more troublesome for management because they understand, again by virtue of their skill, the production processes employers want to control.

If this argument is correct, then employers will economize on the use of skilled labor whenever they can.[1] There are two ways for them to do this. First, they can use what is called the "detailed division of labor." Here the

91

employer studies a particular skilled work task (using an industrial engineer) and breaks the task down into its component parts or details. Consider as an example a skilled metal worker making metal funnels. Suppose the worker has an order for 100 funnels. If we observe the way in which the worker organizes the work, we would see that he or she has broken the job down into steps, and each step is performed 100 times before moving on to the next step. The worker will make a pattern for the funnel, and then, using the pattern, lay out on sheets of metal 100 funnels. Next, the 100 shapes will be cut from the metal. Then, the shapes will be bent to form the funnels. Then the ends of the shaped funnels will be connected. Then the funnels will be smoothed and polished and given whatever finishing touches the worker deems necessary. The reason the funnel maker divides the work into steps and then performs the steps serially 100 times is because it is more efficient to do it this way rather than making one complete funnel then a second and so on up to one hundred.

When employers began to watch how workers like the funnel makers did their job, they hit upon a revolutionary idea. Why not substitute unskilled workers to do the simpler details of the job and use the skilled workers to do only those parts of the job that could not be simplified to the point at which an unskilled worker could do them? This idea, the detailed division of labor, is a ubiquitous feature of capitalist economies, an inevitable outcome of a system in which production is organized by private owners to maximize profits. Its implications for work are profound. Skilled (and therefore more highly paid) workers will always be under attack by employers, and the general trend of capitalist production will be the maximum use of unskilled (and therefore less highly paid) laborers. We should not expect to see a world in which more and more work is skilled and highly paid. On the contrary, we should expect to see a world in which most people labor at unskilled and poorly paid jobs.

Compounding the effect of the detailed division of labor is the second great creator of unskilled labor—mechanization. Throughout the history of capitalism, employers have relentlessly mechanized their production. Neoclassical economists believe that machinery tends to raise the skill requirements of jobs. However, the opposite is generally the case. In a series of studies a generation ago, James Bright of the Harvard Business School examined a large number of the most technologically advanced production sites in the United States. He found that the more sophisticated the machinery used, the lower the skill required of the worker. This is because those aspects of jobs requiring skills have been increasingly incorporated into the machinery. For example, it takes far less skill to operate a numerically controlled machine (which can make complex cuts in metal through the use of a computer program in which the mechanics of the cut are stored) than to do the work of a traditional machinist. It takes more skill to work as a secretary using an old-fashioned typewriter than it does to type using a keyboard and a word processing program. The intelligence is built into the machine and the program. Today, unskilled workers in Mexico can make complex automobile engines for a fraction of the wages received by workers in the United States precisely because the detailed division of labor and machinery have removed the skill content of the job.

Of course, skilled workers might also receive low pay and toil under poor working conditions if there is a large pool of them seeking a limited number of jobs. China and India have trained tens of thousands of skilled computer programmers, so many that they cannot find decent employment. They therefore work for companies in the advanced capitalist countries, and the level of mechanization is such that they do not even have to come to the rich countries to work. They can labor as independent contractors from India, and their product can be transmitted electronically to their employers. Similarly, many college teachers in the rich countries are poorly paid part-timers. More of them have been educated than are needed by cost-conscious colleges and universities, and so they must make a living as poorly paid temporary workers, often working for several colleges at once.

THE WORK WE DO: THE MOST BASIC TRENDS

There are several universal trends in employment in capitalist economies. The first, and most general, is that over time, fewer people are employed in agriculture. This is due to the combined effect of the forcible evictions of peasants from their land, bank foreclosures, falling prices for agricultural commodities, and rapid technological change. The evictions allowed the new land owners to come into possession of large parcels of land that they used to make money through the production of cash crops, utilizing wage labor or, often, especially in the beginning, slave or semi-slave labor. As capitalism developed and spread, people tended to leave the countryside to work in urban areas, either forced out by mass-production technology or drawn by the slightly less burdensome life outside of the rural areas.

In the rich capitalist countries, only a small percentage of the labor force works in agriculture. In the poor nations, a much higher fraction still labor on the land, although the trend is for this fraction to get smaller. Table 4.1 shows this aspect of employment. Although the irreversible trend away from agricultural employment has been evident for a long time, it is remarkable how many people still work in agriculture. In 1990, just twelve years ago, the International Labour Organization (ILO) estimated that 47 percent of the world's economically active population was in agriculture. The estimate for 2000 is slightly over 40 percent, a decline but still a sizable proportion.[2] In numbers, we are talking about more than one billion persons. As the percentages in Table 4.1 imply, the overwhelming majority of these agriculture workers are in the poor countries. In fact, about 60 percent of the world's agricultural labor force is in just two countries: China and India.[3] These workers, many of them children, labor intensively on tiny plots of land, or, increasingly, as wage workers, or as both small-scale peasants and as wage laborers. When the neoclassical economists talk about a future of highly paid skilled workers, they must be talking about the very distant future. For now, we can exclude more than one billion workers from this pipe dream.

It is a curious thing that in the planet's poorest countries, there are hundreds of millions of farm laborers, but these countries cannot feed even the farm workers adequately, much less their urban counterparts. The story is always the same. Peasants lose their land; the land is sown with cash crops for export; some of the former peasants become farm wage workers; and the rest of the former peasants migrate to the cities where they provide a pool of underutilized labor ready to be exploited anew.[4]

The second great labor force trend is the rising labor market participation of women. This trend is tied to the first one. In rural areas, women work more frequently as unpaid laborers, on household plots of land and as homemakers, than do men. But as rural inhabitants move to the cities, women are forced into wage labor as a matter of their own and their family's survival. Here we are talking mainly about the poor countries. Sometimes women move by themselves into urban areas and are expected to remit money to their families back home. Employers in electronics and garment sweatshops, among many others, seek out women employees, believing them to be more tractable than men. As one employer in the film *The Global Assembly Line* said in a matter-of-fact tone of female workers in Manila, "These women can take a lot of abuse." They do, indeed, take a lot of abuse:

abysmal pay, long hours, boring and repetitive motions, noxious chemi-
cals, oppressive heat and cold, and physical and sexual abuse from employers and male workers. However, as we shall see in the last chapter, they also
have begun to organize to prevent abuse and improve their circumstances.   >

TABLE 4.1 Percentage of the Labor Force in Agriculture, Selected Countries

COUNTRY	1990 unless noted	1999 unless noted
Algeria	35.8% (1980)	26.1% (1990)
Bangladesh	66.4	63.2 (1996)
Belgium	3.1	2.2 (1998)
Brazil	22.8	23.4 (1998)
China	53.5	47.5 (1998)
Chad	87.9 (1980)	83.2 (1990)
Czech Republic	12.3	5.1
Denmark	5.5	3.6 (1998)
Ecuador	6.9	7.3
Ethiopia	93.0 (1994)	88.6 (1995)
Germany	3.6	2.8
Guinea	90.9 (1980)	87.2 (1990)
India	69.1	66.7 (1995)
Indonesia	55.9	45.0 (1998)
Japan	7.2	5.2
Netherlands	4.5	3.2 (1998)
Pakistan	51.1	47.3
Philippines	45.2	39.1
Thailand	64.0	48.5
United Kingdom	2.1	1.6
United States	2.9	2.6
Vietnam	74.7 (1991)	68.8 (1997)

SOURCE: International Labour Organization, Key Indicators of the Labour Market 2001-2002
(Geneva, Switzerland, 2002), 110–130.

Of the 180 countries for which United Nations information is available, 122, or 68 percent, show an increase in the fraction of women who were economically active between 1990 and 2000. That is, the labor force participation rate for women increased in most countries over this last decade of the twentieth century. Of the fifty-eight countries that showed either a decrease in this fraction or no change, forty-three were in Africa or in nations that were formerly socialist.[6] In the African nations, the participation rate was typically high to start with. At the same time, economic growth was very low or even negative. These two facts probably combined to drive some women out of the labor market, as women were forced back into the household to devote all of their time to child care and subsistence agriculture. In the formerly socialist societies, there had been a strong emphasis on encouraging women to actively participate in the paid labor market. However, with the destruction of socialism came severe economic

---

CENTRAL AMERICA'S CITIES[5]

Peasants have been flocking to Central America's cities, driven by war, natural disasters, and the growing inability to survive the harsh rural life. It is estimated that by 2010, 55 percent of Central America's population will live in cities. To hear some economists talk, urbanization is itself a sign of economic development. Of course, it is seldom mentioned that the misery of rural life is not something inherent in it, but the result of centuries of imperialism and domestic repression. Even the natural disasters are compounded by the misuse of the land resulting from the same forces.

But while rural life is abysmal, urban life is itself filled with horrors. Here is a description of the life of Armina de Jesus in Santa Tecla, El Salvador: "Here on the western fringe of the capital's sprawl, Mrs. De Jesus and her family have no electricity, running water or title to the land they occupy. Six people sleep on two beds jammed into one room, laundry dangling from a ceiling beam. Her husband has no prospect of steady employment. He does odd jobs to put food on the table." Mrs. De Jesus's life is by no means uncommon; it is the rule and not the exception. If her daughter someday gets a job in one of the garment sweatshops or export processing zones common in her country, is interviewed by a university researcher and says that her life is better than what it was on the farm or in the Santa Tecla shack, we should remember that misery has its degrees but is still misery. No doubt it is better to be in some circles of hell rather than others. But it is still hell. And the prospects of getting out of hell are not very good.

depression and a revival of gender discrimination, and these compelled women to leave the labor force, or that part of the labor force that is officially recorded. If African nations ever start to grow again and if capitalism deepens in the formerly socialist societies, we can expect to see increases in the labor market participation rates for women.

In the rich capitalist countries, the labor force participation rate of women has been rising for many years. The United Nations data show that for the United States, Canada, Norway, Sweden, Finland, Denmark., Iceland, Great Britain, Ireland, France, Spain, Portugal, Italy, Austria, Germany, France, Belgium, the Netherlands, Luxembourg, Switzerland, Japan, Australia, and New Zealand, only Denmark, Finland, and Sweden (countries with already very high female participation rates) did not show an increase in female labor force participation between 1990 and 2000.[7]

It is often argued that the rise in the labor force participation rate of women is an unalloyed blessing for women. Working for wages gives women much greater economic independence and thereby makes them less subservient to their families and husbands. It is, therefore, very often better for women to work for wages than to be homemakers or to be trapped in rural villages. I do not think that such arguments capture what really happens to most women when they enter the paid labor market. It would be more appropriate to say that women trade one kind of exploitation for another.[8]

If women are brutally exploited in the countryside, they are treated none too kindly in the sweatshops of the cities or in the *maquiladora* plants along the Mexican–U.S. border. A 1996 report on women workers in Indonesia's Nike plants describes the women as "walking ghosts in Satan's mills."[9] A supervisor told of his training in such a plant, learning "skills to control women, which usually translated into verbal abuse such as 'fuck you' and 'move, you stupid bitch,' to be used indiscriminately against the workers." What factory work does give to women is a better chance to organize collectively. Workers are massed together in concentrated spaces, and in these places they learn about each other, discovering that what they have in common is that they are all workers, suffering the same fate. But this has nothing to do with any sort of liberating aspect of capitalism. Rather, it has to do with its contradictions.

The third general employment trend, one most observable in the rich capitalist countries, is the shift of labor away from producing goods to the production of services. There are three primary reasons for this. First, there has been phenomenal technological change in the production of goods, that has

allowed businesses to produce a growing quantity of goods with fewer workers. Today many more automobiles can be produced with far fewer workers
than in 1950, and the same is true for most goods, as well as the intermediate
outputs necessary for their production, such as steel, coal, glass, and oil. The
laborers freed from goods production have then provided a large pool of
workers available for the production of services, some of which are essential
for the production of goods. The modern production of goods requires a
tremendous flow of paperwork, and this necessitates an army of clerical
workers. The same can be said for some financial sector workers.

The second reason for a shift of employment away from goods toward
services is the growing tendency of transnational corporations to move production from the relatively high- wage rich countries to the poor nations. As
we saw in the last chapter, a lot of goods production has been transferred
from the United States to Mexico, where wages are less than one-tenth as
high and environmental and other social regulations of production are nonexistent or minimally enforced. All sorts of consumer goods are produced in
poor countries, from most types of clothing and shoes to toys and trinkets.
An indirect proof of the move of manufacturing to the poor countries is that
today there is a negative correlation between the share of manufacturing in
total employment and per capita GDP. Higher income countries no longer
have a high ratio of manufacturing employment to total employment.[10]

A third factor inducing the shift toward service production is the growing wealth of the rich nations. As incomes rise in a country like the United
States, consumers demand more services. They travel more, and this
increases the demand for (and therefore the employment in) all sorts of
travel-related services. The same is true for the demand for health care,
compounded by the fact that the populations of the rich countries are getting relatively older. Service employment is also increasing in the poor
countries, but in them most service employment is in the informal sector.

Table 4.2 provides data on service sector employment for the major rich
capitalist nations. Services include transportation, communication, public
utilities, trade, finance, public administration, private household services,
and miscellaneous services. The period covered is 1960 to 2000, so the
table gives a picture of long-term trends. Data like these are generally
unavailable for the poor nations. Notice that in every country except the
United States (which already had the largest relative service sector employment in 1960 of all of the countries in the table), the gain in service sector
employment is at least twenty percentage points over the forty years.

TABLE 4.2 Percent of Civilian Employment in Service Sector, 1960 and 2000

COUNTRY	1960	2000
United States	58.1%	75.3%
Canada	54.7	74.8
Australia	54.5 (1965)	73.8
Japan	41.9	63.8
France	39.3	72.1
Germany	40.2	63.6 (1999)
Italy	33.4	61.5 (1999)
Netherlands	50.8	75.0 (1998)
Sweden	44.6	72.6 (1999)
United Kingdom	49.2	72.2 (1998)

SOURCE: This chart was constructed from U.S. Bureau of Labor Statistics data available at http://www.bls/fls.

THE WORK WE DO: PLENTY OF BAD JOBS
IN THE RICH NATIONS

Management gurus keep telling us that work is constantly getting better: cleaner, less physically burdensome and dangerous, more demanding of our intelligence, and better paying. The new world of work is that of the knowledge worker, using information to design better products and better workplaces. Of course, there is work like this. Scientists, engineers, artists of all kinds, computer specialists, high-level politicians and bureaucrats, some health care workers like doctors, some lawyers, some college professors, financiers, professional athletes, and a few others—all of these workers get to do that which is fundamentally human: they get to conceptualize their work and then actually execute it. They are relatively well-paid, have considerable job autonomy, and are respected by the society at large. A lot of them are engaged in the production of harmful or trivial products, including those infamous "weapons of mass destruction," and some of them are consummate liars and cheats (think of politicians and financiers), but let us ignore these minor points and concede that, for the most part, these are "good" jobs.

The problem is that, even in the rich capitalist countries, these good jobs constitute a tiny fraction of all jobs. There are, no doubt, millions of "decent" jobs—unionized employment in factories, transportation, and the like, mid-level managers, nurses, public school teachers, civil servants— all the jobs workers say they are satisfied with in opinion surveys. But most of these jobs are stressful, rely on only a fraction of the workers' capabilities, don't pay all that well, and are subject to the deskilling effects of the detailed division of labor and mechanization discussed above. Even some of the good jobs mentioned in the last paragraph—college professors, lawyers, and physicians come to mind—are rapidly being debased by these same factors.

And then there are the dreadful jobs, much more numerous than most people realize. Let us focus our attention on the United States, the quintessential rich nation, the country whose economy is the envy of the world and toward whose structure the other rich countries are rapidly heading. In this high-tech, new economy, the ten occupations estimated by the U.S. Bureau of Labor Statistics to have the largest job growth between 2000 and 2010 are food preparation and service workers, cus-

---

CONSIDER THE WORKERS I

Consider the poultry workers: In the United States there are several hundred thousand poultry factory workers, more than there are steel workers. Typically immigrants, they labor for slightly above minimum wage as "scalders," "eviscerators," and "skinners." The "live hangers" "fasten incoming birds to shackles at the rate of 25 or more per minute." "Workers work quickly and often cut themselves. Motions are fast and repetitive. . . . The noise is overwhelming." "The line is often so fast paced that it looks like chaos. Arms, boxes, and poultry fly in every direction. Fat globules and blood soon speckle glasses, bits of chicken stick to collars, water and slime soak the feet and ankles, and nicks injure the wrists. A woman wraps her forearms in plastic tape because bits of chicken penetrate her wounds and cause infection."[12]

Consider the automobile worker Ben Hamper, who describes a visit to the plant to see what his father does. He says,

tomer service representatives, registered nurses, retail salespersons, computer support specialists, cashiers, general office clerks, security guards, computer software engineers, and waiters and waitresses.[11] A book could be written about the many bad qualities of most of these occupations, Secretary of Labor Reich's paean to cashiering notwithstanding. Among these fast-growing jobs are registered nurses and computer support specialists, jobs most people would consider decent, but both jobs are rapidly sliding down the job desirability scale as they are rationalized by cost-conscious managers.

In 2000, there were approximately 130 million employed persons in the United States. The Bureau of Labor Statistics (BLS) breaks this employment down into several hundred occupations. There are twenty-two broad occupational categories. The five largest broad categories, accounting for nearly 60 percent of all employment, are education, training, and library; food preparation and serving related; sales and related; office and administrative support; production; and transportation and material moving. Let us look at the largest occupations in each of these subgroups and see what they pay per year on average: >

We stood there for forty minutes or so, a miniature lifetime, and the pattern never changed. Car, windshield. Car, windshield. Drudgery piled atop drudgery. Cigarette to cigarette. Decades rolling through the rafters, bones turning to dust, stubborn clocks gagging down flesh, another windshield, another cigarette, wars blinking on and off, thunderstorms muttering the alphabet, crows on power lines asleep or dead, that mechanical octopus squirming against nothing, nothing, nothingness.[13]

Consider the lock box processors: These are mail processors, invariably women. Inside of former warehouses and factories, "long lines of women sit at Spartan desks, slitting envelopes, sorting contents, and filling out 'control cards' that record how many letters they have opened and how long it has taken them." There are quotas: three envelopes per minute or 8,500 keystrokes an hour. "The room is silent. Talking is not allowed. There are no outside windows. . . . Coffee mugs, pictures of kids, or other personal artifacts are forbidden."[14]

TABLE 4.3   Selected Occupations and Yearly Pay, United States, 2000

OCCUPATION GROUP	OCCUPATIONS WITH LARGEST EMPLOYMENT	YEARLY PAY
Education, Training, and Library	Elementary School Teachers (1,409,140)	$41,980
	Teacher Assistants (1,159,110)	18,770
Food Preparation and Serving Related	Combined Food Prep. and Serving (2,159,940)	14,240
	Counter Attendants (2,008,760)	14,750
Sales and Related	Cashiers (3,338,840)	15,730
	Counter and Rental Clerks (3,964,680)	20,260
Office and Administrative Support	Bookkeeping and Related Clerks (1,663,530)	26,950
	Customer Service Reps (1,907,890)	26,530
	Stock Clerks and Order Fillers (1,771,780)	20,650
	Secretaries, excluding Legal, Medical, and Executive (1,698,080)	24,910
	General Office Clerks (2,674,710)	22,290
Production Occupations	First-line Supervisors (769,540)	43,020
	Team Assemblers (1,306,430)	23,490
	Inspector, Testers, Sorters, etc. (571,220)	28,010
	Helpers (533,720)	19,350
Transportation and Material Moving	Truck Drivers, Heavy (1,577,070)	32,810
	Truck Drivers, Light (1,033,220)	24,620
	Laborers and Freight, Stock and Material Movers, Hand (2,120,640)	20,460
	Packers and Packagers, Hand (1,020,640)	17,030

SOURCE: http://www.bls.gov/news.release/ocwage.nro.htm.

Notice the low pay of most of these jobs. Of course, pay does not completely define a job; there are low-paying jobs that require skill and are interesting to do. I once worked as a researcher for the United Farm Workers Union in California for practically nothing, yet this was one of the most exciting jobs I ever had. However, the very names of most of the jobs in the table tell us what kind of jobs they are—boring, repetitive, perhaps dangerous, unskilled, and leading nowhere. For the higher paying jobs above, the average pay is probably misleading. Unionized heavy truck drivers make a good deal more money than do their nonunion counterparts, who drive extremely long hours in often dangerous circumstances and unsafe vehicles. Many first-level supervisors in production make little money and also must put in long hours of labor. Unions in urban areas have made the pay of elementary school teachers high by historical standards, and their pay drives up the average. Thousands of school teachers work for much less than $30,000 per year.

The more than ten million people who toil as teacher assistants, food preparers, counter attendants, production helpers, laborers, and packers have jobs which pay close to or below the official poverty level of income for a family of four. And there are plenty of jobs in occupational categories usually associated with skill and high pay that, in reality, pay little. Nine percent of all management jobs pay less than $13.50 per hour, as do 7.5 percent of all computer and mathematical jobs, 12.3 percent of all legal jobs, 34.4 percent of all education jobs, 40.3 percent of all sports, entertainment, and media jobs, and 20.8 percent of all health practitioner and technical jobs.[15] Can anyone believe that we are rapidly on our way to the elimination of all of these low-paying and relatively unskilled jobs?

It is a bit unfair to use the United States in an analysis of work in the rich capitalist countries. Wages are higher in Western Europe for many of the occupations listed in Table 4.3, and, in countries like Germany, there has been a focus on training skilled and semi-skilled technicians. However, there are plenty of bad jobs there too, often performed by immigrants, and the trend is definitely toward the creation of more of them, as European countries push full throttle to copy the U.S. labor market model. High wages give European employers even greater incentive to use the detailed division of labor and mechanization to avoid using skilled labor.

THE WORK WE DO:

BAD JOBS GALORE IN THE POOR COUNTRIES

In the famous chapter "The Working Day" in Karl Marx's masterpiece, *Capital*, there are numerous heartrending descriptions of work in the factories and shops of England during the first half of the nineteenth century. As a consequence of working-class agitation, the English parliament had appointed a group of factory inspectors to investigate conditions in the "dark satanic mills" and industrial towns of the world's most advanced capitalist country. Their reports were published in what were called "Blue

Books," and Marx was the first social scientist to use them extensively in his work. These Blue Books paint a remarkable picture of human misery. Marx presents reports of children as young as six working twelve and more hours per day; of workers producing "Lucifer matches" in factories that Dante could have used in his *Inferno*; of potters living in towns in which the health of the workers was abysmal but would have been still worse except for intermarriage with "healthier races"; of a town in which the workers petitioned the town's leaders to pass a bill limiting the daily hours of work to eighteen. In one particularly moving passage, Marx describes the death of a garment worker:

> In the last week of June, 1863, all the London daily papers published a paragraph with the "sensational" heading, "Death from simple over-work." It dealt with the death of the milliner, Mary Anne Walkley, 20 years of age, employed in a highly respectable dressmaking establishment, exploited by a lady with the pleasant name of Elise. The old, oft-told story, was once more recounted. The girl worked, on an average, 16 1/2 hours, during the season often 30 hours, without a break, whilst her failing labor power was revived by occasional supplies of sherry, port, or coffee. It was just now the height of the season. It is necessary to conjure up in the twinkling of an eye the gorgeous dresses for the noble ladies bidden to the ball in honor of the newly-imported Princess of Wales. Mary Anne Walkley had worked without intermission for 26 1/2 hours, with 60 other girls, 30 in one room, that only afforded 1/3 of the cubic feet of air required for them. At night, they slept in pairs in one of the stifling holes into which the bedroom was divided by a partition of board. And this was one of the best millinery establishments in London. Mary Anne Walkley fell ill on the Friday, died on Sunday, without, to the astonishment of Madame Elise, having previously completed the work in hand....[16]

When we turn our attention to the poor nations, we find everywhere miserable employment, every bit as bad as that described by Marx nearly 140 years ago. We noted at the beginning of this chapter the children of Pakistan, making rugs and soccer balls and laboring in the fields. Pakistan is no exception when it comes to child labor in poor countries (and child labor certainly exists in rich countries, often in conditions as bad as anywhere in the world. There are about 250,000 farm laborers in the United States. Many of them bring their children with them to work in the fields. Garment sweatshop workers, too, use their children as helpers.).

The International Labour Office (ILO) of the United Nations has done extensive research on the pervasiveness of child labor around the world. It estimates that there are about 250 million children between the ages of five and fourteen working; about half of these children work full-time. Table 4.4 provides some details. The data do not include children who engage in regular unpaid labor. For example, many young girls labor in their own households, taking care of other children and performing basic household duties, usually so that their parents can work for pay. This type of work is just as likely to keep children out of school or sporadically attending school as is paid labor. Also most children work in rural areas, with a rural child being about twice as likely to work as an urban child. However, as societies become more urban, we can expect to see a growing proportion of urban children working.

TABLE 4.4   Some Facts about Child Labor, 1990s

TOTAL NUMBER: 250,000,000

REGIONAL DISTRIBUTION (%)		INDUSTRY DISTRIBUTION	
Africa	32.0%	Agriculture and Related	70.4%
Asia (excluding Japan)	61.0	Mining and Quarrying	0.9
Latin America and Caribbean	7.0	Manufacturing	8.3
Oceania (excluding		Construction	1.9
Australia and New Zealand	.2	Wholesale and Retail Trade,	
		Restaurants and Hotels	8.3
GENDER DISTRIBUTION		Transport, Storage, and	
		Communication	3.8
Boys	56.0%	Community and Personal	
Girls	44.0	Services	6.5

SOURCE: Kebebew Ashagrie, "Statistics on Working Children and Hazardous Child Labour in Brief," at http://www.ilo.org/public/english/comp/child/stats.htm.

These millions of children often work extremely long hours for pitifully low wages. In some studies of particular areas, a majority of children worked at least nine hours per day, and many labored seven days a week, often at night. Children are very frequently injured at work and suffer a wide variety of diseases and illnesses. As the ILO reports:

Recent surveys at the national level have demonstrated that a very high proportion of the children were physically injured or fell ill while working. These included punctures, broken or complete loss of body parts, burns and skin disease, eye and hearing impairment, respiratory and gastro-intestinal illnesses, fever, headaches from excessive heat in the fields or in factories. . . . A large majority of these children had to consult medical doctors and some had to be hospitalized. Many affected children had to miss work for a time, with some stopping work for good.[17]

We shall have occasion to return to the issue of child labor in the last chapter. It is a complex issue, as many families are reliant on the earnings of their children. For that reason, it cannot be approached as if the problem existed in isolation.

We saw above in our discussion of Mexico that unemployment is often disguised as various types of informal employment. The same is true throughout the third world. The activist organization Women in Informal Employment Globalizing and Organizing (WIEGO) tells us that "In 1993 an international definition of the informal sector was adopted, to include those who work in small unregistered enterprises, both employers and

---

CONSIDER THE WORKERS II

Consider the camel jockeys: In early 2002, criminals in Pakistan were uncovered kidnaping children as young as five and transporting them to countries in the Middle East to be used as jockeys in camel races. Investigators found that these hapless children were denied adequate food so that they could maintain a low weight.[18]

Consider the child sex workers: In South Asia, there may be as many as two million sex workers. Mira, a child prostitute in Bombay, was sent, at age thirteen, by her parents from her village in Nepal to work, they thought, as a domestic servant. There are at least 20,000 child prostitutes in Bombay, "displayed in row after row of zoo-like animal cages." We are told,

> 13-year-old Mira of Nepal was offered a job as a domestic worker in Bombay, India. She arrived at a brothel on Bombay's Falkland Road, where tens of thousands of young women are displayed in row after row of zoo-like animal cages. Her father had been duped into giving her to a trafficker. When she refused to have sex, she was dragged into a torture chamber in a dark alley

employees, as well as self-employed persons who work in their own or family businesses."[21] Table 4.5 shows the extent of informal employment in major regions of the world as well as in specific countries.

>

TABLE 4.5 Informal Employment, 1990s

REGION / COUNTRY	nonagricultural employment	new jobs	urban employment
Latin America and Caribbean	57.0%	40.0%	83.0%
Africa	78.0	61.0	93.0
Asia	45–80	40–60	N.A.
Rich nations (including agriculture)	16.0		

	WOMEN	MEN		WOMEN	MEN
Benin	97.0%	83.0%	Bolivia	74.0	55.0
Kenya	83.0	59.0	Colombia	44.0	42.0
South Africa	30.0	14.0	Venezuela	47.0	47.0

SOURCE: http://www.wiego.org/main/fact1.html.

---

used for "breaking in" new girls. She was locked in a narrow, windowless room without food or water. On the fourth day, one of the madam's thugs [called a "goonda"] wrestled her to the floor and banged her head against the concrete until she passed out. When she awoke, she was naked; a rattan cane smeared with pureed red chili peppers shoved into her vagina. Later she was raped by the goonda. Afterwards, she complied with their demands. The madam told Mira that she had been sold to the brothel for 50,000 rupees (about US$1,700), that she had to work until she paid off her debt. Mira was sold to a client who then became her pimp.[19]

Consider the child brick kiln workers: "My master bought, sold, and traded us like livestock, and sometimes he shipped us great distances. The boys were beaten frequently to make them work long hours. The girls were often violated. My best friend got ill after she was raped, and when she couldn't work, the master sold her to a friend of his in a village a thousand kilometers away. Her family was never told where she was sent, and they never saw her again."[20]

While workers in the informal sector contribute a considerable amount of output to their nation's GDP, the conditions under which they labor are usually deplorable. Although precise data are not available, it is safe to say that nearly all workers in the informal sector lack any form of what the ILO calls "social protection." "An estimated 80% of the world's workers [lack] adequate social protection. In many low-income countries 'formal protection for old age and invalidity, or for sickness and health care reaches only a tiny proportion of the population: meanwhile 3,000 people a day die as a consequence of work-related accidents or disease.'"[22] It is important to understand that women are especially likely to be employed in the informal sector. Often women form a special category of informal workers, laboring at home with their children, doing everything from rolling cigarettes to doing garment piecework.

Another type of employment in poor countries is sweatshop labor. A sizeable movement against sweatshop employment has developed throughout the world, including on college campuses in the rich nations. Sweatshops are often defined broadly to include not just relatively large factories, such as the infamous Nike plants in Indonesia and Vietnam, but also small shops and even home work. If we include the latter, we are going to have a lot of overlap with informal employment. So it is impossible in reality to know how many sweatshop workers there are. What is more, there are plenty of sweatshops in the rich countries. In New York City alone there are tens of thousands of garment and restaurant workers, earning as little as two dollars per hour and working for as many as 100 hours per week.

While it is impossible to give a breakdown of the poor world's labor force similar to that constructed for the United States by the Bureau of Labor Statistics, our descriptions so far tell us that the overwhelming majority of poor nation workers are toiling at exhausting and relatively unskilled jobs. The one billion openly unemployed and underemployed workers in the world's labor force are mostly from the poor countries, as are the millions of informal sector workers and child laborers. There are skilled and highly paid workers everywhere in the world, but if these are a small minority in the United States (and a somewhat less small minority in Western Europe), they are a very tiny minority in the poor countries. And they are not growing as a percentage of the labor force. On the contrary, the informal sector, child labor, sweatshops, and unemployment are the most "dynamic" parts of the poor countries' labor forces. A study done by Jacques Charmes found that in North Africa, Sub-Saharan Africa, Latin America, and Asia informal employment grew as a percentage of employment between the 1980s and the 1990s.[23]

To conclude our overview of work in poor countries, let us briefly consider India and China. India has a labor force of nearly 400 million persons, about 13 percent of the entire world's labor force. In India, inequality is growing, and people at the bottom of the economic ladder are actually getting absolutely poorer. More than 70 percent of the nonagricultural labor force is in informal employment; if we include agriculture (more than 60 percent of the labor force still works in agriculture), this figure rises to perhaps over 90 percent. All sorts of informal employment are commonplace, including various types of debt bondage and self-employment. Nearly all of the work done in India is unskilled, requiring little education and training, of which insignificant amounts are available in any event. India's vaunted engineering and software industries absorb a tiny fraction of the labor force. Open unemployment is at 12 percent. Thirty- six percent of the population lives below the completely inadequate official poverty level. A household engaged in farming, with two adults and two children, earned a meager $130 a year in 1995.[24] India is often described as the world's largest democracy. Unfortunately, it is a democracy of misery.

In China there are not even the trappings of democracy. Chinese peasants, still the majority of people in the country, made great economic strides, especially in health and education, after the Communist revolution in 1949, but as China has moved inexorably toward capitalism, these gains have been lost. Amid the small but growing number of rich and middle- class businesspeople (who have gained their riches largely through corruption and influence peddling), we see growing numbers of unemployed and marginally employed workers. In urban areas, perhaps 10 percent of the more than 200 million workforce are unemployed, and tens of millions more eke out a living in informal employment. More than 100 million peasants are now moving around the country seeking employment. Robert Weil tells us, "On the streets that I had walked innumerable times [in Changchun] during 1993–94 without observing a single person standing around aimlessly or looking for work, there were now [1999] at corner after corner groups of mainly male workers, laid off from state enterprises in the city. Lounging on the sidewalks or playing cards or chess to pass the time, they waited all day for the possibility that someone would come by willing to hire their labor, rushing at every car or truck that pulled up to the curb. In more than one conversation, these newly unemployed members of the working class literally pointed to their stomachs while stating, 'We have no food.'"[25]

Women have been especially hard hit, as gender discrimination has returned with a vengeance along with private enterprise. Many older women have lost jobs and will never work again in regular employment. Young rural women are brutally exploited in China's many export processing zones, set up by the state to attract foreign capital. Prostitution has grown rapidly. Dissidents are jailed, executed, or put in mental hospitals. Convict labor is widespread.

India and China alone contain about 30 percent of the world's labor force. When we confront the extent of unemployment and underemployment, along with extraordinarily low wages, we can see at once that any talk of rapid improvement in the lives of the world's workers is premature, to say the least.

THE WORK WE DO: WAGES

Just as there are hierarchies of GDP per capita between countries and individual wealth and income within them, there is a hierarchy of wages. Average wages vary greatly among countries, and there is a wide range of wage rates within every capitalist nation. In addition, there are varying trends in wage rates among national economies. Wage rates are critically important for two reasons. First, workers' wage rates tell them what part of society's output they can buy with each hour of work. Second, labor is an obviously important cost of production to employers. Given that the detailed division of labor and mechanization have advanced to the point at which employers can have increasingly larger amounts of production done in may parts of the world, wage rates play an important role in determining where production will actually be located. It used to be that wage rates in the rich countries could be much higher than in poor countries, but employers would still maintain production in the rich countries because labor productivity was so much higher there. This kept the unit cost of production (the total cost per automobile, for example) competitive in the rich countries. Today, this is less likely to be the case.

Before we take a look at wage rates around the world, we must make a distinction between wages and compensation. Compensation is a more inclusive measurement; it includes not just the hourly (or weekly or monthly) wage but also any additional costs, such as fringe benefits. The most important benefits are health care and pensions. In much of the world these are very low or nonexistent, so, in effect, wages and compensation are about the same. In the rich countries, benefits are often significant, so it is necessary to make a distinction between the two.

The International Trade Administration, a U.S. government agency that promotes U.S. exports, has made estimates of average manufacturing wage rates, converted to U.S. dollars for a large number of countries. Table 4.6 shows these wage rates, along with the GDP per capita, for the year 1997. The countries are listed in the order of their GDP per person, from the lowest to the highest.

TABLE 4.6 Manufacturing Wages and GDP per Capita in U.S. Dollars, 1997

COUNTRY	average hourly wage rate	gdp per capita	COUNTRY	average hourly wage rate	gdp per capita
Bangaldesh	$0.21	$335	Croatia	1.87	4,246
Kenya	0.49	365	Mexico	1.02	4,250
India	0.19	374	Trinidad & Tobago	3.40	4,510
Pakistan	0.34	449	Malaysia	1.97	4,688
Sri Lanka	0.31	816	Chile	2.36	5,275
Philippines	1.34	1,119	Seychelles	2.59	6,910
Egypt	0.63	1,253	Malta	3.62	8,838
Ecuador	1.05	1,520	Argentina	4.03	9,111
Jordan	0.96	1,583	Slovenia	3.88	9,142
Guatemala	1.23	1,584	South Korea	7.26	9,620
Jamaica	0.73	1,609	Bahrain	2.77	9,850
Dominican Rep.	1.51	1,855	Portugal	3.07	10,275
El Salvador	0.90	1,890	Greece	5.39	11,700
Tonga	1.00	1,908	Spain	9.37	13,541
Paraguay	1.52	2,002	Israel	10.15	16,812
Colombia	2.25	2,516	New Zealand	10.46	17,651
Thailand	0.99	2,542	Ireland	10.43	17,821
Fiji	1.60	2,578	Canada	12.13	20,145
Costa Rica	1.69	2,714	Australia	12.13	21,323
Turkey	1.16	2,980	United Kingdom	13.97	21,864
Panama	3.39	3,034	Netherlands	15.42	23,117
Botswana	0.90	3,358	Finland	11.25	23,320
South Africa	3.81	3,371	France	8.95	23,750
Poland	1.58	3,510	Austria	13.87	25,548

COUNTRY	average hourly wage rate	gdp per capita	COUNTRY	average hourly wage rate	gdp per capita
Germany	10.73	25,552	Japan	12.36	33,234
Sweden	15.19	25,741	Norway	15.00	34,840
United States	13.17	29,278	Switzerland	20.07	35,894
Singapore	8.72	31,161	Luxembourg	13.72	40,211
Denmark	24.54	32,153			

SOURCE: See http://ia.ita.doc.gov/wages/97wages/97wages.htm.

These wage rates do not tell us what an hour of labor buys for the workers in these countries; to find this out we would have to know about prices in each country. However, these wages do give us some insights into why manufacturing is leaving the rich countries and moving to the poor ones. The average wage rate in Denmark manufacturing is more than 100 times higher than in Bangladesh. As modern technology and the detailed division of labor make it possible to use relatively unskilled labor in modern high-tech facilities, corporations will find the cheap labor irresistible.

To give the reader some idea of what wages will purchase, consider some examples taken from the activist organization Sweatshop Watch. The garment industry is populated by hundreds of thousands of classic sweatshops around the world. In U.S. dollars, the hourly compensation (wages plus benefits) rate in apparel manufacturing in 1998 ranged from $0.15 in Indonesia to $8.00 in the United States. No wonder Nike loves Indonesia! Sweatshop Watch then gives the following examples of how far some of these (and other countries') sweatshop wages go:

> Fundacion Nacional para el Desarolla . . . an NGO research organization in El Salvador, establishes the basic basket of necessities for the average sized Salvadoran family (4.3 people) to survive in "relative poverty" as $287.21 per month. In El Salvador, workers at Doall Enterprises make $0.60/hour. This meets only 51% of a basic basket of goods necessary to survive in relative poverty.
>
> According to a U.S. Commerce Department Report, "The minimum wage [in Honduras] is considered insufficient to provide for a decent standard of living for a worker and family." $0.43 per hour, or $3.47 per day, is the base wage for garment workers in the Evergreen factory in Honduras, meeting only 54% of the cost of survival. . . . When transportation to and from work, breakfast and lunch costs $2.59, that leaves only $0.80 a day for families' other basic needs.

According to independent labor rights activists in Hong Kong, a living wage in China would be about $0.87/hour. Minimum wage rates vary as they are set by each provincial government; however, they do not meet this living wage. Shanghai's minimum is $0.21/hour, and Guangzhou's $0.26/hour.

Garment workers in Los Angeles, California, who are mostly paid a piece-rate average $7,200 a year, less than 3/4 of the poverty level income for a three- person family.[26]

Wage rates are so low in many parts of the world that an analysis of trends in wage rates is not very meaningful. However, in many countries inflation has eroded wage rates and made them even lower in terms of what they will purchase. In Mexico, a severe financial crisis in late 1994 and 1995 drove the exchange value of the Mexican peso sharply downward. This meant that it took many more pesos to buy a dollar or some other foreign currency than it did before. The result was a sharp rise in the price of imported products. Since Mexico, like nearly every other poor country, has shifted means of production from production of goods and services for domestic use to production for export markets, its people are more reliant on imports than ever before. The increase in import prices thus caused a steep decline in the purchasing power of the wages of Mexican workers and a fall in their real income.

Trends in wages in the rich capitalist countries have varied over the past twenty years, although in general this has been a period of wage austerity as employers have gone on the offensive against their workers. Workers in the United States have faced the greatest slowdown in wage growth during the period since the early 1970s. For all production and nonsupervisory workers (roughly speaking, the working class), real average hourly earnings rose by 2.3 percent per year between 1947 and 1967. This means that real wages more than doubled in these twenty years. However, between 1979 and 1999, real wages actually fell by 0.2 percent per year, meaning that they were considerably lower in 1999 than twenty years earlier. The major benefits, health care and pensions, also showed a significant growth slowdown after the mid-1970s, and fell for parts of the past three decades.[27]

The situation in the other rich capitalist countries has not been nearly as bad. The countries whose economic policies have been most like those of the United States have seen the biggest slowdowns in wage and benefit growth, while those which have not, mainly those in Western Europe, have seen slowdowns for the most part, but not as sharp. Workers in the other rich capitalist nations, again mainly those in Western Europe, are provided much better social welfare programs and legally mandated benefits than is the case for the United States. As the authors of the excellent book *The State of Working America, 2000–2001* point out, "One important reason for international differences in hours worked [is that] statutory annual vacation policies in European countries . . . exceed the average days provided, on average, by U.S. employers. The U.S. average, about 16 days per year, is below the legally required minimum in all of the countries in the figure [the authors show a chart of legally mandated holidays in Sweden, Spain, Denmark, Austria, Finland, France, Ireland, Portugal, Netherlands, Belgium, Norway, Switzerland, and Germany]."[28]

As with unemployment, underemployment, and jobs, it is important to understand that average wages, as bad as they might be, hide a great deal of disparity within the working class. Throughout the world, women almost always earn less than men. In the United States, for example, women still earn less than three-quarters of the wage earned by men.[29] Women are invariably segregated in certain types of occupations and these are typically the poorest paid and the least prestigious. It is even the case that as women increase their employment in an occupation, the relative wage rate of that occupation usually falls. What is true for women is also true for racial and ethnic minorities. Wherever in the world we see the most burdensome work, with the lowest pay and the most dangerous conditions, we also see racial and ethnic minorities doing this work.

THE WORK WE DO: HOURS

A trend that has been occurring in both rich and poor countries is the spread of what is called nonstandard work. We have already seen that in the poor countries, informal employment is very common, even the norm in many places. In rich countries, there is growing evidence of increases in part-time work, independent contracting, home work, and temporary work.

In some cases, informal and nonstandard work involve short hours of work, while in others they mean extremely long hours of labor. In India, informal sector workers engage in what has been called "self exploitation"; they work extraordinarily long hours selling things on the street, for example, because only long hours allow them to live at all.[30] We have already seen that restaurant and garment sweatshop workers in Manhattan's Chinatown routinely put in nearly 100 hours of work a week. Although good data are not available, it is safe to say that when they can, workers in the poor countries put in exhausting days of hard work, but these days are often interspersed with no work or part-time work. This is the clear implication of the ILO estimate that there are perhaps one billion unemployed and underemployed people in the world today. As an El Salvadoran urban slum dweller put it, "Life is hard here, but we're accustomed to it now. . . . We're living a little, working and waiting. But we've been working since the day we were born."[31] It should also be noted that in poor nations, hours away from paid labor are not spent in leisure. In the Bolivian mountains, there are tin mines, once employing many thousands of workers but now not so many. The male miners labor long and hard in the mine, spitting out their lungs and soon enough dying of lung diseases. They chew coca leaves to keep from feeling hungry. Their wives or widows scavenge scrap tin on the gigantic piles of poisonous waste heaped outside the mines. When they are not thus earning their daily bread, they and their older children are waiting in interminably long lines for food or cooking, cleaning, and taking care of the younger children in an endless cycle of work and poverty.[32]

In the rich capitalist countries, hours of work vary considerably. For years, Japanese workers toiled for more hours than workers in any other advanced capitalist economy. Workers in Japanese factories were pressured not to take vacation and to put in hours of "voluntary" overtime. The stress from this overwork resulted in rapid increases in stress-related illnesses and alcoholism. Workers literally died from overwork, a phenomenon that resulted in the invention of a new word for it: *karoshi*. The Japan Occupational Safety and Health Resource Center has reported on court-certified deaths from overwork, typically taking the form of suicide.[33]

As Table 4.7 shows, the United States has now surpassed Japan in yearly average hours of work. While not shown in the table, the hours of paid labor done by women in the United States has increased by many hundreds of hours per year since the late 1960s, generating what economists like Juliet Schor have called the "time crunch."[34] While men have taken on a larger share of household duties, these still fall mainly to women, who like so many of their sisters in the poor countries, work a "double day," working for a wage in the marketplace and for their families at home.

These data show that only in Sweden and the United States did average yearly hours of work rise in this period, although Swedish workers still labored in 1998 average yearly hours lower than in any country in the table except Norway. As I pointed out above, workers in most other rich capitalist economies are the beneficiaries of public policies that reduce hours of

work. These, in turn, are the consequence of much stronger labor movements. However, it should be noted that part-time work is becoming
increasingly common in Europe, with part-time employees making up
significant shares of total employment in Great Britain, Spain, and the
Netherlands, among others.

Some economists have observed a connection between underemployment and overwork in rich countries. Employers find it cheaper to increase
the hours of their regular employees. Compulsory overtime, even though it
might have to be paid at a premium wage rate (for example, in the United
States, most nonsupervisory workers must be paid at one and a half times
their normal hourly wage rate for all hours worked in excess of forty hours
per week), is cheaper than hiring new workers, who have to be trained and
for whom there are hiring costs and fringe benefits. Fringe benefits payments do not increase if a regular worker works overtime, but they do rise
if a new worker is employed. The use of overtime work then makes it
difficult for new workers to find full-time employment, and these workers
form a pool of exploitable part-time workers.[35]

The increased demand for overtime work by employers is heightened by
the increased willingness of workers to take on overtime. Workers who

TABLE 4.7 Annual Hours of Work, Rich Countries, 1979–1998

COUNTRY	1979	1998
United States	1,905	1966
Japan	2,126	1898 (1995 data)
Germany (Western only)	1,764	1,562
France	1,813	1,634 (1997 data)
Italy	1,788	N.A.
United Kingdom	1,821	1,737
Australia	1,904	1,861
Finland	1,868	1,761
Norway	1,516	1,401
Spain	1,988	1,821
Sweden	1,451	1,551

SOURCE: Lawrence Mishel, Jared Bernstein, and John Schmitt, The State of Working America 2000/2001
(Ithaca, NY: Cornell University Press, 2000), 400.

experience increases in family income quickly raise their expenditures for all sorts of consumer goods and services. They increase their use of credit and get caught in what Schor calls a cycle of "getting and spending." To pay their bills and maintain their increased consumption, they work as much overtime as they can get. I once taught groups of automobile workers, employed at a parts plant near Pittsburgh, Pennsylvania. In addition to their employer's demand for forced overtime and the get-and-spend cycle, many of these workers had also experienced extremely insecure employment as plants in the industry shut down in the 1980s and 1990s. They were "willing" to work long hours today in part because they might be victims of another plant shutdown tomorrow. During breaks, some of them would tell me that they had been working twelve hours a day seven days a week. At the funeral of my grandfather, my uncle told my wife that he had been working twelve-hour days for more than twenty years!

The plight of people doing long hours of involuntary part-time work in the rich countries pales in comparison to the working lives faced by the third world proletariat (including the components of this proletariat sweating it out in the rich countries). For these workers, labor is a matter of life and death, all day, every day.

There are significant segments of the working population in the rich countries that are reasonably well off. Elementary school teachers in the United States, for example, who are as a group averaging more than $40,000 per year, are not suffering privation, irrespective of how burdensome their work might be. Even unemployed workers in a rich country like Germany are incomparably better off than most fully employed workers in India or China. In the poor countries, especially those that have enjoyed rapid GDP growth, certain strata of workers have been able to afford consumer goods like televisions and even cars and small houses. But these are a distinct minority. In much of the world, life is still, as the philosopher Hobbes put it, "nasty, brutish, and short." And as workers in the rich countries find that the economic gains they made in the three decades after the Second World War are under attack and have gradually eroded, what can the vast underpaid, underemployed, and overworked mass or workers in the poor countries expect to happen to them? A friend of mine told me that an elementary school teacher in South Africa, whose classes are enormous and whose access to teaching resources are meager, thinks a good workday is one in which she can prevent the female students from being physically injured.

CHAPTER FIVE: The Neoclassical/ Neoliberal Dogma

WHAT MUST BE EXPLAINED?

The last two chapters have highlighted certain features of contemporary global capitalism. At least four of these characteristics stand out. First, the capitalist world economy is divided into a relatively few rich countries and a large number of poor countries. In addition, the gap between the per capita incomes of the two groups of countries has shown no sign of diminishing over a long period of time, and, in fact, has risen for perhaps over a hundred years and certainly since 1980.

Second, there is great inequality in wealth, income, and various social indicators among individuals, households, and families within every capitalist country. Again, these inequalities show no sign of disappearing. Not only are there significant overall inequalities, but throughout the capitalist world, women and racial and ethnic minorities are overrepresented at the bottom of the various distributions—more likely to be without wealth, unemployed, poor, and sick.

Third, capitalist economies are frequently plagued by unemployment and underemployment. In the poor countries these are endemic and have been for a long time. In both rich and poor countries, economic crises are recurring events, driving up the rates of unemployment and underemployment, sometimes with catastrophic results.

Fourth, the overwhelming majority of workers in the capitalist world perform work that is physically or mentally debilitating, often both. Unskilled work, informal employment, child labor, sweatshops—these are the lots in life for most people. What is more, work is often insecure, unsafe and unhealthy, and only nominally free.

These four features of contemporary life under capitalism pose questions that any economic theory has to explain. Economic theories must be tested on the basis of their capacity to explain why capitalism has these features. Put differently, they must say why more than three hundred years of capitalism has raised the world's output to unimagined heights and fostered truly astonishing technological advances yet left more than two billion persons subsisting at the dawn of the twenty-first century on less than two dollars a day.

In this chapter, we will look at the answers to these questions given by mainstream or neoclassical economics. The neoclassical theory enjoys the allegiance of most professional economists, whose training in graduate school was steeped in this theory. It is the economic theory presented in nearly all introductory textbooks, so it is the only theory to which nearly all college students (and elementary and secondary students if they are taught any economics) are exposed.[1]

Strictly speaking, neoclassical economics originated in Europe and England in the 1870s and was developed in part as a response to the radical economics of Karl Marx and Frederick Engels and the working-class movements that drew inspiration from this new school of economics. However, the neoclassical economists drew much inspiration, as did Marx, from an earlier group of economists sometimes called the classical economists. This earlier group includes such great economists as Adam Smith and David Ricardo. I am lumping together in what follows all those aspects of classical and neoclassical economics that today form the corpus of the standard economic wisdom. This is a bit of a disservice to Smith, Ricardo, and all of their predecessors and progenitors who saw matters more clearly and realistically than do modern neoclassical economists.[2]

THE NEOCLASSICAL THEORY

It Is Not from the Benevolence of the Butcher and the Baker

In neoclassical economics, the individual is the primary unit of analysis. Society is seen as the sum of the individuals in it; social outcomes are the result of the decisions made by individuals. Economics is then conceived as the study of the individual decision maker. Neoclassical economics is basically the "science" of making economic choices. Since economic choices are primarily market choices, neoclassical economists study the choices that the participants in the market make. Neoclassical economists have also examined individual behavior outside of the market—inside a business firm or inside a family, for example—but the analysis generally presumes that the individuals inside the firm or family act as if they were operating in markets.

We argued in Chapter One that a scientific investigation begins with assumptions. We have already mentioned that the primary assumption of neoclassical economists is that all persons act out of self-interest. To allow us to meaningfully trace out the logic of this assumption, the neoclassical economists argue that acting out of self-interest means that each person is a maximizing agent, trying single-mindedly to obtain the maximum amount of something.

The main actors in the marketplace are business firms (which sell outputs and buy the means of production), consumers, and workers. Each business firm, consumer, and worker is assumed to be a maximizer. The business firm is assumed to be trying to maximize its profits. The consumer is assumed to be trying to maximize his or her "utility," the subjective satisfactions that are obtained by consuming the goods and services purchased. A consumer faced with two bundles of goods that yield the same utility will always choose the cheaper one. If the two bundles of goods have the same price, the consumer will always choose the bundle yielding the most satisfaction. Workers are assumed to maximize their utility, by allocating their time between wage labor (which is presumed to yield negative satisfaction, that is, to be "painful") and not working (taking what the economist calls "leisure") in such a way that they are subjectively better off than if they had chosen any other combination of work and leisure.

When all of the economic actors are busy pursuing their self-interests, they create both demands for and supplies of every conceivable type of good and service. The interaction of all of the buyers and sellers in the marketplace generates a certain amount of production of any particular good or service and a price for it. The amount of a good supplied by business firms will tend to match the consumer demand for it. And the amount of labor supplied by workers will tend to be matched by the demand of the business firms for that labor. To see why this is so, we can ask what will happen in a world ruled by self-interest if the supply of something is larger than its demand or vice versa. When prices are too high, selfish business firms supply too much of it, looking toward the high profits they can make if they can sell a lot at a high price. Consumers, on the other hand, see the high price as a sign that they should look for cheaper substitute products. So suppliers, unable to sell all that they have supplied, lower their prices, and this drives some suppliers out of the market. But consumers now demand more since the prices are lower. Eventually, the supply and the demand become equal, or as the neoclassical economists put it, there is an "equilibrium" between supply and demand.

This same sort of process is presumed to work in all markets. When prices are too high, supply is greater than demand. This surplus of output forces prices down until demand and supply are equal. If prices are too low, the opposite occurs. Demand is greater than supply and prices rise until the two are equal. The higher prices reduce demand but attract supply. In a labor market, for example, if workers supply more than employers demand, a surplus of labor will exist in the market (unemployment) and wages will fall, attracting demand but repelling supply ("leisure" will become more attractive to some workers the lower the wage rate) until demand and supply are equal.

To sum up, we can say that, according to neoclassical theory, all economic outcomes—the amount of each output produced, the price of every output, the amount of labor and the nonhuman means of production utilized, the wages of workers—are determined by the forces of demand and supply. If the GDP of the United States is many times larger than that of Ethiopia, this must be a matter of supplies and demands in the two countries. The same must be true for any other differences between the two countries, from school attendance to infant mortality. If there are inequalities of wealth, income, jobs, wages, and hours within a country, these must also be connected intimately to supply and demand. Supply and demand must be at the root of unemployment, as well as differences in unemployment among various groups or countries and the sharp increases in unemployment associated with economic crises. Since both supply and demand are but the expression of the self-interested (maximizing) behavior of the individual actors in the marketplace, neoclassical economists hold that ultimately all of these phenomena are the consequence of individual choices made by buyers and sellers to maximize profits or utility.

Besides explaining economic outcomes as the result of self-interested individual choices in markets (supply and demand), neoclassical economists also argue that, if a society is willing to allow individuals to make their choices with a minimum of interference, the economic results will be a social optimum. What they mean by interference is intervention in the operation of markets by the government. By and large, governments should not do things such as setting maximum prices for outputs or minimum wages for workers. They should not alter prices by placing taxes on outputs, and above all they should not impose restrictions on the mobility of any of the means of production. No nation should place a tariff, for example, on the import of another nation's output.

The notion that a social optimum can be achieved by allowing each person to act in a self-interested manner when making economic choices was put into a famous maxim by Adam Smith, author of *The Wealth of Nations*. He said, "It is not from the benevolence of the butcher, the brewer and the baker that we expect our dinner, but from their regard to their own interest."[3] In other words, we get what we want and need because everyone acts out of self-interest. Society as a whole benefits when each person looks only to his and her individual gain. We do not intend that society benefit but that is the result that the market gives us. The market harnesses our "greed" and turns it into a gain for society.

A concept that neoclassical economists use to illustrate the power of the market to benefit society is "consumer sovereignty." When markets are free of control, and when consumers are free to choose the outputs they want, then the market gives them just what they want. Suppose that a market, say for pizza in a large city, is in equilibrium, that is, the supply of pizza is roughly equal to the demand for pizza. For some reason (consumers have higher incomes or the prices of other fast foods have risen), consumers now want more pizza. What will happen? The existing pizza shops will not be able to keep up with the increasing demand—long lines will be seen at the entrances to the shops or they will be uncomfortably crowded. Observing this higher demand, the pizza shop owners will find it advantageous to raise the price of pizza pies (remember, they are profit maximizers). The pizza business will now be more profitable than before. Seeing this, the existing shop owners will start to enlarge their shops or open new stores, and budding young entrepreneurs will begin to open new shops. The rising competition in the marketplace does two things. It increases the supply of pizza and forces the price of pizza down. But lo and behold, pizza consumers get exactly what they wanted—more pizza! And this took place without any sort of government planning, indeed without any planning at all. As Ronald Reagan was fond of saying, this is the "magic of the marketplace."

We could have worked the above example backward and shown that when consumers want less of a product, the market gives it to them, this time by forcing less profitable firms to leave the market. Furthermore, when consumers tell the market (through their purchases) that they want more of something, the market also goes to work to make sure that the needed means of production are channeled into the market in which demand has increased. If the demand for pizza rises, so too will the demand for pizza shop workers. The higher demand for the workers will push the wage rate up, and the higher wage rate will attract the necessary labor to this market. So the market not only gives consumers what they want (making them sovereign in the market), it also places (allocates) society's means of production right where they are most needed.

And we are still not done with the wonders of the market. Suppose that an enterprising pizza maker invents a more efficient pizza oven and installs it in his store. This owner can now produce pizzas cheaper than his rivals. He can make higher profits because his costs per pizza are now lower. However, over time, his rivals will be forced to implement the new technology, and this will increase the supply of pizza, lowering its price (to the delight of pizza lovers) and returning everyone's profits to rough equality. The implication of this example is that a competitive market will be very inducive to rapid technological development and that this is ultimately to the benefit of consumers.

Our pizza example can be extended almost infinitely. Suppose that workers demand more pleasant jobs. Just as in the pizza case, the increased demand for more pleasant jobs will raise the "price" of such jobs. That is, employers supplying less pleasant jobs will not be able to attract an adequate supply of workers. Wages for the less pleasant jobs will rise. The higher cost to employers supplying less pleasant jobs will encourage them or new employers to start supplying more pleasant (and temporarily less costly) jobs. Just as in the case of our pizza consumers, the workers get what they want. According to the neoclassical theory, they are sovereign in the market.

Market Failures

Neoclassical economists recognize that there are situations in which the pursuit of self-interest does not necessarily lead to socially desirable outcomes. Such situations are called *market failures*. There are quite a large number of these. Let us briefly describe five of them. First, some socially useful outputs will not be produced in an economy where self-interest rules. If a shipping company builds a lighthouse along the ocean to protect its ships, it will not be able to prevent its rivals from using the light once it is turned on. Therefore, no shipping company will build a lighthouse, despite the obvious usefulness of lighthouses. Similar arguments apply to the national defense, general education, roads, bridges, and the like.

Second, if there are pervasive and severe inequalities in wealth and income when a market economy begins, these inequalities will be maintained by the normal operation of the markets. Markets are impersonal mechanisms, and they can make no judgments about what is right or wrong or good or bad. The example given in Chapter Two of the two children born in Pittsburgh illustrates the problem. If everything needed by a person has to be purchased in the marketplace, those with a lot of money to start with have an obvious advantage. Rich parents will be able to buy the things necessary for their child to face the labor market with good prospects while poor parents will not be able to do so. Inequality can be socially and politically destabilizing, and we are now learning that it can, by itself, produce many bad social outcomes, including more crime and sickness. Inequality also takes some of the shine off the notion of consumer sovereignty. Those with the most money will be most sovereign.

Third, in a market economy, businesses must pay for their means of production, that is, they must bear certain costs of doing business. They must pay their workers, buy materials, supplies, machinery, and equipment, pay for advertising, transport, and a host of other necessary inputs. However, the production of most outputs also generates other costs to which the market does not automatically attach a price. The coal mining company in the village of my birth dumped its waste water into the nearby river, its waste by-products into a ravine across town, and its noxious smoke into the air above the town. The residents, therefore, had to bear the costs of these corporate actions: rusty cars, infected lungs, poisoned water, dirty houses and laundry, and the debased natural beauty of the place. These costs, for which the mining company was not liable, are called "social" costs or "spillover effects." Their existence means that, from society's point of view, too much of the product that generates these costs is being produced. If these costs had to be taken into account when production decisions were made, the producer would find that some output was no longer profitable to produce.

Fourth, our example of consumer sovereignty assumed that when the existing pizza shops raised their prices and made higher profits, new businesses would open, and the increased supply from this new capital would give consumers what they wanted and lower the price at the same time. But what if the existing pizza shop owners could somehow prevent new shops from opening? In the case of a pizza shop, with its relatively low startup costs, this seems unlikely, barring some sorts of criminal actions (which, of course, are not unknown). However, there are many examples of large companies successfully preventing new capital from entering a market. In automobiles, for example, the startup costs are so large that new entry is very unlikely even if demand is high and profits are large. The size of the existing firms acts as a "barrier to entry." If barriers to entry exist, the notion of consumer sovereignty falls to the ground. Consumers will face higher prices and smaller outputs than they desire, and the suppliers will enjoy price and output setting power.

Fifth, there may exist what neoclassical economists call "involuntary" unemployment. The supply of available jobs might not be large enough to absorb all of those seeking employment. Certainly this has happened in market economies, most notably during economic depressions. We have already discussed the considerable social costs of such unemployment, so suffice it to say here that involuntary unemployment is a market failure. This is because, once a depression begins, market forces can make a crisis worse. In 1932, for example, business firms could have hired workers at bargain basement wage rates, and they could have borrowed money from banks at near zero interest rates. Had they hired workers and used borrowed money to build new plant and purchase new equipment, output would have risen and unemployment fallen. They did neither of these things. They believed that if they did do these things, they would have made themselves vulnerable to bankruptcy and competitor takeover if the crisis did not end. Since they could not possibly know if it would end, they took the prudent path of putting whatever money they had in safe places and waiting. This action made the crisis long-lasting and showed that markets can produce socially undesirable outcomes in the form of widespread involuntary unemployment.

Neoclassical Solutions to Market Failures: The Libertarian View

Since the market mechanism does not itself solve these market failures, the neoclassical economist is compelled to admit that some force outside of the marketplace must try to solve them. That is, there must be some entity in a market economy that looks out for the society as a whole. In all modern societies, of course, this entity is the government. The neoclassical position is that it is the duty of the government to combat market failures so that society's interests are served.

Having said this, I must immediately add that neoclassical economists are not in agreement about either the severity of the market failures or the best methods of dealing with them. Although this simplifies a little, I think it is fair to say that neoclassical economists can be divided into two camps: the libertarians and the liberals. These names sound similar, as both camps claim to be champions of liberty, but the differences between them are significant. Except for the period from the Great Depression until roughly the end of the 1960s, the libertarian camp has been the dominant one, and it certainly is the predominant group today. In the United States, for example, a look at President George W. Bush's chief economic advisers tells us immediately that they espouse libertarian positions and are deeply imbued with a strong antipathy for all things liberal.

The libertarian view is that, first, none of the market failures seriously challenge the overwhelming superiority of capitalism as a system of production, and second, that to the extent the government must take actions to resolve them, it should do so in ways that intrude upon markets as little as possible. The government's duty is to prevent interference in the workings of the market and to expand the sphere of the market whenever possible. Sometimes governments try to curry public favor by implementing rules that interfere with the marketplace. Libertarians see such rules as grave errors, ones that governments should avoid in the first place but rectify wherever they find them already in existence. Here is a representative list of market interventions that libertarians oppose:

1. PRICE SUBSIDIES. A government should not place controls on prices such that they are below the level which would be set by self-interest driven supply and demand. Suppose a government sets a maximum price for milk below what the market price would have been. It does this with the goal of helping poor families who perhaps cannot afford to buy certain basic necessities. The artificially low price of milk does not really help the poor, says the libertarian. The low price creates a shortage (demand larger than supply), and this shortage will give rise to various undesirable situations. Those with political influence will get the scarce milk first. More well-to-do people will be best able to wait in the long lines that shortages always precipitate (or hire others to do so). Black markets will develop as self-interested individuals see that a higher price will be paid by some people rather than going without milk. To feed these black markets, people with influence will buy up the available milk and then resell it on the black market. In the end, those who the government aimed to help will still not get the milk. And suppliers who would enter the market if the

price were higher will not do so. What is true for milk is true for any product for which the government sets an artificially low price—electricity, bus fares, cooking oil, etc.

2. MINIMUM WAGES. A similar argument applies to minimum wages. If the government sets a minimum wage above that which would prevail in the marketplace, the result will inevitably be a surplus of labor (supply larger than demand), that is, unemployment. The people presumably helped by a minimum wage are the people unable to find work at the artificially high wage rate. Needless to say, libertarians also oppose "living wages," which have been proposed for and implemented in a number of U.S. cities. The "living wage" mandated by such proposals is always higher than the minimum wage set by the federal government.[4]

3. INCOME SUBSIDIES. Many countries have provided income to people who find themselves in unfortunate circumstances such as extreme poverty, unemployment, illness, or disability. Libertarians take a dim view of such income subsidies.[5] Outright grants to the poor are especially criticized. In the United States, for example, certain poor persons, mainly single women with children, were once eligible for public assistance in the form of monthly cash grants. Some poor single men were also eligible. Libertarian neoclassical economists are opposed to these grants. They argue that they encourage idleness by providing income without work effort. Just as we expect a person who hits a large lottery to quit working (because the demand for leisure will rise as income rises), so too we can expect the poor to work less or not at all when they get cash grants not tied to work effort. With respect to unemployment compensation, the libertarians reason that such compensation will create a certain amount of voluntary unemployment by encouraging the unemployed to take longer to find new jobs than would otherwise be the case. Payments for disability, especially if they are generous, will simply encourage workers to fake injury and illness to collect the subsidy. Again, the society loses valuable labor. We have already had occasion to examine the hostility of libertarians to social security (in Chapter One, although there we did not identify Professor Feldstein as a libertarian, just as a neoclassical economist).

4. MARKET-REGULATING LAWS. Libertarians ordinarily also take a dim view of laws aimed at regulating markets. In addition to minimum wage and price support laws, they oppose laws which protect workers' right to unionize. For them, unions are by their nature inimical to the smooth functioning of markets. Unions use their power to force wages above their equilibrium levels, generating unemployment in a manner similar to legally mandated minimum wages. The workers shut out of unionized markets must seek employment in an overcrowded nonunion market, meaning that if they obtain work, it will be at wages lower than those that would prevail in the absence of unions. Unions can also make domestic products uncompetitive on world markets, thereby reducing both exports and employment.[6]

Other regulating laws are seen as unnecessary, in the sense that the market would accomplish the same things as the laws set out to do. Consumer sovereignty will drive unsafe and unhealthy products out of the market, so why bother to regulate them? Free workers will best be able to decide whether to work in certain unsafe jobs or unhealthy work environments. If they freely choose not to, employers will have to make the jobs safer and healthier to obtain a sufficient supply of workers. Similar arguments can be made for banking regulations, indeed for any type of business regulation.

5. PUBLICLY SUPPORTED PRODUCTION. Neoclassical economists agree that certain production can only be done under the auspices of the state. The building of basic infrastructure like roads, bridges, airports, and the like is not going to be undertaken by private businesses, and the same is true for the national defense, the court system, and other needed government functions. However, if at all possible, the actual production of roads, bridges, planes, government buildings, etc., should be undertaken by private companies. It is legitimate for the government to levy and collect taxes (though not progressive taxes, which might interfere with various kinds of individual initiative—entrepreneurs might not be willing to take risks if the income they get when a risky venture pans out is taxed too heavily) to pay private businesses to supply the government with outputs. But actual government production should be avoided. Government production is bound to be less efficient than private production because competition will be lacking. Without competition there will be no incentive for a government-run operation to be efficient or for public employees to work hard. Actual public enterprise should be strictly limited to things like the armed forces, the courts, and certain police, such as border guards. All else should be contracted out to the private sector.[7]

6. RESTRICTIONS OF FOREIGN TRADE AND CAPITAL FLOWS. There is a strong presumption among neoclassical economists that nations should not impose constraints on the buying and selling of goods and services across their borders. Nor should they place restrictions on foreign capital, whether this capital is in the form of money or capital goods. Tariffs and quotas on foreign output prevent the world's economy from operating as efficiently as it otherwise would. If each country specializes in those things it does best (in those for which it has what mainstream economists call a "comparative advantage") and trades with other countries for the things these other countries produce relatively efficiently, both nations will gain, that is, they will get a greater output than they would have had they tried to be self-sufficient. Consumers in each country will also pay lower prices if imported goods and services are freely available and untaxed. When a nation place a tariff on, say, foreign steel, consumers must then pay higher prices for every product that uses steel. The domestic steel industry will also not have to face full international competition and will, therefore, not be as efficient as it would otherwise be.

Placing restrictions on the movements of foreign capital also denies people the benefits of higher production and lower prices. The more money available in domestic markets, the easier it will be to find financing for any number of production projects. Poor countries, for example, are often starved for capital (at least this is what the economists tell us). So foreign capital fills a void and allows these nations to begin to develop their economies.

The libertarian neoclassical economists advise governments, then, to eliminate whatever restrictions they have placed on the free operation of markets. But how should a government handle the market failures? We have hinted at the answers above. If the market will not allow the production of certain useful goods and services, the government should provide for their production. The government should strictly limit public production; whenever possible, it should use tax revenues to contract out with private companies. It is acceptable for soldiers to be public employees, but the weapons they use should be produced by private corporations.

Libertarian neoclassical economists do not take the market failure of inequality very seriously. In fact, they usually argue the contrary: that inequality is a socially desirable thing. Inequality gives those with lower incomes an incentive to work hard and achieve, while it gives everyone the hope that they might accumulate very large sums of money and enjoy the life that money makes possible. Without the possibility of great riches, people would not be willing to take risks and innovate production. The only role the government might play here is to provide for those few people who, because of physical or mental disabilities, cannot possibly work. Private charities should be encouraged to help the less fortunate, and the government must strictly monitor the recipients of any aid to prevent cheating. Libertarian neoclassical economists are not opposed to public incentive schemes to encourage those who are poor to obtain education and training, the results of which will make them productive enough to earn more money. Some programs that might help are school vouchers to help families to pay for school, perhaps low- interest loans for school or training, and tax credits or wage subsidies to private employers to encourage them to hire the poor.

Social costs such as environmental destruction are best handled by extending the market mechanism rather than by legislation. The libertarian neoclassical economist points out that the reason a private business pollutes the air and water is because the water and the air are not private property. Thus, there are no costs the company must pay when it pollutes. The water and the air belong to no one; they can be used "free of charge." What needs to be done is to place a price on the use of the water and air. This could be done through the creation, by the government, of what we might call "rights to pollute." Such rights would have to be purchased by a company that wanted to dump a certain amount of a particular pollutant into the water or air. Once a business had to buy a pollution right, it would try to economize on its expenses, either by producing (and polluting) less or by finding a way to control pollution cheaper than the cost of the pollution rights. The production of pollution control devices would be encouraged, since this would create a demand for them. Companies that purchased rights they did not use could sell them to any company that needed to pollute more than its own pollution rights allowed. All in all, this pollution rights scheme is another example of the "magic of the marketplace."

Libertarian neoclassical economists suggest that, while barriers to entry in markets might be a short-term problem, they should not be a long-term issue. Barriers to entry result in abnormally high profits for those businesses creating the barriers. High profits, however, serve as an exceptionally strong incentive for capital to find a way into a market. In the 1950s, for example, the U.S. automobile and steel industries dominated world automobile and steel markets. Moreover, only a few giant firms dominated each industry in the United States. Very few cars were not produced by General Motors, Ford, and Chrysler. U.S. Steel and a handful of smaller but still large-scale producers made most of the world's steel. Automobile and steel corporations were extremely profitable. General Motors achieved a rate of profit on invested capital of 20 percent, a phenomenally high rate of return at that time. Yet despite the massive amount of money necessary to enter these markets and compete effectively, these corporations could not prevent rivals from entering their markets. Today, there are numerous Japanese, Korean, French, German, Swedish, and Italian automobile companies, and there are scores of competitors in the steel industry. Consumers have benefitted from this competition, and, at the same time, the efficiencies (called "economies of scale") of large-scale production made possible by companies like Ford have been maintained.

With respect to involuntary unemployment, libertarian neoclassical economists were shocked by the Great Depression. They had held the view that market forces would quickly bring a return of prosperity to a depressed economy. When a crisis strikes an economy, unemployment will increase as businesses cut back production or close. At the same time, the demand for bank loans will fall for the same reason. The growing unemployment, however, will put downward pressure on wage rates, and this will encourage firms to begin hiring again. The fact that bank loan demand diminishes means that banks now have excess money to lend out. Banks will be forced by market competition to lower their loan interest rates, and this will encourage borrowing. As newly hired workers spend their paychecks and borrowers spend the proceeds of their loans, business will begin to pick up, and the crisis will soon come to end.

During the Great Depression, wages and bank loan rates fell dramatically, but businesses did not hire more workers and no borrowers showed up at the banks. The Great Depression just dragged on. At first, the libertarians were dumbfounded, but in the years since the 1930s, they have put forth the position that the great crisis was the result of bad policies followed by governments in most of the world's market economies. One public (or quasi-public as is sometimes the case) institution that all neoclassical economists believe is necessary in modern economies is a central bank and a central banking authority. In the United States the bank is the Federal Reserve System, and the authority is the Board of Governors. One function of a central bank is to regulate the availability of credit. Central banks do this by engaging in activities that put upward or downward pressure on interest rates. They can also serve as "lenders of last resort," making money available to troubled sectors in the market. Had the Federal Reserve put more downward pressure on interest rates as soon as the downturn began in late 1929, and if it had made funds available to cash-strapped businesses, banks, and brokers, the downturn would not have been nearly so severe and the upturn would have taken hold in a relatively short amount of time. In addition, most nations responded to the depression by placing high tariffs on imports. The resulting slowdown in international trade only made the depression worse. One country's exports are another country's imports. If the United States levies a high tariff on foreign goods, as it did in 1932 with the notorious Hawley-Smoot law (which imposed tariffs as high as 100 percent, doubling the price of some imports), other countries will not be able get the revenue necessary to buy U.S. exports. The inability of U.S. exporters to sell their wares means that U.S. residents won't be able to buy another country's exports. A vicious spiral will drive output down in all countries. So the libertarians say that had countries not reacted to the 1930s crisis with such high trade barriers, the crisis would not have been as severe as it was.[8]

In general, libertarian neoclassical economists believe that prompt actions by central banks can either prevent recessions or depressions altogether or end them soon after they begin. No other government action is needed. If a government reacts to unemployment by increasing its own spending or cutting taxes, it will only waste money or cause total spending in the country to increase by too much, causing inflation. Sometimes libertarian neoclassical economists favor tax cuts when a recession begins, but this is usually done for the strategic purpose of forcing the government to spend less money in the future. By reducing public revenues, a tax cut puts pressure on the government to curtail its spending or risk running a budget deficit.

Neoclassical Solutions to Market Failures: The Liberal View

Liberal neoclassical economists share a faith in the goodness of markets with their libertarian counterparts, but the liberal faith is tempered by an understanding that market failures can seriously undermine the well-being of society. Their solution to market failures is a more activist government. It is important to note here that liberals are not radicals; they do not aim to overthrow existing social arrangements. Like the libertarians, they believe that capitalism is far superior to any alternative mode of production.[9]

A good way to contrast the two groups of neoclassical economists is to run through each of the market failures again. Liberals are not in principle opposed to the public production of goods and services the market will not provide. For example, they generally support public education. They point out that the social security system, administered by the federal government, is operated in an extremely efficient manner, with administrative costs of about 1 percent. In the liberal view, there is no inherent reason why private production of social goods and services is superior to direct public production. They might point to the defense contractor scandals—private defense contractors bilked the government out of many millions of dollars.

Liberals are more concerned about the problem of inequality than are the libertarians. Liberals ask how equality of opportunity, one of the bedrock goals of modern capitalist economies, can be maintained if there is great wealth and income inequality. It is perfectly legitimate for the government to use its power to redistribute at least some income, to give those with the smallest share of the economic pie a little larger slice. This might be done by progressive taxes and progressive spending, government outlays that benefit the poor more than the rich. Such expenditures might include subsidized health care, free school lunches, and subsidized schooling. Liberals would also be inclined to support a decent minimum wage and a strong labor movement, the latter seen as a "countervailing power" to that of large corporations.[10]

Regulatory laws are not necessarily anathema to liberals. Environmental laws, strictly enforced, are seen as superior to pollution rights schemes by many liberals. Laws are also needed to prevent the most predatory practices of businesses and to protect consumers, borrowers, investors, the elderly, the sick, and the young.

The problem of involuntary unemployment shows the greatest divide between liberals and libertarians. In fact, the liberal neoclassical perspective was developed in large part as a response to the Great Depression. When the economies of the major capitalist countries failed to rebound as the most respected neoclassical economists of the day believed they would, a large rift developed within mainstream economics. Until the Great Depression, nearly all neoclassical economists were what I have been calling libertarian neoclassicals. However, the inability of economists to adequately explain one of the most significant episodes in the history of market economies led some of them to speculate that something was wrong with the accepted economic wisdom. The need to find answers was made more acute by the growing anger of workers and the poor, matched by new interest in the radical ideas of Karl Marx (see Chapter Six).

A group of economists at Cambridge University in England, led by John Maynard Keynes, began to put forward arguments today associated with modern liberalism. In the mid- 1930s, Keynes was already a famous economist and public intellectual. Interestingly, he had not studied economics at university, although he had been tutored by friend of his father, himself a noted economist.[11]

Keynes's upheaval of neoclassical orthodoxy is laid out in his magnum opus, *The General Theory of Employment, Interest and Money*, published in 1937.[12] In this dense and much-interpreted book, Keynes argued that full employment was not a natural state of affairs in a capitalist economy. If the economy suffered a shock that spawned a depression, market forces might act in a perverse way and deepen the downturn in output and employment rather than putting the economy back on the path toward full employment as Keynes's neoclassical predecessors had argued. Keynes' ideas are complex and not easily put into a few words, but the main idea is straightforward. When the economy goes into a slump, business managers and owners might become so pessimistic about the profitability of prospective investment spending (and consumers about consumer spending) that they will not spend money no matter how low interest rates fall. Businesses will not hire workers no matter how low wages fall, and consumers will not raise their spending no matter how low prices fall. Thus, the increase in investment and consumer spending necessary for an economic recovery does not transpire, and the economy stays in a slump, trapped, as it were, by the fears of investors and consumers about the future. Whatever money investors and consumers have beyond that needed for essential maintenance and consumption will be hoarded and not spent. Keynesians say that this is precisely what is happening in Japan today.

Keynes was not a radical; he strongly endorsed capitalism and was a foe of socialism. He believed that his theory provided a fairly simple way out for capitalist economies stuck in depressions. The problem in a depression is not enough spending, or, as the economist would put it, insufficient aggregate demand for newly produced output. Put another way, in a slump the amount of money saved by businesses and consumers is larger than the amount businesses are willing to invest. If allowed to persist, this situation will give rise to a decline in both output and saving. The solution is for the state to take away some of the private sector's savings and make public investments—that is, to spend the money itself. The government could get private savings through taxation or borrowing. If taxation is used, the taxes must be levied on those with relatively high incomes, since the well-to-do can pay the taxes out of money they would otherwise have saved. Taxes could also be levied on corporate profits, since it is the hoarding of these profits that is one of the sources of insufficient spending in the first place. If borrowing is employed, the government will issue bonds and sell these to the public, banks, and other businesses. The government bonds might appear to be a wise use of unspent savings because they yield interest and, at least for an advanced capitalist economy, are relatively safe.

Once a government has collected money through progressive taxation and/or borrowing, it must spend the money. It could transfer the money directly to the unemployed and the poor, who will immediately spend the money and stimulate businesses to produce more output and hire more labor to meet the higher demand. Or, better, the state could make public investments, such as in public housing, infrastructure, health care, and many other socially useful projects. Not only would these public investments put people directly to work (either employed directly by the government or by private contractors), but they would also generate much needed spending on output. The improvement in the economy's performance, primed by the government's initiatives, would then create an environment conducive to optimistic expectations about the future of the economy, and this would spur private investment and consumer spending. The upturn would feed on itself until full employment was achieved and the downturn was over.

The Second World War seemed to vindicate Keynes's theory. Governments everywhere in the advanced capitalist world sharply raised taxes and issued bonds. They used the proceeds to finance the war. Military spending increased enormously, as did the investment spending needed to produce war materials. Governments themselves built entire factories to make the planes, tanks, and guns needed to prosecute the war. Amazingly, unemployment soon disappeared; in the United States, the Great Depression was but a memory by 1943. Labor shortages replaced surpluses; everyone who wanted a job could easily get one.

After the Second World War, Keynesianism became part of economic orthodoxy. Capitalist nations like Sweden utilized the Keynesian techniques of progressive taxation and public investment and employment to achieve extremely high average standards of living. In no rich capitalist economy did government spending and tax revenues fall back to their prewar levels. Governments also implemented automatic tax and spending mechanisms so that downturns would be immediately counteracted without any conscious policies. Unemployment compensation, for example, automatically helped to maintain consumer spending when workers lost their jobs during a slump. So too did progressive taxation; as incomes fell in a recession, tax payments fell faster, thus helping to stabilize consumers' disposable incomes.

Liberal economists often combined their Keynesian economics with the promotion of policies aimed at reducing inequality, such as higher minimum wages, poverty programs, and support for unions. Not only were these seen as just programs; they also stimulated spending and employment. This was so because poorer persons would spend all of any increase in income they received, whereas the rich would save part of theirs.

The period between the end of the Second World War and the end of the 1960s was the heyday of Keynesianism. There were differences of opinion about how the government should spend the money it raised from taxes and debt. In the United States, military spending dominated, giving rise to the term "military Keynesianism."[13] Other Keynesians decried the growth of military spending, contending that such spending might give the economy a one-time boost but would not raise the long-term productiveness of the economy. One of Keynes's disciples, Joan Robinson, called what the United States was doing "bastard Keynesianism."[14] Strictly speaking, however, it does not matter what the government spends on. All that matters is that it spend and use its taxation, debt, and spending policies to manage the macro economy.

THE TRIUMPH OF THE LIBERTARIANS

Today, liberal neoclassical economics is in disarray, and the libertarians dominate the mainstream of economics. Libertarians believe that the increasing globalization of capital, fueled by the electronic revolution, has made Keynesianism irrelevant. In addition, they argue that the liberal economic project, with its insistence on large-scale government intervention into the economy, was profoundly wasteful and undemocratic.

Globalization has rendered the Keynesian economic stabilization remedies useless. Suppose, for example, that a government decides to strongly stimulate a national economy through government spending, progressive taxation, and low interest rates. The greater interconnection among national economies, through trade in goods and services as well as various kinds of money flows, greatly reduces the expansionary effects of such a program.

First, as incomes increase, so too do imports, moving spending out of the country and lowering the increase in domestic demand. The increase in imports tends to create a deficit in the country's balance of trade (exports minus imports), and this, in turn, puts downward pressure on the national currency's exchange rate. That is, if the United States imports more than it exports, the demand for dollars relative to other currencies falls, and this makes the dollar worth less in relation to other currencies. It now takes more dollars to buy yen or euros than before. This raises the price of imports, and in countries that are import dependent, inflation becomes a problem.

Second, rich individuals will begin to move their funds out of the country seeking lower taxes and higher interest rates. The same might be true for domestic businesses. Third, currency speculators, sensing a decline in the exchange value of the currency, might begin to speculate in the curren-

---

MONETARY AND FISCAL POLICY [15]

Two types of macro economic policy are available to governments trying to stabilize their economies, that is, keep their outputs high or make them higher if the economy has slumped. Libertarian economists say that a government can rely solely upon monetary policy. Monetary policy aims at regulating the availability of credit. This policy is overseen in the United States and in most other rich capitalist countries by a relatively autonomous monetary authority. This authority controls a nation's central bank, which is not a normal bank but one that regulates the commercial banks that most people and businesses normally deal with. In the United States, the central banking system is called the Federal Reserve system, and the central banks are called Federal Reserve banks. The banks are located around the country, with the most important one in New York City, the country's financial center. The agency charged with operating the central banking system is called the Board of Governors. There are seven governors, appointed by the president for overlapping terms of fourteen years. One of the seven is made chair, also by the president. Today the chair is Alan Greenspan, the world's most powerful central banker.

The Federal Reserve has a number of tools it can use to make more or less credit available. In a slump, it would want to make more available, so it would do things that would put downward pressure on interest rates. Lower interest rates would encourage businesses and consumers to borrow and spend more money, and the increased spending would, in turn, lead firms to produce more output and hire more workers.

cy. They can do this by borrowing dollars (if we are talking about the United States) and selling them. This further drives the exchange value of the currency down and worsens inflation. The speculators will then buy the dollars back at a lower exchange value at some time in the future, pay back their debt to the lender of the dollars, and so become richer by the fall in the exchange value.

Now the country is faced with inflation and capital flight. To combat the inflation and to get money flowing back into the country, the central banking authorities engage in actions that push interest rates up. This may reduce the inflation, but it will curtail consumption and investment spending, counteracting the effects of the expansionary fiscal policy. The government will also face strong pressure to reduce the progressivity of the tax structure. In the end, market forces conspire to defeat the good >

The actual ways in which the Federal Reserve puts pressure on interest rates are complicated, but the basics are not overly difficult to grasp. Commercial banks (Chase Manhattan, Wells Fargo, etc.) that join the Federal Reserve system must keep a fraction of their deposits on reserve at their Federal Reserve bank. (Membership confers considerable advantages to banks: they can borrow money from their Federal Reserve bank; they can get expert advise from Federal Reserve economists; and the Federal Reserve clears their checks.) Mellon Bank in Pittsburgh, Pennsylvania, for example, must keep its required reserves in the Federal Reserve bank in Cleveland, Ohio. The reserve fraction, known as the reserve ratio, is set by the Board of Governors. Money on reserve cannot be loaned out by the commercial bank. So the Board could encourage borrowing by lowering this ratio, giving the banks more money to lend out and forcing them to lower interest rates to get prospective borrowers to actually borrow money.

Banks can also borrow money from their Federal Reserve banks. The interest rate on these loans is called the discount rate (because the asset the commercial bank puts up as collateral for the loan is discounted, that is, the interest is taken out in advance). The discount rate is set by the Board of Governors. A lower rate sends a signal to the financial community that the Federal Reserve wants to stimulate the economy. A third tool of monetary policy is open market operations. The Federal Reserve banks own large quantities of federal government bonds, bonds issued to pay for past government spending. These old bonds are frequently bought and sold, just like stocks. Federal Reserve buying or selling of old bonds is called open market operations. In a recession, the Board of Governors would order the Federal Reserve

intentions of the Keynesians. The libertarians take all of this to mean that a government cannot really expand the economy through fiscal policy.[16]

In the face of Keynesianism's failure, libertarians recommend that the best thing to do is rely upon the markets' tendency to generate socially desirable outcomes. The entire Keynesian experiment left capitalist governments with bloated public bureaucracies and wasteful public spending projects. High taxation served as a strong disincentive to hard work and investment, slowing down the growth rate of the economy. Large budget deficits meant that governments were competing with private businesses for loans (deficits mean that a government has issued bonds to pay its bills), driving up interest rates and further depressing private investment. The same was true for the myriad government rules and regulations, which only compelled businesses to devote precious resources to satisfying the bureaucrats.

banks to buy old bonds. The money used to pay for these bonds comes from the reserves deposited by member banks, the interest received by Federal Reserve banks on their own bond holdings, and the newly printed money made by the U.S. Mint, which is deposited in Federal Reserve banks. When the money enters the private sector, some of it will be spent, directly stimulating the economy. Some of the money will become deposits in banks, and the banks will try to lend this money out, lowering their interest rates to do so.

The central bank does not itself set interest rates, except for the discount rate. But what it does puts pressure on market interest rates. For example, commercial banks loan money to one another on a daily basis. The interest rate on these overnight loans is called the federal funds rate, and it is one of the first to change when the central bank makes a move. Another commonly reported interest rate is the prime rate. This is simply the interest rate the nation's largest banks charge their biggest and most favored customers. It is, therefore, the lowest of all market loan rates. If the Federal Reserve is trying to stimulate the economy, you will see these interest rates falling.

The central bank has still greater powers. It can serve as a "lender of last resort," making money available to corporations facing extreme financial distress, to brokerage firms unable to get money from clients who have bought stocks on credit, even other countries in economic distress. The central bank is the society's ultimate source of "liquidity," that is, of cash needed in emergencies.

Libertarian economists believe that if any government policy is needed to stabilize the economy, monetary policy is all that is needed. Liberals, however, are less sanguine

Libertarians believe that the Keynesian experiments were monumental mistakes, attempts to defy the logic of the market and subvert its beneficence. They had some short-term good effects, but over the long run they caused capitalist economies to become much more inefficient, and, therefore, in the long run, hurt those they aimed to help. Now globalization has forced a rethinking of Keynesianism and a welcome return to the old-time religion of the marketplace.

The turn away from Keynes and toward the market is today called *neoliberalism*. It is nothing more than what I have called libertarian neoclassical economics. The use of the word *liberal* in neoliberalism refers to the nineteenth century usage of liberal, which then meant what today is called libertarian. Neoliberalism reflects the belief that nations should pursue economic policies first enunciated by Adam Smith, David Ricardo, John >

---

about central bank policy. First, they point out that in a severe downturn, monetary policy may be completely ineffective, as argued by Keynes in the 1930s. If businesses and consumers become so pessimistic about the future that they seek safety above all else, they will not borrow and spend no matter how much interest rates decline. In this case, the government must execute fiscal policy—its control over taxes, debt, and spending—to increase spending, output, and employment. In other words, monetary policy works only indirectly to energize the economy. What might be necessary is a direct stimulus in the form of public investment financed by either progressive taxes or bond sales.

Second, liberals note the inherent conservatism of central bankers. The Federal Reserve system in the United States operates with considerable autonomy; it does not need either congressional approval or funding for what it does. Yet this independence, combined with the fact that those who serve on the Board of Governors or as Reserve bank officers invariably come from the business community or are academics sympathetic to the business perspective, ensures that monetary policy will have a bias toward controlling inflation rather than reducing unemployment. Banks, the society's primary creditors, hate inflation because rising prices make their customers' loan repayments worth less in terms of purchasing power than the money loaned out in the first place. The central banking authorities, arising as they do from the banking and business community, are much more comfortable pursuing a contractionary economic policy, one that pressures interest rates up to reduce spending and weaken inflationary pressures. Therefore, monetary policy cannot be trusted to stimulate the economy enough during an economic contraction.

Stuart Mill, and all of their heirs apparent in the neoclassical pantheon.

Before we turn at last to the neoclassical analysis of the data we have examined in Chapters, Two, Three, and Four, let us see exactly what neoliberalism means in terms of what countries should do in terms of their economies. An exceptionally clear summary can be found in Thomas Friedman's much-publicized book *The Lexus and the Olive Tree*:

> . . . a country must either adopt, or be seen as moving toward, the following golden rules: making the private sector the primary engine of its economic growth, maintaining a low rate of inflation and price stability, shrinking the size of its state bureaucracy, maintaining as close to a balanced budget as possible, if not a surplus, eliminating and lowering tariffs on imported goods, removing restrictions on foreign investment, getting rid of quotas and domestic monopolies, increasing exports, privatizing state-owned industries and utilities, deregulating capital markets, making its currency convertible, opening its industries, stock and bond markets to direct foreign ownership and investment, deregulating its economy to promote as much domestic competition as much as possible, eliminating government corruption, subsidies and kickbacks as possible, opening its banking and telecommunications systems to private ownership and competition, and allowing its citizens to choose from an array of competing pension options and foreign-run pension and mutual funds.[17]

INEQUALITY AND WORK IN THE GLOBAL ECONOMY: NEOCLASSICAL EXPLANATIONS

How do neoclassical economists explain the inequality, underemployment, low wages, and overwork that plague so much of the world? Let us take each subject in turn.

Inequalities among Nations

Why are there rich countries and poor countries? Why are some countries poor? What is missing in them that is present in the rich countries? The neoclassical answer to these questions has various strands.[18] Since neoclassical economists see capitalist economies as much more productive than any prior economic system, they contend that one reason why some countries are poor is that they are as yet insufficiently capitalist. We saw in Chapter Four that 40 percent of the world's workforce is still in agriculture.

In the poorest nations, much of this agriculture is relatively primitive, labor-intensive farming. This agriculture is inherently inefficient; a large outlay of hard labor is necessary just to feed rural families. There is little surplus to feed urban dwellers, much less trade with other countries.

What is true for agriculture is true of much of the rest of the poor economies. The main problem is low productivity. What makes an economy productive, capable of raising its output with fewer inputs, is capital. Poor countries are poor, the neoclassical economist tells us, because they lack capital. Without capital, they cannot use modern capitalist techniques of production and must resort instead to highly labor intensive work processes. Capital is not just machinery and modern technology, however. It is also a trained and skilled workforce. Poor countries lack what the neoclassical economist calls "human capital." Poorly educated and trained workers are bound to be relatively unproductive.[19]

The poverty of a nation, deriving from the lack of capital, in turn impoverishes the government, which cannot perform certain vital functions, such as maintaining the law and order necessary for smoothly operating markets. People unable to support themselves adequately otherwise will try to use the government for their own advancement. Thus poor countries show a marked proclivity for public corruption, and this makes the economy still less productive, as valuable resources are stolen or used to support a swollen state bureaucracy.

A look at the rich countries reinforces the neoclassical arguments. In the rich countries, almost all economic activity goes through markets and is subject to competitive market discipline. Only the efficient survive in such markets. Agriculture takes up a tiny fraction of the labor force, and farming is ultramodern, with the ubiquitous use of sophisticated machinery and equipment. As a consequence, agriculture is extremely productive, producing a large surplus over basic consumption needs, both for rural communities and the population as a whole. The labor displaced from agriculture provides workers for industry, and capitalist competition soon develops industry, providing a surplus of labor for work in the service sectors now dominant in the rich capitalist countries.

The governments of rich countries have sufficient resources, because incomes are high, to finance infrastructure and the institutions necessary to make the economic system still more efficient. Workers are highly educated and trained to be ever more productive. The chance to move up the economic ladder—absent in poor countries—keeps workers on their toes, working hard, and making their economies productive. In the rich countries, fully developed markets create an environment in which prosperity feeds on itself. Wealth creates opportunities, the seizing of which creates more wealth: a virtuous circle of growth, opportunities (realizable through market competition), growth.

What does the neoclassical economic advisor recommend to the poor nations? First and foremost, a poor nation must attract the requisite capital. Since the rich countries have the capital, the poor countries must obtain capital from them. This means opening up domestic economies to foreign capital. Any barriers to foreign capital, such as rules that limit foreign ownership or access to domestic currency, must be eliminated. Strong government structures must be put in place to guarantee the safety of foreign (and domestic) capital. Capital must be assured that it will not be nationalized or otherwise expropriated, and assured that it will get to keep whatever profits it makes, minus a fair share for domestic taxes. Capitalists must not be forced to pay bribes to operate. Tariffs on foreign products must be speedily eliminated, so that cheaper foreign goods can get into the country and benefit domestic consumers.

To make economic progress, a country must be willing to specialize in those goods for which it has a relative cost advantage. In poor countries, labor is cheap, so specialization can begin in those areas where foreign capital is looking for relatively cheap labor. In addition, many poor countries are especially suited for the production of certain agricultural commodities and minerals. Foreign capital should have access to the land and mines (through purchase on the market, of course). These enterprises could then hire the abundant labor to help produce crops and minerals for export. The foreign exchange earned from the exports could finance imports of other necessary capital equipment. As these sectors develop, they will naturally become more modern and capital intensive, freeing labor for production of manufacturing goods in urban areas. Then a similar process will occur there, and eventually production will shift to services as the poor country comes more and more to resemble the rich nations.

Poor countries can be helped along through foreign aid from rich countries and loans, perhaps on favorable terms, from multinational agencies like the World Bank and the International Monetary Fund. These can help governments to build the infrastructure necessary for efficient market operations, from roads and dams to modern financial markets. Along with taxes from rising wage incomes and business profits, loans can help nations build modern state bureaucracies, uncorrupted and responsive to democratic processes. Money can be spent for education and training, so that workers can take advantage of the growing demand for skilled labor that neoclassical economists assume accompanies economic growth.[20]

If poor nations actively encourage the development of markets, open up their economies to foreign capital, and build modern state structures, the neoclassical theory predicts that over time there will be a convergence between per capita incomes in the poor and rich nations.[21] The demand for labor in the poor countries will be relatively greater than the demand for labor in the rich countries, and this will cause wages in the poor nations to rise relative to wages in the rich nations. The relatively greater investment in the poor countries, attracted initially by the high rates of return, will cause the poor nations' economies to grow relatively more rapidly than the rich ones. This means a convergence of GDPs per capita, assuming that population growth is not larger in the poor countries. This should not be the case, however, since higher economic growth rates will discourage large family size as they have in the rich countries. In addition, some persons will emigrate from the poor countries, attracted by higher wages, and this will further reduce population growth.

Inequalities and Poverty within Nations

The various types of inequalities among people within nations that we studied in the last two chapters are analyzed by neoclassical economists in much the same way as the inequalities among nations. The same is true for poverty. We must note at the outset that neoclassical economists take the initial distribution of wealth in a capitalist economy as a given. They do not analyze how historically this initial distribution came to be what it was, although they admit that wealth inequality will, in and of itself, generate income inequality.

Implicit in their analysis of income and wage inequality and poverty is the notion that wealth inequality is the result of different maximizing decisions made by the participants in the marketplace. For example, those with high wealth must be persons who have had a stronger propensity to save large shares of their incomes, using the savings to purchase income-bearing assets like stocks and bonds. Or they must have had a higher tolerance for risk and used their savings to start businesses. Naturally, to maintain the argument that there is a fundamental equality between the participants in the market, each person must have roughly the same chance to save money, purchase assets, and take risks.

If we set aside questions of wealth distribution, we can explain the neoclassical analysis of income distribution and poverty in a straightforward manner.[22] According to the theory, the owners of the means of production are rewarded—that is, receive a price in the market—in proportion to their productivity. Consider workers ranked in order of their productivity to a prospective employer. Each will, other things equal, add some amount of output to the firm's total output, and, at the market price for the product, this added output will add an amount of extra revenue to the firm's total intake of money from sale of the product. The firm, if it is a profit maximizer, will hire workers as long as the amount they add to revenue (their productiveness) is greater than the amount they to add the firm's cost (their wage). The last worker hired will have a productiveness just about equal to the worker's wage.

It follows from this analysis that if one group of workers has a productiveness greater than that of another group of workers, the first group will receive a higher wage than the first group. Inequality in wages is simply a matter of unequal productivities. It also follows that the surest route to higher wages is greater productiveness.

Just as labor is productive and the market dictates that labor will be rewarded according to the level of its productivity, so too is capital productive and the market dictates that its owners will be rewarded according to its productivity. The high incomes of some of the owners of capital are due, therefore, to the great productivity of the capital they have put into the market place. If financier George Soros gets a yearly income of one billion dollars, it is because of the great productiveness of his capital, which he has risked on the market.

Poverty and unemployment receive exactly the same treatment in neoclassical economics as does inequality. The only difference is that the willingness of workers to supply their labor enters into the discussion as well as the employers' demand for labor. People are unemployed, according to the neoclassical economist, for one or both of two reasons. They may not be productive enough to be hired at the lowest wage rate they will accept. If I will not work for a wage rate less than $5.00, but I add a maximum of $4.50 per hour to an employer's revenue, I will not be hired. It could be said either that I am not productive enough to be hired or that I am asking for too high a wage rate. Another way to put this second point is to say that at the going wage rate, I have a preference for not working (leisure) which outweighs my preference for the goods and services I could purchase with the income from working. The conclusion of all of this is simple: I am unemployed but this unemployment is voluntary. I choose to be unemployed. Likewise, I choose to be poor. So some unemployment and poverty are due to insufficient productivity, but this is just another way of saying that the unemployed and the poor are insisting on a wage rate that is too high.

The solution that flows from the neoclassical analysis of inequality, poverty, and unemployment is for the society to implement policies that will raise the productivity of those at the bottom of the income and wealth distributions, the poor and the unemployed. Policies that should be avoided are those that will encourage people not to work or that will price them out of the labor market. Minimum wage laws should be avoided, since their inevitable effect will be to price less productive workers out of the market. Similarly, welfare programs that pay people without demanding that they also work should be avoided. These will just encourage people with higher leisure preferences not to work and therefore not gain the job experience so critical to becoming more productive. Unemployment compensation and disability programs should not be overly generous for the same reason—they discourage work effort.

Education and training should be promoted, because these are seen as productivity enhancers. Neoclassical economists have noted the strong positive correlation between earnings and education and training. This must mean that education and training improve worker productivity, since it is productivity that primarily determines income. Mandatory schooling, a focus on training for work in the schools, scholarships and low-interest loans for higher education, subsidies to employers for hiring less productive workers and training them, workfare programs in which those who receive welfare subsidies must work to get them—all of these, the neoclassical economist argues, can reduce inequality, poverty, and unemployment. If economic difficulties are caused by an economic downturn, monetary policy will be sufficient to get the economy back on track again.

What I have just offered as the neoclassical solutions to problems of inequality, poverty, and unemployment speaks primarily to the libertarian neoclassical position, far and away the predominant way of thinking among neoclassical economists. Two points must be added. First, the vast majority of libertarians are not concerned about inequality. They say that inequality is the price we pay for capitalism's fantastic productivity. What must be done is to strengthen the markets that are the source of this productivity. If an economy grows rapidly, all boats will rise, including those of the poor and unemployed. Why worry that a few persons are extraordinarily wealthy, as long as the majority of people experience rising incomes? Equality is the real problem: too much of it stifles productivity by denying the creative the rewards of their creativity.

Second, liberal economists are in basic agreement with their libertarian colleagues on these issues. They might still argue that some fiscal policy will be needed to end a severe economic downturn. They might say that too much inequality cannot be tolerated, so it is good to have some progressiveness in the tax structure and some concentration on the poor and unemployed in government spending programs. They might favor a higher minimum wage on the empirical grounds that most studies show relatively small job loss when the minimum wage has been increased in the past. They might also favor subsidization of things like health care for the very poor, because decent health is a prerequisite for productive labor.

Testing the Neoclassical Predictions

The neoclassical theory is the intellectual foundation of neoliberalism. If poor countries follow the neoliberal program outlined by Thomas Friedman above, they will, according to the neoclassical economists, someday become rich countries. If poor persons make appropriate investments in their "human capital," they will become richer persons. The same is true for those who are unemployed or underemployed. People work long hours largely because they choose to do so. When people acquire skills, employers will be compelled to create enough skilled jobs to match the higher demand for them. If, once people do the things necessary to improve their economic circumstances, they want to build up their wealth, they will start to save part of their income and use this saving to obtain wealth.

It is not always easy to devise tests of the neoclassical predictions, for reasons described in Chapter One. But the evidence from tests that have been done does not conform to their hypotheses. Let us look at several examples.

If markets are competitive, if nations specialize in areas where they have a comparative advantage, and if capital is free to move around the world without restraints, neoclassical economists argue that poor economies should grow more rapidly than rich ones. There should be a gradual convergence of per capita Gross Domestic Products. The evidence here is completely contrary to the neoclassical theory. We have already seen that the per capita GDPs of rich and poor nations have been diverging since at least the end of the nineteenth century.[23] With very few exceptions, the original rich capitalist countries are still rich, and the countries initially colonized and molded to shape the needs of the rich nations are still poor. It would take a kind of mindless optimism to believe that the countries in sub-Saharan Africa are going to become rich, no matter how "free" they make their economies and no matter how far into the future we make our projections. The reasonably optimistic assumptions made for India in the example in Chapter Two show a GDP convergence with the United States twelve generations from now![24]

The neoclassical economist could contest the data on divergence by saying that the poor nations had not made their economies sufficiently reliant on "free" markets. That is, in the comparisons between rich and poor countries, other things have not been held constant so that the comparison is an objective one. Had the poor nations done what they should have done, their growth rates would have been much greater, and there would have been convergence of per capita GDPs. This is a common tactic used by neoclassical economists. It is trotted out every time neoclassical expectations are not confirmed by actual events. Since it is difficult to imagine that any economy could be structured exactly according to the neoclassical assumptions, it is always possible for the economists to say that events do not really contradict the theory's predictions. This becomes a kind of quasi-religious argument. There is always at least one of God's rules that imperfect humans have violated, and this transgression can be used to "explain" why human beings have come to ruin.

It is possible to use recent history to provide a test of the convergence hypothesis. Between 1980 and the present, most of the world's poor nations have introduced much of the neoliberal regimen of open markets, deregulation, privatization, austere public budgets, and encouragement of foreign investment. According to neoclassical theory, such a long period of neoliberal reforms should have brought about high GDP growth rates. Exactly the opposite was the case, as shown in Table 5.1. The growth rate of per capita GDP in the developing countries (what I have called the poor countries) was much lower between 1980 and 1998 than it was in the earlier period, 1960–1969. In fact, the growth rate was zero! While growth rates also slowed in the rich countries, they were still much higher than in the poor countries, and the amount of the decline was not as large. Therefore, per capita

GDPs continued to diverge. The evidence against convergence is so over-whelming that neoclassical economists have begun to tweak their models so that, under certain assumptions, even competitively organized economies might diverge.[25] When theorists resort to such devices, however, they are admitting that their basic model is inadequate. And it is always the basic model that informs the public policies promoted in the name of the theory.

It needs to be stressed that the poor countries that most fully embraced neoliberal programs were the most likely to suffer severe financial crises. There are many examples here. Thailand in the late 1990s and Argentina in 2001 and 2002 come immediately to mind. Both economies experienced rapid GDP growth—though not development in the sense of a widely shared general increase in social welfare—and were christened by mainstream economists as the latest economic miracle. When Thailand opened up its economy, doing all of the things Mr. Friedman tells us poor nations must do, foreign money literally flew into the country, attracted by low wages, high interest rates, and eager borrowers. Stock market and real estate booms ensued, and all sorts of businesses began operations, often in newly constructed buildings. But then Japanese banks raised their interest rates and investors began to realize that the boom had played itself out. Money began to leave the country as fast as it had entered. As the Thai currency, the baht, was sold to purchase dollars and yen, it fell in value. Stocks and real estate were sold and the money sent out of Thailand. Speculators went to

TABLE 5.1   Table 1. Median Average Annual Per Capita Income Growth Rates, OECD and Developing Countries[a]

	1960-1979	1980-1998
OECD[b]	3.4	1.8
DEVELOPING COUNTRIES[c]	2.5	0.0

a   The numbers shown in this chart represent median values for average annual per capita income of countries over the years indicated. The median value is the point at which half of all countries in the group are above the average growth rate indicated while half are below.

b   These are the leading industrial economics in Europe, plus the United States, Japan, Canada, Australia, and New Zealand.

c   Developing countries here encompasses all developing countries, including China and ex- Communist states in Eastern Europe and Central Asia.

SOURCE: This table is taken from The Editors, "The New Face of Capitalism," Monthly Review 53 (April 2002): 3.

work, selling short, and this drove the prices of everything inexorably down-ward. As the value of the currency sank, the price of imports, upon which the country was dependent (it was following the export model of economic growth, ignoring production for domestic markets), rose dramatically, >

SUMMERS'S INFAMOUS MEMO [26]

Lawrence Summers is the president of Harvard University. A well-respected econo-mist, very much committed to the neoclassical model, he served as President Clin-ton's Secretary of the Treasury and before that as chief economist at the World Bank. In 1991 he issued a memorandum concerning industrial pollution. In it he said, "Shouldn't the World Bank be encouraging more migration of dirty industries to the third world?" His argument is a classic example of neoclassical reasoning. We know that industrial pollution causes sickness and death. This sickness and death have costs, which can be measured by the forgone earnings of those who get sick (and cannot work) and those who die.

According to Summers, forgone earnings will be higher in rich countries, where wages (and therefore productivity) are higher, than they will be in poor countries, where the opposite is the case. Since the loss in rich countries outweighs the loss in poor countries, the world will gain if polluting industries are moved to poor countries. In addition, since some poor nations have more pristine environments (because they have less pollution-generating industry), the initial pollution from industries will do relatively less environmental damage than it would in environments already heavily polluted. A little bit of smoke in clean air will hardly be noticed, whereas more smoke in dirty air might be the straw that breaks the camel's back. Finally, pollution will cause cancer and other diseases that might only affect people in their old age. In poor countries life expectancies are low, so people won't live long enough to get the diseases, again a good reason to encourage the building of polluting industrial facilities in poor countries.

Nowhere in Summers's memo does he point out how it is that the poor countries came to be poor. The fact that much of the rich countries' wealth was simply the result of the force and violence wreaked by the rich nations upon the poor countries does not enter into his analysis. This is not his concern. He just takes the conditions of the poor countries as a given. Then his marginal analysis of costs and benefits appears impeccable in its logic. A poor life is indeed worth less than a rich one. If he were to see the plight of the poor countries as the consequence of deliberate actions taken by the rich nations, of the money in the rich man's pocket as intimately con-nected to the emptiness of the poor person's pocket, he could not have written his memo. Instead he would have had to talk about debts and reparations.

badly hurting ordinary Thais. As construction ground to a halt and business in general went into a slump, unemployment and misery mounted.
Neoclassical apologists began to say that the Thai government was corrupt.
It practiced "crony capitalism," and was therefore not a true model of
neoliberalism. No wonder the economy failed.[27]

Reality also dealt a serious blow to neoclassical economics with respect
to the North American Free Trade Agreement (NAFTA). This treaty, supported by virtually all neoclassical economists, was supposed to raise the living
conditions of workers in all three treaty nations: Canada, the United States,
and Canada. Yet research shows that NAFTA's promises have not been realized. Research done by economists at the Economic Policy Institute in the
United States indicates that NAFTA is partly responsible for growing
inequality in all three signatory countries. NAFTA has caused significant job
loss in high-wage manufacturing industries in the United States.[28] This by
itself lowers average wage rates in the United States, but it also lowers wages
by increasing the supply of labor seeking employment in the already low-
wage service sector. We have already noted the treaty's devastating impact
on Mexican peasants.[29] I am not aware of any study showing that NAFTA
raised the per capita GDP growth rate of any of the three nations. In fact,
right after passage of NAFTA, the Mexican economy went into a tailspin.

If the neoclassical theory fares poorly in explaining inequality among
nations, its performance is strikingly bad in unraveling the causes of
inequality, poverty, wages, and underemployment within countries.
According to the theory, inequality in income is simply the monetary
reflection of inequality in productivity. This notion can be challenged on
both theoretical and empirical grounds. Although capital in the form of
machinery, buildings, and equipment is productive in the sense that, other
things equal, the more capital per worker, the more output is produced,
the ownership of capital is not a productive act. Therefore, income from
the ownership of the nonhuman means of production cannot be justified
on the grounds that the means of production are productive. A significant
fraction of the nonhuman means of production become the private property of individuals through inheritance, and in these cases the argument
that the inheritors are productive is particularly ridiculous. Neoclassical
economists do not seem to be capable of the realization that if Bill Gates
went into a coma, he would still collect billions of dollars of income every
year, despite the fact that whatever productivity he once had had was now
reduced to zero. It is ownership that generates income, not productivity.[30]

The neoclassical explanation of wage inequality is likewise suspect. If we say that wages reflect productivity, we must be able to measure the productivity of individual workers. This, however, is for the most part impossible. The output of many workers, particularly those in the burgeoning service sector, cannot be measured in any meaningful way. What output does a teacher produce? A policeman? A doctor or nurse? In industrial settings, work is not an individual process; it involves the necessary cooperation of large groups of workers. The productivity of an individual worker is a meaningless concept.

But even if we use indirect measures of productivity, such as years of schooling and years of experience, and hold these constant across samples of workers, we find that wages are still unequal. Workers can do exactly the same kind of work and have equal productivity (as measured indirectly) and still earn different wages. All workers know of situations in their own workplaces in which one worker works harder and with greater diligence in the same job and gets less pay than another.[31]

The most damaging studies for the neoclassical wage analysis have been those dealing with wages by race and gender. Nearly all studies show that equally situated black and white workers do not earn the same pay; black workers always make less. The same is true for women; no matter how many factors we hold constant, women earn less than men. Neoclassical economists have devised several ingenious theories to explain racial and gender differences. Nobel award winner Gary Becker has hypothesized that some employers have a "taste for discrimination," that is, these employers are willing to pay—by making lower profits—to satisfy this taste, which leads them to pay black workers who are as productive as whites less money. But what Becker does not seem to be able to explain is why some nondiscriminating employers would not then hire black workers at a wage less than their productiveness, lower their product prices, and drive their racist rivals out of business.[32]

The neoclassical theory predicts that equally productive workers will make equal wages. This is manifestly not the case. If we look at workers across the world and observe the astronomical differences in wages among workers, this prediction looks increasingly preposterous. The Mexican workers making car engines for General Motors or Ford are as productive as their Detroit counterparts, but the pay of the former is a small fraction of that of the latter.

On a macroeconomic level, there is no direct connection between productivity and wages. In the United States, for example, productivity in the economy as a whole rose steadily between 1973 and 1998. Yet median compensation (compensation equals wages plus benefits) fell in real terms throughout most of this period.[33] If productivity is the major wage determinant, these trends are very difficult to explain.

There have been many other, indirect, tests of the neoclassical explanations of labor market outcomes. We have already noted the minimum wage studies by Card and Krueger. Contrary to the prediction of the neoclassical theory, a government increase in the minimum wage does not lead to losses of employment, at least not in the United States. Instead, an increased minimum wage has ordinarily been associated with increases in employment, as well as some reductions in poverty and income inequality. There is also some evidence that so-called living wage laws, enacted by local governments in the United States to provide certain employees with a wage that will keep a family above the poverty level of income, have not caused any job losses.[34]

The neoclassical theory predicts that rising wages will cause unemployment. This can be explained neoclassically in two ways. First, as wages rise, insufficiently productive workers will be priced out of the labor market. Employers will be forced to cut back employment or risk losing money. Second, if we consider two parts of a country, one with a low and one with a high unemployment rate, we could argue as follows. Suppose that a worker living in the low unemployment area is contemplating moving to the high unemployment area. He or she will require a higher wage to move, since in the new location the risk of unemployment is higher. Two British economists put this hypothesis to the test in an exhaustive study involving millions of wage and unemployment observations worldwide. What they found was that, other things equal, the relationship between wage rates and unemployment is inverse. High unemployment rates are associated with low wage rates and not vice versa as the theory predicts. Unemployment may be due to many things, but it does not appear that high wages are one of them.[35]

Finally, neoclassicals have always argued that some unemployment and poverty are voluntary, the result of high leisure preferences among some persons. Again, the empirical evidence for this is weak. In the United States, the federal government conducted an income transfer experiment in the 1970s. Two groups of families were selected in a number of eastern cities. One group was given an income subsidy each month for three years, and the other group was not. Using statistical techniques to hold other variables constant, researchers studied the labor market behavior of the two groups. Neoclassical theory predicts that the families receiving the subsidy would be more likely to drop out of the labor force or reduce their hours of work. This was not the case, especially for Black and Hispanic men, who actually increased their labor market activities. The wives in the families did reduce their labor market activities, but they substituted greater child care and more schooling for this. The behavior of both wives and husbands in this study hardly fit the neoclassical stereotype of leisure-seeking poor people, loafing more because they get money from the government.[36]

THE ECONOMICS OF THE ISOLATED INDIVIDUAL

Neoclassical economics is the economics of the isolated individual. Social outcomes are hypothesized to be the results of all of the maximizing decisions of buyers and sellers in the marketplace. In this theory the individual is prior to society, so it is not necessary to ask what effects social circumstances might have on individual behavior. Society is never to blame for anything in this theory, precisely because it is not in any sense outside of and acting upon the individual.

It is no wonder the theory does not test well when it comes to inequality among nations, inequality within countries, poverty, underemployment, and overwork—the subjects of this book. How a nation's economy performs has everything to do with the position it holds within the ranks of the world's nations. The extremely poor nations of sub-Saharan Africa have been forcibly underdeveloped by the rich nations for centuries. Unless this relationship, one of imperialism, changes, there cannot be much hope that these nations will develop, regardless of what their governments decide to do. Certainly, if they pursue neoliberalism, they just reinforce the conditions that got them into such a fix in the first place.

Similarly, those at the bottom of the income distribution, those who are poor, those without wealth, those who are underemployed, those who are overworked—none of these people are likely to improve their circumstances much through individual maximizing actions. Nor will we be able to explain their conditions by looking at individual maximizing behavior. Their difficulties are structural; they find themselves locked into a set of structures beyond their individual control. To say that the thousands of people living and working in the garbage dumps outside of Manila in the Philippines have made a set of poor maximizing choices is to say nothing at all. To say that they should get more schooling is naive beyond words. To say that they are unproductive is equally unhelpful. To say that they are voluntarily underemployed is preposterous on its face. To say that they will be helped if the government embraces neoliberalism is simply wrong; their plight and the plight of most of the world's poor have worsened precisely as their leaders have opened their economies to foreign capital.

While libertarians rule the neoclassical roost, there are still some liberal economists who have taken issue with the libertarians. They do not believe that all unemployment and poverty are voluntary; they still hold to Keynes's view that unemployment is, for the most part, involuntary. Aggressive fiscal policies are needed to combat this unemployment, and various types of capital controls (see the last chapter for more on these) must be put in place so that the expansionary impact of fiscal policy can be realized.

Another group of liberal economists have pretty much abandoned strict neoclassical arguments and concentrated upon empirical investigations. Good examples are the minimum wage studies of Card and Krueger and the wage/unemployment rate studies of Oswald and Blanchflower. U.S. economists Richard Freeman and James Medoff have done important empirical work on the real-world effects of unions on wages, employment, prices, and equality. Their conclusions are much more sympathetic to unions than is the neoclassical theory itself.

While the liberal economists represent a more humane outlook than the libertarians, it is important to understand that only another theory, better able to explain the economic world, can supplant the neoclassical theory. And, for reasons made clear in Chapter One, only a strong social movement aimed at radically altering the societies that gave rise to neoclassical economics can ensure that a new theory will have a chance to survive.

CHAPTER SIX: A Radical Economic Perspective

WHY IS NEOCLASSICAL ECONOMICS SO PERVASIVE?

When capitalist economies were new, the writers who attempted the first analyses of these economies were, for the most part, driven by a desire to understand things. They did not stand to gain anything by their studies, such as academic appointments, government commissions, or money. They weren't trained as economists and thereby subject to the prejudices of their teachers; indeed there was no such person as an economist nor a field of university study called economics. Adam Smith was a professor of philosophy and David Ricardo was a financial speculator and businessman. Because they were relatively objective, they could learn some fundamental truths about capitalism. Smith could see clearly the tendency, inherent in the normal operation of the new system, for employers to find ways to destroy their competitors and monopolize markets. Ricardo could see clearly that profits are not a cost of production but a surplus.

Neoclassical economics can make no claim to objectivity. Its analyses of inequality, underemployment, poverty, and wages are manifestly incorrect and fail nearly every test to which they have been put. Yet each year scores of new textbooks appear on the market presenting the same worn analysis as if were God's truth. Inequality reflects productivity differences. Minimum wages, living wages, union-negotiated wages, all cause job loss. Welfare and social welfare programs drive people out of the labor force. People are poor or underemployed because they are unproductive. Their lack of productiveness is the consequence of the choices they made in the past. Jobs are what they are because workers want them to be that way. We are all free to choose, and therefore we are all responsible for the outcomes of those choices. Poor nations will become rich nations if they embrace the neoliberal program of free markets, deregulation, privatization, foreign investment, and free trade.

All of this is the stuff of the most commonly adopted textbooks. All of this is the stuff of the public pronouncements and daily actions of economists. Go to Harvard University, or the University of Chicago, or Stanford University and you will find Nobel Prize winners in economics galore. But try to find five economists on any of these campuses who oppose the North American Free Trade Agreement, the World Bank, or the World Trade Organization. Try to find five economists on any of these campuses who champion labor unions, who are fighting on behalf of living wage campaigns, who believe that there is such a thing as imperialism and are willing to use their skills against it, or do not make some sort of excuse for sweatshops and child labor. Try to find five tenured economics professors at those prestigious universities who have not done lucrative consulting for the rich and powerful.

The fact that neoclassical economics is so wrong yet so powerful tells us that it is not a science but an ideology. As we have suggested in previous chapters and will make manifest here, capitalist economies are expansionary by their nature. There is no place on earth or any aspect of life that will not become subject to the rule of the market. This is true in both a direct and an indirect sense. In a direct sense, capitalism puts everything everywhere up for sale: anything that can be done profitably, anywhere in the world, will be taken over and subordinated to the needs of profit. And the commodification of everything, everywhere will be presented as natural, inevitable, and good.

Neoclassical economics dominates not because it relentlessly pursues the truth. It certainly does nothing of the kind; if it did, the same tired textbook clichés constantly contradicted by the evidence of testing could not survive. A scientist who maintained that the earth was flat would not even be considered a scientist, much less get a scientific forum from which to speak. Yet an economist like Martin Feldstein, whose views on social security have no scientific basis whatever, is not only considered to be an eminent economist but can, whenever he wants one, find a venue in which to speak. What is more, he will be loudly applauded for what he says and handsomely paid. Why?

The most important reason why neoclassical economics dominates the field is because it is so very favorably disposed toward capitalism. It might be attractive to some students because it is elegant. Its precise mathematical formulations, in fact, do appeal to a good number of dropouts from the natural sciences. A popular joke among economists has it that a good economist will be reincarnated as a physicist, while a bad one will come back as a sociologist. But neoclassical economics' elegance cannot explain its dominance. The economics of Karl Marx is elegant; Marx was once called the "poet of commodities."[1] But Marx is not taught in the economics classroom.

Capitalism seeks out those who love it. Neoclassical economists love capitalism; their theory is one long hymn of praise to capitalism. No wonder then that the media, themselves organized as powerful capitalist enterprises, seek them out and publish their phrases. No wonder that textbook publishers pay them large advances to write the textbooks. No wonder that corporations, think tanks, governments, and international financial institutions hire them. Could Lawrence Summers have been hired by the World Bank if he had previously led large demonstrations of the poor against the rich and powerful? Could Gregory Mankiw have been paid a seven-figure advance to write an introductory economics textbook if his text had called for the abolition of the World Trade Organization and insisted upon a rationally planned economy? Could he have gotten a column in *Fortune* magazine? Could an economist who served as an economics adviser to any of the many national liberation struggles of the past and present obtain a good job in an economics department anywhere in the capitalist world?

Neoclassical economics is an important part of the belief system that makes the maintenance of capitalism possible. Capitalism must beat people into submission when necessary, but it is far better to win the hearts and minds of the people who live and work in capitalist societies. If they come to believe that capitalism is the best economic system or at least the only one that can be made to work in the modern world, they will be unlikely to spend time and energy seeking alternatives to it. They will find it in their own best interests to just accept it. Perhaps they will think it necessary to try to correct some of its weaknesses, but these efforts will be seen as working within the system and not against it.

Neoclassical economics does its ideological job well. It claims to show that an economy based on self-interest will be one that satisfies society's most pressing needs and does so better than any other system. By preaching this simple idea repeatedly, endlessly, in textbooks, in front of classrooms full of eager students, in the media, in public debates, always to high praise from presidents, congresspersons, and corporate leaders, neoclassical economics has succeeded in helping to create a capitalist society. So well has it succeeded that studies have shown that students who take a course in economics are more likely to behave selfishly than those who have not.[3]

Our interest does not lie in simply exposing the weaknesses of neoclassical economics. We want to find out what really causes the problems examined in Chapters One through Three of this book. It is not enough to know that unemployment is not caused by low worker productivity compared to wage rates. We need to know what does cause unemployment. In this chapter we lay out another theory of economics, a radical theory, first developed by Karl Marx and Frederick Engels.4 As we will see, this theory offers a much better fit with capitalist reality.

Another reason for the dominance of neoclassical economics is the bad name that has been given to socialism both by its enemies and some of its supposed friends. Before the 1990s, there were many economies that were not capitalist. In fact, far more people lived in socialist economies than lived in capitalist ones. The challenge to capitalism implicit in the Soviet Union, China, Cuba, and the economies of Eastern Europe gave rise to the Cold War

---

A PERSONAL STORY

I chose to major in economics by accident. I had to choose a major to get a scholarship, so I had my father read down the list of majors. When he got to "Economics," I said, "Put that down." I diligently studied neoclassical economics for the next six years. I was impressed by its formal elegance and by the sense of its professors of the superiority of economics to the other social sciences. Once I had mastered some of it, I felt that I had joined an elite club. Not for us the fuzzy thinking of political science and sociology. This was science, complete with theorems and mathematical precision.

In graduate school, I had my first doubts. The economists and most of the students seemed either oblivious to the horrible war in Vietnam or, worse yet, they supported it. When my favorite professor devoted a class to a discussion of the war, he was roundly criticized by the students for wasting their time. How could they pass their comprehensive exams when their instructors behaved so irresponsibly? Most of the students just wanted to learn about general equilibrium analysis, Cobb-Douglas production functions, the Slutsky equation, and all of the other staples of formal economic analysis. If we could only master the advanced works of Paul Samuelson, we'd be in heaven.

The war ultimately ended my graduate career. I got drafted three times, fought against the Selective Service system, and eventually found a safe haven as an instructor at a branch campus of my university. It was here, as a teacher, that I really became enlightened. As I began to teach neoclassical economics, I had to force myself to

of U.S.-led aggression toward the socialist economies. This war was waged on many fronts, not least of which was an ideological front.5 Neoclassical economics was an important element in the anti- socialist ideological war. The neoclassical economists railed against the lack of market freedoms in socialist economies; there was no consumer sovereignty in them. Dictatorial planners made all of the basic decisions in socialist economies. There were never enough goods to go around, as evidenced by long lines at stores and rationing schemes. Staunch neoclassical economists such as Friedrich Hayek and Ludwig von Mises insisted that planning was inherently irrational and incapable of effectively directing a complex modern economy.

Since the name of Karl Marx was often invoked by the socialist societies' leaders, all of the alleged evils of these societies were associated with Marx and kindred theorists. Radicals of all stripes were lumped together as defenders of the godless and anti-democratic socialist states. >

make sense of it, so that I could explain it in plain English. This I found impossible to do. The neoclassical answers to the questions I now had were just not adequate. Why was the United States destroying Vietnam? Why were Blacks rioting in the streets? Why were economists so hostile to people in poor nations trying to liberate themselves? My neoclassical colleagues did not think it odd that Milton Friedman and his "Chicago boys" were urging the fascist government of Chilean General Pinochet to use "economic shock treatment" (their phrase for neoliberalism) in Chile right when the general's thugs were using real shock treatment and murder on the supporters of democratically elected supporters of Salvador Allende, whom these same thugs had just killed.[2] Similarly, they did not see why the university should sell its stock holdings of those companies that did business in apartheid South Africa, another place where neoclassical economics reigned supreme.

One day in class my first year, I became so disgusted with the sterility of what I was teaching that I threw the textbook and my notes to the floor. "We're going to talk about the real world today," I said. I then led a spirited discussion of the war in Vietnam, poverty in the United States, and racism. I found by accident some radical magazines in the library, including Monthly Review, and began to read them voraciously. One article led to other articles and books. Discussions with some of the more progressive students and teachers led to others. Within a year, I was a confirmed radical. I never again taught neoclassical economics without at least criticizing it and suggesting alternative ways to look at production and distribution.

Not coincidentally, they were also declared enemies of the "free world," in other words of capitalism, since in the minds of the champions of the "free world," including the neoclassical economists, freedom and capitalism went hand in hand.[6]

Given the ferociousness of the Cold War, it is not surprising that those opposed to neoclassical economics had a hard time getting an audience for their views. Radical economists were fired from universities and ever after unable to earn a living as teachers. Radical ideas were expunged from the economics curriculum, except as objects of scorn. Radical economics was, according to the neoclassical economists, an exercise in dogma, not science. By 1960, there was exactly one radical economist tenured in a U.S. university, the outstanding scholar of economic growth and development, Paul Baran. But Baran was completely isolated and driven to sickness by the persecution he faced. Radical economists were forced, like their counterparts in the entertainment world, to write under assumed names and to earn their living far from their chosen fields.[7]

This situation changed somewhat as a consequence of the rebellions of the 1960s, but the Cold War certainly continued. Today, however, the Cold War is over. The socialist economies, with but a couple of exceptions, most notably Cuba, have collapsed and are rushing pell-mell toward capitalism. This has redounded even more to the advantage of neoclassical economics. With the triumph of capitalism over its socialist rivals, neoclassical economists could say, "See, we told you so." Since the radical alternative to capitalism failed so miserably, it is evident that the radical theory of capitalism that formed the foundation of socialist economic thinking must itself be worthless. Of course, a moment's reflection tells us that the radical analysis of capitalism need have nothing at all to do with the failure of the socialist economies.

CAPITALISM'S EARLY CRITICS

From their beginnings several centuries ago, capitalist economies have had their critics as well as their champions. The feudal economies directly preceding capitalism were traditional societies, in the sense that people in them had fixed, more or less hereditary, roles to play. A lord was a lord, a serf was a serf, and both held their social places directly from the will of God. Capitalism, by contrast, is most untraditional; the untrammeled pursuit of money, in fact, tends to burst apart all fixed relationships. As Karl

Marx put it so famously in the *Communist Manifesto*, "All that is solid melts into air."[8] Unless a traditional way of doing things can be fitted into some money-making enterprise, it must disappear.

The constant flux and change inherent in capitalism is profoundly disorienting to many people and is at the heart of what we might call the "reactionary" critique of capitalism. Some members of the European nobility found capitalism distasteful because it disdained tradition. Merchants, for instance, were not happy to pay taxes and tolls to the nobility and otherwise show servility toward them, certainly not if these cost them money. Accordingly, some nobles criticized capitalism, but with a hopeful eye turned toward the past, to which they hoped to return. Today, certain religious fundamentalists criticize capitalism in the same vein, except that they say capitalism demeans religion with its money. For example, a business person will not be keen to honor too many religious holidays, because such holidays impede the business person's ability to make money.

The impersonal nature of markets gives rise to a moral criticism of capitalism. If children are cheap and productive enough, capitalists will employ them. The same goes for their mothers and fathers. The early factories and the towns in which they were located were places of abomination—filled with filth, noise, smoke, disease, and death. What capitalism did was turn human beings into commodities, "things" bought and sold in a cold and heartless market. Many people found this repulsive and castigated the new economic system as immoral The moral critics of capitalism made many recommendations for alleviating the worst abuses of the new system, though few of them thought in terms of transcending capitalism and building a new economic system. Some of them recommended education; others proposed "model" factories; a few proposed the establishment of entirely new communities run on a less competitive and more cooperative basis.[9]

The critique of capitalism was profoundly affected by an important development. The new economic system had brought forward a new class of persons: wage laborers. Prior to capitalism, those who labored were in one way or another attached—connected—to the nonhuman means of production. Gatherers and hunters roamed the land freely and used it as they pleased, getting their food by direct appropriation. Slaves and serfs were not free, but they were definitely attached to the means of production. Wage workers, however, are "free" of the nonhuman means of production; they have no access to them unless they can sell their ability to work.

Commandeering the notion of "freedom" being used by the new capitalist class to their own ends, the newly created wage laborers began to organize themselves collectively, so as to secure a more meaningful freedom than that given to them as "free" wage laborers.[10] This organization of wage laborers forced intellectuals to look more carefully at the new capitalist economic system. Attention was shifted away from the market, where, it was claimed, the workers and their employers met as equals before the impersonal market, and toward the workplace, where, as the new workers' organizations made clear, workers were eminently not free. This look inside the workplace helped to give Marx and Engels their great insight into the nature of capitalism. They came to see that markets, although ubiquitous, were superficial aspects of capitalism, hiding what was most critical—the inherently unequal relationship between capitalists and wage laborers.

The organization of workers had a second, and equally profound, impact on the critique of capitalism. In previous class societies, those who labored faced insurmountable barriers to any struggle they might mount against their masters. Slaves did revolt, but they did not often succeed. The power of the slave owners was too great. Much the same was true for serfs in feudal society. In addition, neither slaves nor serfs are "universal" classes; they often coexisted with other forms of freer labor, such as independent peasant farmers. Slaves and serfs could not easily communicate across estates and manors, making their existence completely localized. With wage laborers, however, we have something different. Capitalism tolerates no rival mode of production, and this means that over time nearly everyone who works has to sell their labor for a wage. By definition, capitalism is not a localized system; we have already seen that it has a global impulse. As capitalists relentlessly shift their capital everywhere and anywhere, workers are pitched from pillar to post. They intermingle across countries and eventually across the globe. Furthermore, they are herded into factories, again mixing with other workers, not all of whom will be of the same religion, race, gender, age, or ethnicity as themselves.

Capitalism, in other words, creates a universal class of persons, all sharing the same status: propertyless and unfree. As they came to understand their situations, might it not be possible that they would also come to realize their enormous potential power? They alone produced the world's wealth, and there is no substitute for them. They could, through universal collective organization, win control of society's productive mechanism and produce for themselves, which, given their overwhelming numbers relative to the whole of society, would mean that, for all practical purposes, they would be producing for all humanity. Combined with Marx and Engels's radical insight into how capitalism worked, this notion of an organized working class fighting to liberate itself, and by extension all of us, has formed the basis for the many anti-capitalist movements that began to develop as long ago as the French Revolution.

THE TWIN FACES OF CAPITALISM

Radical economists grant that capitalist economies are engines of economic growth. After all, the industrial revolution occurred in capitalism, not in feudalism or slavery or gathering and hunting societies. By unleashing, indeed glorifying, self-interest, capitalism paved the way for a dizzying array of technological innovations and rapidly rising output. We have seen that this output growth never happens without periodically slowing down or even going into reverse, during the periodic recessions and depressions that have marked capitalism's history. We have also seen that growth is uneven among nations, with most of the growth concentrated in a few rich capitalist countries. Finally, we have observed that the output produced in capitalist economies need not be useful in any meaningful sense and can, in fact, be harmful to human beings and the natural world. Yet it is still true that, compared to other economic systems, capitalism can and often does deliver the goods, lots of them.

The question that radicals ask is what makes the growth of output in capitalist economies possible. Their answer to this question is one of the major points of difference between neoclassical and radical economics. What makes the growth of output possible in a capitalist economy is the profits of the capitalists. Only if capitalists make profits will they produce output; only if they make profits will they invest these profits in new means of production and cause the economy to grow. Therefore, the question of the growth of output is really the question of profits. How is it possible for capitalists to make profits? How can they begin with one sum of money and end up with a larger one?

The radical answer to this question is that profits are made possible only by the exploitation of wage laborers.[11] Capitalism can be described as a system whose motor force is the *accumulation of capital*, the ceaseless drive by individual capitalists to make money and achieve growth. However, this accumulation of capital is predicated upon the extraction of a surplus from the labor of the workers. In order for wealth to be created, suffering, in the form of exploitation of labor, must also exist. Marx portrayed this as the simultaneous development of poles of riches and misery. In other words, and to put it bluntly, the conditions of life and labor investigated in Chapters Two and Three are not accidental or due to poor maximizing choices made by working people. They are the necessary conditions for the accumulation of capital. Wealth and poverty go hand in hand in capitalism; you cannot have one without the other.

Before, we delve into the details of the radical theory, it is important to grasp what we are saying here. We are stating unequivocally that capitalism cannot possibly liberate the masses of people from their poor circumstances. It is the creator of these circumstances, and no amount of reform whether it be neoliberal or old-fashioned liberal can alter this fact. We shall see in Chapter Seven that if workers are well organized, they can achieve certain, usually temporary, gains within the confines of capitalism. But they cannot win what is most necessary—an end to their dependence on capital and their exploitation by it.

THE ACCUMULATION OF CAPITAL

In *Capital*, volume one, Karl Marx devised a letter scheme to help us analyze capitalism. The scheme is M-C-C'-M'. Suppose that we imagine a typical capitalist business. Any one will do, but let us use a large flower farm on the outskirts of Bogotá in the South American country of Colombia. The rich farm land outside of Colombia's capital city has been transformed into enormous agricultural "factories" devoted to the production of cut flowers for export to the rich countries. Today, for example, 47 percent of Canada's imported cut flowers come from Colombia.[12] As might be expected, working conditions are horrendous: long hours, low pay, and constant exposure to dangerous pesticides. A perpetual cloud hangs over the area from the spraying of the crops.

To become a cut flower capitalist, the first ingredient is money. Capitalist enterprises cannot be started without money; money is always the starting point of capitalist production. The letter, M, in the above schema stands, therefore, for *money capital*. Note that this is not just money but money that is going to be used to organize the production of output. This money functions as capital and not as money to be used to buy consumer goods. How capitalists get their hands on the money is not relevant here.

The money capital must now undergo a series of transformations, the ultimate aim of which is to convert the original sum of money (M) into a large sum of money (M'). The first transformation occurs as a result of a set of market transactions. Our cut flower business must use its money capital to buy the means of production, all of the inputs needed to produce the flowers. Let us assume that the owners pay whatever the market prices are for these inputs and that these inputs are sold on reasonably competitive markets. These inputs are called *commodity capital (C)*; through their purchase the money capital has changed form. We still have capital because the means of production are not purchased for their own sake but for their further conversion into output, in this case, cut flowers.

There are two types of inputs needed. The first type consists of all of the nonhuman means of production: land, buildings, tools, machinery, and raw materials. These are called *constant capital*; some of them are long-lasting (the machines, etc.), while some will be used up in each production cycle (the raw materials like seed and fertilizer). The second type of commodity capital is the labor power of the workers, without which, of course, there can be no production. This labor power is purchased as a commodity like any other commodity. Remember that labor markets are one of capitalism's three essential features. We call it labor power rather than labor because the employer does not buy the laborers themselves, but only their potential to work, to exert their power to labor. The labor power purchased in the market is called *variable capital*.

Once the requisite amounts of constant and variable capital are bought, they must be combined, under the strict control of the capitalist, to produce the desired output—cut flowers. The cut flowers are the C' in the letter scheme, and we can call them *commodities for sale*. We must note that the transformation of commodity capital into commodities for sale does not occur in the marketplace. Instead it takes place inside of the workplace, in this case on the farm. It is here, inside the workplace, that our capitalist comes into direct contact with the workers whose labor actually produces the flowers. The employer will have to insist on tight control over what happens inside the workplace, over what we call the labor process. This is because the workers are the only active agent in production, and therefore they are the only means of production that could interfere with the capitalists' aim of making money. We will have much more to say about this later.

Finally, after the commodity capital has been changed into commodities for sale, our capitalists are ready for the last step. The commodities now return to the market for sale. The money obtained from the sale of the cut flowers is represented by the M'. If the process has been successful, the

M' will be larger than the M. The difference between the two Ms is the profit—or loss, if M' is smaller.

Will our capitalists, delighted at having made some money, be content just to spend the money, perhaps on luxury consumption? Will they, in an act of generosity, share out the profits with their hard-working laborers by raising wages or improving working conditions? Radical economists say no; businesses must use as large a part of the profits as possible to begin the M- C-C'-M' process again, but on an expanded basis. That is, capitalists must not only make profits, they must see to it that their capital grows. The reason for this is simple. It is not because the capitalists are greedy, though they probably are, but because they face strong competition. If our cut flower capitalists do not invest profits in expanded production and any of their rivals do, they will not be able to compete effectively over the long haul. They will not be able to purchase the best new equipment, or develop a research facility, or enlarge their advertising budgets enough, or get bank loans on favorable terms. After a while, they will be undersold and driven from the market, losing all of the amenities that come one's way when one is a successful capitalist—prestige, high incomes, and political power. Competition forces each capitalist, on pain of death in the marketplace, to make profits and grow, to, in a word, *accumulate capital*.

Marx called the twin process of profit maximization and growth the accumulation of capital, and it is this that drives the capitalist economy forward. It is this that gives capitalism its dynamic character, and it is this that differentiates it from all previous modes of production. The growth of investment and output is built into the nature of the system. The accumulation of capital knows no bounds. Capital is always looking for ways to expand. First local markets are conquered, then national, and finally global markets. First one sphere of life provides opportunities for capital accumulation, then another, then nearly all of life. Today, our births, our upbringing, our schooling, our religions, our work lives, our leisure, and our deaths, all provide ample opportunities for making money, and each, in its turn, becomes a platform for the accumulation of capital.

THE LABOR THEORY OF VALUE

While the accumulation of capital is the goal of all capitalists, it remains to discover how this accumulation is possible. How precisely is the M converted into the M'? Marx's answer to this question forms the heart of the radical theory of capitalism. In a capitalist economy, production and distribution are organized around markets, that is, most aspects of production and distribution involve the buying and selling of commodities. In the labor market, workers and employers do not appear to actually face each other but rather each faces the market. Since the market is impersonal and not controlled by either the worker or the employer, it appears that the two parties face each other as equals. Each is free to either reach or not reach agreement. No worker is bound to any employer, and no employer is compelled to hire any worker. It does not appear that the workers are exploited by the capitalists; profits then do not appear to result from any exploitation. They appear to be the consequence of the sale of output in the marketplace. It is obvious in a slave society that slaves are exploited, that their labor is the source of the output that forms the basis for the slave owners' wealth. Similarly, in a feudal society, we could see the serfs delivering up their surplus output to the lords as rent. And we could see the serfs laboring on the lords' fields, all of the output of which goes directly to the nobility. Clearly, serfs are exploited. But with capitalism, things appear to be different.

Marx argued that markets represented capitalism's appearance but not its ultimate reality. Underneath the market was a reality of exploitation of labor by capital. The market served as a veil, a cover we have to remove if we want to see capitalism's reality. Workers are exploited just as certainly as slaves and serfs, but the way in which this occurs is much different. Workers are cheated behind their backs, so to speak.

The key to Marx's theory lies in the movement from C to C' in the letter scheme. Remember that this transition takes place inside of the workplace. It is here that the workers confront the capitalist. They have the potential to labor, and the capitalist has the "duty" to convert this labor power into actual work. Let us use an example to see what happens. Each day our cut flower company employs some average number of workers. Assume that this number is 1,000 employees. Furthermore, these 1,000 workers use up a certain amount of constant capital each day. Assume that each day, 500 "units" of constant capital are used up along with the 1,000 units of labor power. Each "unit" consists of an amount of raw materials plus some fraction of the long-lasting constant capital. (A bit of the machinery is used up or depreciated every day, along with a bit of the land, buildings, and equipment). That is, each "unit" of constant capital consists of a composite of raw materials and long-lasting constant capital.

How much will the cut flower employer have to pay for the constant and variable capital used up each day? Marx employed a device known as the *labor theory of value* to answer this question. The labor theory of value says that in competitive markets, commodities that can be produced over and over again are exchanged in the marketplace according to the amount of average work time of the same quality that it takes to produce them. Adam Smith has a simple example in *The Wealth of Nations*. Suppose we have a simple economy in which only two animals are hunted, and the hunters use only their hands to capture the animals. Smith used beaver and deer in his example. Let us say that an average quality hunter requires two hours of work to capture a beaver but four hours to get a deer. If beaver and deer are traded, it is clear that in equilibrium, two beavers must exchange for one deer. This is because what is really exchanging are the labor times: four hours for four hours. No person would trade three beavers for one deer, because in the six hours it takes to capture three beavers, it would be possible to get a deer on your own (or hire someone to get one for a "price" just a bit above two hours) for four hours and have two hours left over. If deer and beaver have prices, it is clear that the price of a deer must be twice that of a beaver.

If we make our example more realistic and allow for a weapon to be used in the hunting, the example becomes more complicated because the time required for a capture must now include some small part of the time it took to produce the weapon (a small part because the weapon can be used to hunt many animals before it wears out). However, this complication does not alter the principle that, in equilibrium, equal labor times must exchange. In any event, let us assume that the labor theory of value is correct, and commodities exchange in proportion to the average quality labor time it takes to make them.

Our cut flower employer has to purchase, given our assumptions, 500 "units" of constant capital each day. The price paid will depend on the labor time embodied in each unit. Assume that it took six hours of average quality labor to produce each unit. This means that the cut flower employer will have to "pay" 3,000 hours for the 3,000 hours of constant capital (remember that equal labor times exchange in the market). The 1,000 workers employed on average each day will have to labor 3,000 hours to produce the cut flowers that, when sold, will pay for the constant capital used up each day. Each worker will have to labor for three hours per day (3,000 hours divided by the 1,000 workers). What is true for these workers is true for all wage workers; part of their workday pays for the constant capital used up by their employer.

The variable capital presents a problem for this analysis. It is clear that the machinery, raw materials, and other forms of constant capital were actually made by workers somewhere in the world and thus have definite amounts of labor time embedded in them. However, labor power itself is not produced in factories like tractors and shipping crates. An employer cannot go to a labor power factory and order so many units of it. So how can the labor theory of value apply to the price of labor power? It can be applied, but in a round-about way. Marx argued that workers produce their own labor power, and they do this by consuming a definite quantity of goods and services. In order for workers to get to work every day and work with an average intensity over their work lives, they must obviously eat a certain amount of food, obtain an adequate amount of shelter and clothes, and consume whatever else is necessary to continue to work. In other words, reversing the way we usually think of it, workers must eat to work and not the other way around.

Put simply, there is some "basket" of necessities that an average worker must consume to maintain his or her labor power. Now, this basket of goods and services took labor time to produce. Some definite amount of labor power must be exerted to produce the basket of necessary goods and services. This means that, on average, an employer must pay workers a wage that will purchase this basket; otherwise, the workers will not be able to maintain their labor power, much to the detriment of both parties. Assume that the basket of necessary daily consumer goods and services takes five hours to produce. Each worker's wage must then be equivalent to five hours of labor. The 1,000 workers will have to work 5,000 hours (5 hours per worker per day) to produce the cut flowers that, when sold, will pay them wages just sufficient to buy the basket of needed consumer goods and services. The minimum long-term wage rate is the equivalent of 5 hours of labor time.

We have, then, our employer purchasing the requisite amounts of constant and variable capital each day: 3,000 hours' worth of constant capital and 5,000 hours' worth of variable capital. The total "cost" is 8,000 hours' or 8 hours per worker per day. For our employer to break even, to just cover costs of production, the workday must be exactly 8 hours long. Notice that these 8 hours are indistinguishable from the employer's point of view. The constant capital is not paid for in the first 3 hours of the workday and the labor power in the next 5. Whatever length the workday happens to be, 8 hours of it are necessary to pay for the constant and variable capitals.

The question is: how long will the workday be? Whether we think back to the time of Marx, when expropriated peasants were flocking to the towns and cities desperate for work or we think of conditions prevailing in most of the world today, it is clear that employers have the power to set the length of the workday. This power is rooted in their monopoly ownership of the nonhuman means of production. If workers do not get access to these means of production, they will die, so the employer has great lever-age over them. They must work on the employers' terms or not at all.

Employers will make the workday as long as their power allows them to make it, consistent with their drive to accumulate capital. They cannot make the workday 24 hours long for each worker, but as the history of capitalism shows, they can make it very long indeed. Let us suppose that employers, including our cut flower capitalist, are powerful enough to set the average workday at 12 hours. What we immediately see is that there are 4 more hours than the 8 hours it takes to pay for the capital used up each day. These extra hours Marx called "surplus labor time." What distinguishes these from the other 8 is that there are no costs of production associated with them. They are "free" to the employer. One-third of the workday is surplus for the

---

EVERY SOCIETY NEEDS A SURPLUS

It is important to understand that, when we say that profits in a capitalist economy are a surplus extracted from the workers by their employers, we do not mean to imply that, in the absence of this exploitation, workers' wages would rise by an amount equal to the profits. Suppose we imagine an economy completely con-trolled by those who actually did the work, one in which the nonhuman means of production were owned collectively and not individually as in capitalism. This economy would need a surplus of production over consumption (in money terms, the total revenue generated in production would have to be greater than the wages paid the workers). This is because machinery and equipment wear out and have to be replaced, and because new equipment and machinery have to be built if the economy is to grow. It is also because there must be money to fund various types of collective consumption such as schools, health care, roads, public trans-portation, etc.

In our imagined society, the surplus would be controlled by the people them-selves. They would determine both how large it should be (in percentage terms, that is, its share of total output) and how it is to be utilized. They could decide to have more consumer goods and services produced and forgo some future growth (this would be so because the surplus would be smaller). Or they could decide to

employer. However, these hours are not free for the workers. They are expected, indeed compelled, to labor as hard in these hours, producing cut flowers,
as they do in the other 8 hours. Therefore, the output they produce in the
surplus labor time is surplus as well, "surplus value," as Marx called it. When
the capitalist returns to the marketplace and sells the surplus output, the
money returned to the employer is profit.

Marx's great insight was to see that profits derive from the surplus of the
workers inside of the workplace. They do not derive from market transactions; the market just allows the surplus already created to be realized in a
money form. Paraphrasing Marx, workers go into the workplace with only
their hides, and what they get inside of them is a "hiding." Our cut flower
workers get paid for 12 hours of labor if they are paid by the hour. But their
pay is not the equivalent of 12 hours of output, only 8. The market makes it
appear as if they are getting the market wage for all 12 hours, that they are
not being cheated. However, they are being cheated in advance, so to speak;
surplus labor is forced from them inside their workplaces.   >

---

save a lot (have a larger surplus) and use the funds for the production of capital
goods for higher future growth. They could decide to focus production on collective consumption by devoting a larger share of resources to the production of outputs such as public transportation, schooling, child care, health care, and the like.

In a capitalist economy (and in all societies in which one group owns or controls
the nonhuman means of production), the owners "own" the surplus and they alone
decide what to do with it. Human needs will have nothing to do with their decisions; all that will matter to them is that they use the surplus in such a way as to
maximize the likelihood that future surpluses will be still greater. Workers can only
try to shift some of the surplus to themselves in the form of higher wages, but short
of workers controlling production themselves, they cannot get all of it. And if they
did control production, then they would have to decide how much surplus would
be necessary to ensure that worn out capital is replaced and new capital produced
for future growth. In a capitalist society, workers can build their political power to
pressure the government to take some of the surplus and use the proceeds for
socially desirable purposes, but there are bound to be limits to their ability to do
this as long as the means of production themselves are the private property of a
minority. As we saw in the last chapter, when this minority does not like what the
government is doing, it can take action to force a government to reverse course.

THE RESERVE ARMY OF LABOR

The labor theory of value is important for a good understanding of capitalist economies, not because it is a theory of the exchange value of commodities, but because it tells us that the source of profits is the exploitation of workers by their employers. It tells us that at the heart of capitalist economies is an antagonistic social relationship. What is in the interest of employers is not in the interest of their employees. If, for example, workers struggle collectively and win a shorter workday, the theory shows us clearly that, other things equal, the surplus labor time will decrease and so will the profits. If the workers win higher wages, it will take more labor time to produce the output that, when sold, will pay their wages, and this too will reduce the surplus labor time and the profits. From the perspective of the radical theory, there is no such thing as the society's best interests, as the neoclassical theory suggests. Rather, there are *class* interests: those of workers and those of employers.

Workers eventually catch on to the fact that they produce all of the output but get back a wage equal to only a fraction of that output. As they become conscious of their exploitation, they begin to organize, first forming various types of self-help organizations, the most important of which are labor unions, and then progressing to political organizations, such as labor political parties. Since workers comprise the overwhelming majority of all persons in advanced capitalist countries, it is conceivable that they will organize so effectively that they will permanently threaten the ability of capitalists to accumulate capital. This is the worst imaginable possibility for capitalists. What will they do about it? The history of capitalism shows that they will resort to violence, either their own direct violence or coercion solicited from the government. However, Marx argued that there is a mechanism within capitalism itself, one stemming directly from the accumulation process, that limits the ability of workers to threaten capital accumulation.

Marx's study of the capitalist workplace taught him that employers were constantly revolutionizing the way in which the actual work was done. Modern radical economists call this the reorganization of the *labor process*.[13] This reorganization is undertaken so that the employers can maintain as much control over the workers as possible, the better to insure the existence and expansion of the surplus labor time, the source of capital accumulation. Historically the labor process has been subjected to various managerial control mechanisms. First, the workers were herded into central locations; the factory system replaced the exploitative but less easily controlled outworking system, in which workers borrowed the raw materials and sometimes the necessary tools (raw wool and looms, for example, in the production of cloth) from the capitalist and then returned the finished product for a wage. Outworkers often lived close to starvation, but the pace of the work and the techniques of labor were controlled by them and not their employer. In addition, the raw materials and tools were not in the direct possession of the employer, and this opened up the possibility of various kinds of theft by the workers. Finally, machinery obviously could not be used in the outworking system.

Employers began to abandon outworking (it never completely disappeared and still exists throughout the world today, used wherever the supply of labor is high enough and the workers desperate enough) and concentrate production in central locations. The new factories were such horrible places to work that employers had to resort to using convicts and orphans to do the work. Soon, however, factories were ubiquitous and commonplace, because their advantages were so great. Workers could be forced to adhere to fixed work schedules, called to work by factory whistles and monitored carefully during the workday. What is more, employers could observe how workers actually did their work, especially the relatively skilled workers, and use their observations to engineer radical changes in the labor process. First, as we noted in Chapter Four, they used the skilled workers' division of work into steps (to save time in doing large jobs) to begin to break down jobs into unskilled details. Unskilled workers—women and children, for example—could be employed to do the unskilled labor. In addition to increasing managerial control and power, this "detailed division of labor" greatly expanded the number of persons who could do any given job. In one fell swoop, the detailed division of labor expanded the supply of potential laborers, what Marx called the *reserve army of labor*. Detail workers could easily be replaced by other detail workers, and this reduced the potential power of the workers to reduce the length of the work day and increase the wage rate. Children could not do the most skilled labor, but they could carry out routine tasks. Employers were quick to employ children and the early factories were filled with children as young as six, kept to work for long hours and denied the right to naturally develop their bodies and minds. Just like the millions of child workers around the world today.

A second advantage of concentrating workers in factories and a direct consequence of the detailed division of labor is the rapid introduction of machinery. Machines also swell the reserve army of labor. Directly, they replace workers whose jobs can now be done more efficiently by machines. As Marx put it, living labor is replaced by the past or dead labor embodied in the machines. Indirectly, machine production creates a vast army of unskilled machine tenders, reducing the skill requirements of many jobs and thereby compounding the labor-surplus-creating effects of the detailed division of labor.

A third source of the reserve army of labor, and historically the primary source, is capitalism's inevitable destruction of prior modes of production. We have seen that wherever capitalism goes, peasants lose access to their land as it is forcibly converted into private property. Peasants are forced to leave the land and go to the towns and cities seeking work, compelled by events beyond their control to enter the reserve army of labor.

Today, with the perfection of certain types of machinery, capital has become much more geographically mobile. As capital is exported from the rich to the poor countries, workers in the rich countries are driven into the reserve army of labor. Autoworkers in Germany and the United States are in competition with autoworkers in Mexico. Clerical work of

TIME IS MONEY

Most workers have a good intuitive grasp of the labor theory of value. They know that employers are in a war with them each day at work, and they know that this war is all about time. When employers purchase the labor power of workers, they see this labor power as their property and assume that they have the right to get as much labor out of this labor power as they can. Most workers also know that employers will go to any length to extract labor from labor power. They will threaten, bribe, maim, and sometimes murder to get it.

There are many examples of the time war. Industrial engineers design work-places so that rest areas are located where the distance between workers on average and the rest areas is a minimum. Workers on automobile assembly lines have to ring a bell to go to the bathroom. Some employers impose a rule of silence, so that workers don't get distracted from their work. Elementary school teachers have to take their students with them when they (the teachers) have to go to the bathroom. In a Nabisco plant in California, some workers had to wear depends (diapers designed for the elderly when they become incontinent) because they could not go to the bathroom at all while the assembly line was moving.[14]

Japanese automobile manufacturers have pioneered techniques of managerial control known as "lean production." They have managed to speed up assembly line

many kinds can be done anywhere in the world thanks to high-speed electronic data transmission. We have learned that worldwide there may be as
many as one billion underemployed workers, nearly one-third of the
world's labor force, a vast reserve army of labor, willing to do most anything to obtain employment.

The process of capital accumulation creates its own protective mechanism by dividing the working class into two groups, those who are
employed and those who are in the reserve army of labor. Well before workers can shorten the workday or raise wages enough to truly threaten capital
accumulation, the reserve army swells and saves the day for the capitalists.

THE STATE

Today there are many social scientists who believe that capitalism is gradually transcending government, meaning that governments can no longer regulate and control capital accumulation.[16] This view is incorrect. Capitalist   >

---

work so much that workers now work fifty-seven out of every sixty seconds they are
on the line. We should keep these examples in mind when we hear economic experts
talk about the need for continuous increases in labor productivity. The Japanese
managers have a name for this as it applies to what workers do in the workplace.
They call it *kaizen* or constant improvement.

What they mean by this is that work can always be sped up, another fraction of a
second can always be stolen from the workers. In one particularly insidious tech-
nique of lean production, workers are divided into teams, with each team responsible for a certain amount of work. A light system is placed above the work space. If all
of the lights are green, this means that all is going well. To the lean production manager, however, this means that there is some slack in the system. The teams are then
denied some materials, or the assembly line is made to run faster, or a team is
reduced in size. As the workers become unable to do their work, the lights begin to
turn from green to yellow or red. Some sort of music begins to play incessantly, perhaps a nursery rhyme like "Mary Had a Little Lamb." Managers rush to the problem
team and demand that the team fix the situation and get the lights green again. They
must *kaizen* until the problem is solved. Once everything is running smoothly again
(that is to say, the workers are working more intensively), the process begins again.
When does it end? Never. Such are the ways of capitalism. This is what we see when
we stop looking myopically at the market and get up close to the labor process.[15]

economies developed alongside of strong central governments and cannot exist without them. Capitalist production and distribution occur within markets marked by intense competition and extreme individualism. Without some sort of central control, markets would devolve into chaos as rampant cheating and violence erupted over market control.[17] A central government is needed to make laws and rules for the smooth operation of markets: laws to compel contracts to be honored, laws to ensure minimal product purity, a bureaucracy to enforce laws and rules, and so forth. Governments are also necessary for the production of certain outputs essential for capitalist production but that the markets themselves will not cause to be produced. Either because no capitalist could be sure of reaping the reward of a particular investment or the investment is beyond the means of any single capitalist, the state must undertake certain investments. It must provide for the national defense, build roads, bridges, lighthouses, port facilities, airports, railroad lines, and provide for the general education of the workforce.

Of still greater importance, a strong government is needed to keep the struggle between workers and capitalists within bounds. Workers are ultimately the major roadblock to capital accumulation. At any point in time, the reserve army of labor may be insufficient to contain the power of the working class. There have even been times when the employed and the unemployed joined hands in collective struggle.[18] Today in Argentina, for example, there is a strong mass movement of the unemployed who have been blockading highways across the country and bringing transport and much related economic activity to a halt. Should the movement of the unemployed join the movement of workers, the whole system of capital accumulation in Argentina would be severely threatened.[19]

To prevent workers from using their ultimate powers of general strikes, the governments of all capitalist economies have put in place laws and a police power to uphold the laws that make many types of working class activity illegal and subject to the state's use of violence to suppress it. Examples here are legion, as a reading of any capitalist country's labor history will make clear.[20] In addition, the governments of the rich countries have tried to strangle every anti- capitalist movement in the poor countries, and they have often succeeded, almost always with violence.[21]

We will have more to say about the state in the next chapter. Suffice it to say here that the radical view of the state is one that argues that the state is primarily an instrument of class rule, a weapon used from the dawn of capitalism by employers to help them accumulate capital and suppress the working class. Neoclassical economists never tire of equating capitalism with freedom and democracy. Nothing could be further from the truth. The rich capitalist countries are set up as representative democracies, but this has little to do with capitalism. Workers fought to extend the bourgeois notions of freedoms to include freedoms relevant to them, and to the extent that modern capitalist governments guarantee some of these freedoms, this is due to the efforts of workers and not to capitalism. (Once certain freedoms become more or less universal, the state begins to propagandize this universality as an inevitable feature of capitalism.) Furthermore, those who own the means of production have managed to subvert representative democracy everywhere it exists through the power of their wealth. In the poor capitalist countries, even representative democracy is rare. Capitalism has had no problem existing in harmony with the most repressive forms of government and all forms of absolutely unfree labor, including slaves. We should also not forget that capitalism accommodated fascism in Western Europe without difficulty.

MONOPOLY

The accumulation of capital takes place in an environment of intense competition; it is the competition of the many capitals that, in fact, drives the accumulation process forward. Yet as businesses seek profits, they see that one way to make more money is to find ways to deny new entrants into their market. A process of centralization of capitals begins to occur to accomplish this. More successful capitalists buy up or drive out of business the less successful ones. Large powerful capitals merge into giant corporations, and these few firms use their leverage over supply to keep prices and profits high. Monopolization of production thus becomes a tendency of capitalist production. (The process can more accurately be described as oligopolization—an oligopoly is an industry in which a few gigantic firms dominate production. Actual monopolies, in which one firm has the market to itself, are rare.)

While there is a tendency toward centralization of production, this does not mean that competition ceases to exist. New capital does enter even the most concentrated markets, as evidenced by the automobile and steel industries. U.S. firms once completely dominated these markets, but this is not the case today. Entire new industries are constantly being formed, and competition typically rules in the early stages of the industry's development. In addition, capitalist enterprises are always centered in particular countries and rely upon their government for help in competing with capitals centered in other countries. And even when an industry is marked by oligopoly, this does not mean that the firms are not in competition with one another.

The tendency for capital to become more concentrated, for an increasing share of production to be controlled by a decreasing percentage of all firms, has important consequences. Large firms in oligopolistic markets make greater profits than firms in more competitive markets. They can therefore keep some of their productive capacity in reserve and still have high profits. They would do this to be prepared for sudden increases in demand without having to make new investments. By the nature of large companies, new investments are very expensive, and they add to the firms's capacities to produce output, an added capacity that may or may not be needed. Better to keep some capacity in reserve. In addition, oligopolistic firms, because their capital investments are very large, will not quickly scrap capital even if more efficient capital is available. This also slows down the rate of capital investment as large firms wait until their capital stock is fully depreciated before embarking on new capital spending.[22]

CRISES

Neoclassical economists see economic crises—recessions and depressions—as caused by some sort of external shock to the economy, such as a war, a sudden business failure, a stock market panic, catastrophic weather, etc. The libertarians believe that the impact of the shock on various prices (wages and interest rates) will quickly get the economy back on track, with perhaps a little help from the central bank's monetary policy. The liberals say that some fiscal policy might be needed as well, in the form of tax- or debt-financed government spending.

Radical economists argue differently. They hold that crises come from within; they derive from the process of capital accumulation itself. Marx put forward a fundamental form of crisis: the tendency of the rate of profit to fall as capital accumulation proceeds.[23] He posited that over time, capitalists would make production more reliant on constant capital; they would substitute the dead labor embodied in the constant capital for the living labor of actual workers. Relatively speaking, this would mean a decline in the mass of current workers, the source of surplus value and profits. With relatively less living labor to exploit, downward pressure would be put on the rate of profit, unless the living labor could be more intensely exploited.

But during an economic expansion, it may become more difficult to raise the rate of exploitation. The reserve army of labor shrinks, and this not only puts some upward pressure on wages, but also may make workers more aggressive and less productive in their workplaces. Without as much fear of becoming unemployed, workers may be more willing to stand up to their bosses—taking longer rest breaks, skipping work more often, even forming unions. The combination of rising wages and falling productivity pushes the unit cost of production up and this squeezes profits. Falling profits make capitalists less willing to put there money capitals onto the market, and when they act on this unwillingness, the economy goes into a slump.

But the nature of economic expansion or contraction is unpredictable. We only know that capital accumulation is self-limiting; the accumulation process runs up against an internal contradiction—an inability to increase the rate of exploitation of workers fast enough to compensate for the fall in the relative mass of exploitable living labor. However, it is not just a matter of expansion coming to an end. The crisis serves a necessary purpose, in that it gets the economy prepared for the next expansion. During a slump, workers are disciplined by employers as the reserve army of labor swells and the fear of unemployment takes the steam out of the workers' fight against their employers. Wages fall, or at least the rise in wages levels off, and productivity begins to rise again, both factors lowering unit costs and helping to restore profit margins and business confidence.

Each expansion and each contraction will have unique characteristics, and these will help to determine how long each lasts and how deep or severe each is. For example, the United States came out of the Second World War with tremendous advantages over the other rich capitalist nations. The United States lost none of its productive capacity, whereas that of the countries of Western Europe and Japan were physically devastated. This meant that U.S. manufacturers had a near monopoly of world production. In addition, consumer spending was brisk after the war as people spent their forced wartime savings. Businesses added productive capacity rapidly, both to replace that used up in the war and to meet the foreign demand for U.S. products. These factors, combined with a boom in housing and automobile production, fueled by consumer debt spending and government loan guarantees, generated the great postwar boom in the U.S. economy.[24]

Another factor that might influence the strength of an economic expansion is the aforementioned tendency of capital to become more concentrated. The more monopolized is production, the less robust an expan-

sion might be, because large firms might be unwilling to make new investments when they already have a good deal of excess capacity. Their market
power might make it more difficult for new capital to enter the market as
the economy grows, and this slows down the recovery from a slump. Large
firms in oligopolized markets might simply raise their prices as demand
increases, just as in a downturn they might shed workers rather than
lower their prices, since their large capital investments make price wars
too risky to begin.

Each downturn is likewise unique. Perhaps during an expansion consumers and businesses, caught up in the optimism that often accompanies
such periods, take on very large amounts of debt. They think that it is safe
to do so as long as the economy is growing; the growth in income gives
them the ability to pay back the debt and still prosper. However, when the
expansion ends, the debt still has to be paid, and the payments on the debt
deepen the slump. Consumers have to devote a higher fraction of their
(reduced) incomes to debt repayment rather than spending on consumer
goods and investing.

Can a government use Keynesian economic policies to end a slump? In
some circumstances, yes, although we have seen that in today's less regu-
lated global economy Keynesian policies can be foiled by the actions of
consumers (increasing their demand for imported goods and services),
businesses (refusing to make domestic investments), and speculators
(selling the domestic currency). But even supposing that the government
could bring a slump to an end, it must be remembered that, according to
the radical theory, governments normally act in the general interest of
the capitalist class. They will not normally want to push unemployment
too low for fear that this will ultimately push down profits. It has frequently been the case that governments pursue policies that raise unemployment, pushing the economy toward a slump, for the express purpose
of reducing the potential power of workers and their collective organizations. During the early 1980s, when the U.S. economy was mired in its
deepest crisis since the Great Depression, the Board of Governors of the
Federal Reserve system, under the chairmanship of Paul Volcker (current-
ly appointed to head an advisory group trying to resurrect the Arthur
Andersen accounting firm after the Enron debacle), pushed interest rates
up to nearly 20 percent. This caused the failure of many businesses and
the unemployment of millions of workers, including thousands of steel
workers in my then hometown of Johnstown, Pennsylvania.

TESTING RADICAL PREDICTIONS

What makes the radical theory so different from the neoclassical theory is that it is both historical in its analysis and based upon the notion that classes rather than individuals are the best theoretical building blocks. The neoclassical theory sets up a completely abstract model of capitalism, devoid of any connection to reality, and then proceeds to trace out the logic of this abstract model and make predictions about the real world. In the process, >

ALTERNATIVE CRISIS THEORIES[25]

There has been a long-standing and ongoing debate among radical economists concerning the nature of economic crises in capitalist economies. It is beyond the scope of this book to provide the details of all of these theories. However, two theories deserve some attention.

First, some radical economists have argued that prosperity so increases the power of workers that it is possible that this power will, itself, translate into lower profits and set off a crisis. During the post–World War Two boom, workers unionized and formed political organizations that raised their wages and benefits and forced employers to pay taxes to the government to fund various worker-friendly programs. The growing security that both private and public power gave to workers made them still more aggressive vis-a-vis their employers. Ultimately, employers experienced rising wages and taxes as a "squeeze" on their profits, and they responded by reasserting their own economic and political power.

A second theory is the theory of monopoly capitalism associated with the magazine, Monthly Review. This theory was developed in the book Monopoly Capital written by Monthly Review founder Paul Sweezy and the late radical economist Paul Baran. Sweezy and Baran noted that one of the most important features of modern capitalist economies is the rise of giant corporations, created through mergers that destroy competition and replace it with oligopolistic markets in which a few large firms are able to set prices by restricting output. These firms constantly strive to cut costs, and the combination of higher than competitive prices and falling costs generates ever-higher profits or what Sweezy and Baran call the tendency of the economic surplus to rise (surplus is larger than reported profits because it includes the large depreciation funds of corporations, funds that bear no connection to the wear and tear on machinery and that are available to finance corporate expenditures).

most neoclassical economists seem to lose sight of the difference between their model and the real world. They say, in effect, that the real world must be made to conform to their model if we are to reap all of the good consequences of an economy that operates on the principles elucidated in the model. But then they turn around and evaluate real world phenomena as if we were actually operating in their model economic world. They do not, for example, analyze an increase in the minimum wage in the context of the

---

For capital accumulation to continue without crisis, the growing surplus must find spending outlets. Baran and Sweezy argue that the oligopolistic structure of modern business slows down investment spending, as we argued above in the section on monopoly. This implies that there will be a tendency for the surplus to grow faster than the investment outlets for it. This cannot continue indefinitely, because what will happen is that the shortfall in investment spending will cause total demand in the economy to fall short of supply. Insufficient demand will lead to a stagnating economy.

Two things can keep the system afloat in such conditions. First, history indicates that some earth-shaking innovation, such as the railroad or the automobile, might come along and generate an explosion in investment spending, absorbing for a time the rising surplus. The automobile, for example, not only required vast amounts of capital for direct production, but also necessitated large investments in the steel, rubber, glass, oil, and related industries. Furthermore, the automobile completely revolutionized social life by increasing our mobility, and this led to huge investments in residential housing, motels, roads, and much more.

Unfortunately, "epoch-making innovations," as Baran and Sweezy call them, cannot be guaranteed and, in any event, the investment boom they cause eventually peters out as the world becomes saturated with the product (there will be many people in the world who will never be able to buy it) or as its production produces tremendous social costs, as is clearly the case with cars. Then, the dearth of investment opportunities must be compensated through various forms of wasteful and socially destructive spending (the profit demands of business do not permit spending on more useful outputs such as publicly produced affordable housing, health care, schooling, and transportation). Baran and Sweezy point to the growth of military spending and the explosion of corporate spending to promote sales, from advertising to packaging. Unfortunately, these serve as only temporary palliatives, since both increase the surplus (military spending is very profitable, as is advertising), the growth of which makes the economy unstable to begin with.

actual world in which it occurs. Rather they examine this in the context of their model world. The fact that an increase in the minimum wage leads to undesirable results in their model world is given as evidence that it will do real harm in the real world. No wonder the theory's predictions do not test well. What the neoclassical economists have is not really a scientific theory at all. What they have is an ideology, a belief system that they use to evaluate the world. It is remarkable that this is precisely what they accuse radical economists of doing, though nothing could be further from the truth.

Several predictions can be derived from the radical theory of capitalism. Marx predicted that, once capitalism took hold, it would know no bounds. It would spread outward from its starting points in Europe to eventually encompass the globe. This is exactly what has happened. Radical economics posits a capitalism that is radically inequitable. This inequality is rooted in the concentrated ownership of the nonhuman means of production. From this ownership flows the income that is the "reward" for the exploitation of labor.

Without the development of a strong workers' movement, aware of its exploitation and determined to do something about it, the inequality of and income inherent in capitalism will, the theory predicts, increase. We have seen this prediction verified throughout the world during the last three decades. The triumph of neoliberalism has been made possible by the thorough defeat of working-class organizations in nearly every rich and poor capitalist country. Workers were left completely subjugated by the naked force of capital accumulation, aided and abetted by the police power of the state. The data we provided in Chapters Two through Four give evidence of what Marx called the "immiseration of the proletariat." Without strong organization, the logic of capital accumulation demands constant cuts in wages, detailed division of labor, mechanization, overwork, and underemployment. While the neoclassical theory makes these dependent on the maximizing choices of employers and workers, the radical theory situates them in the nature of the capitalist system itself.

Once capitalism took hold in Europe, it was inevitable that it would spread. As Canadian economist Sam Gindin notes, "Globalization is not new. A century and a half ago, Karl Marx noted the inherent capitalist drive to '. . . nestle everywhere, settle everywhere, establish connections everywhere. . . . In place of the old national seclusion and self-sufficiency, we have intercourse in every direction, the universal interdependence of nations.'"[26] How does the radical theory predict this would play out?

Could it have been peaceful? Could the wealth of nations have been shared? This would appear to be impossible. Capitalism requires the privatization of the nonhuman means of production; in the case of early capitalism, these consisted mainly of the land. In the first capitalist countries, peasants were ruthlessly deprived of their land rights; they were driven off the land and compelled to become wage laborers, sometimes, ironically, on the lands they had once had a right to use but that have now been converted into sheep farms. Once expropriated and subjected to capitalist exploitation, it was not possible for them to gain a large share of society's wealth and income. Only their collective organization, over many decades, won for them some improvements in their life circumstances.

When capitalism began to spread, to Africa, Asia, and Latin America, European capitalists had already learned the art of property theft. Aided by better ships and arms, themselves the product of capitalist enterprise, they violently subjugated peasants around the world, converting capitalism early on into a system of imperialism. The degree of destruction of indigenous peoples was unprecedented in its magnitude. Millions were murdered and millions more died of diseases. Millions were enslaved. Wealth was looted as fast as it could be taken and put on ships bound for Europe. This stolen wealth—not just gold and silver but human beings—had a double effect. In Europe, this wealth greatly stimulated capitalism, creating the conditions for further exploitation of workers at home and abroad. To a certain extent, the exploitation of the poor countries allowed capitalists in the rich nations to pay better wages and set better conditions for their workers (though not ordinarily without great struggle by the workers). One advantage of this was that workers in the rich countries could be more easily coopted to support imperialism, even to the point of becoming soldiers in imperialist armies. At the same time, in the rest of the world massive poverty and misery swelled. The stage was set for a future of rich nations and poor ones.

Mainstream commentators and propagandists often ask why, after so many years, the poor nations aren't richer. Just as they ask why black people in the United States haven't done better. After all, the poor nations ended their colonial status many years ago. Slavery for blacks in the United States was abolished with the Civil War of the 1860s. In the world of opportunity capitalism creates, these pundits ask, why haven't poor nations and black people seized upon the opportunities so obviously available and bettered themselves? The clear implication of such musings is that there is something wrong with the poor countries and the black people. Poor countries are full of corruption and ignorance. Black people are lazy, too much into present-day consumption rather than the more arduous tasks of saving money or going to college.

To give readers an idea of how wrong this line of "reasoning" is, suppose we imagine two equally strong persons. One of them would like to take advantage of the other. He borrows a weapon and robs the other man. Then he shoots the other man and cuts of his arms and legs and leaves him to die in the street. Suppose that by a miracle the injured man survives. He endures several years of painful rehabilitation, but when he is released to the streets again, he has no money nor any place to live. His assailant, meanwhile, has used the stolen money to establish a business. Would anyone wonder why, twenty years later, this man was not as well off as his attacker had become? Would anyone be surprised that the material gap between the two had grown larger over time? The assault by the rich nations on the poor ones and the enslavement of people from Africa by plantation owners in the United States were no different than the brutal attack by the one man on another. When slavery ended in the United States, the larger society left the former slaves to fend for themselves. The white brutality that had marked slavery continued in new guises. Without wealth or access to it, condemned to the worst kinds of employment and beaten down with extreme harshness anytime they insisted on being treated like human beings, how exactly were black persons supposed to accumulate? It was not until the 1960s, just forty years ago, that Blacks in the United States started to enjoy the right to vote anywhere in the country, and it was in that same decade that the last terrorist lynching of a black man took place.

The radical theory predicts that capitalist economies cannot be full-employment economies. The theory posits the necessity of a reserve army of labor, as well as the necessity of periodic crises. A crisis-free and full-employment capitalism is a contradiction in terms. Certainly this insight of the theory has been borne out by the entire history of capitalism. A very few capitalist economies managed after the Second World War to achieve high growth rates, low unemployment rates, rising real wages for workers, and decent provision of social welfare for most people. However, given the constant propaganda about what a wonderful system capitalism is, what is remarkable is how narrow these achievements were—how few of the world's workers benefitted. What is also remarkable is the extent to which working people had to fight to win entry into what had always been a small elite of persons who could afford such amenities as vacations, cars, and college for their children. And most remarkable of all is how fast these gains have been eroded, as capitalist economies entered a long-term crisis in the middle of the 1970s.

In this context, Sam Gindin tells us something important when he says,

> Capitalism, as a social system, could not live with the rise in equality and security for workers. The working class victories and concessions from business were not calming but raising expectations, and they were undermining discipline: they were threatening profits, class power, and class rule. What were earlier viewed as measures of progress—higher wages, better social programs, greater security—were redefined as barriers that blocked capitalism's own needs. And it was those needs which demanded the deepening and expansion of market-logic known as neoliberalism.[28]

The radical theory of capitalism postulates a mechanism—the accumulation of capital—as central to an understanding of the system. It lays out the features of this accumulation and asks how it is possible. Using the labor theory of value, it concludes that accumulation can only take place if

---

A POOR NATION IN AFRICA[27]

Equatorial Guinea is a small country on Africa's west coast. Its population is about one-half million. While the GDP per capita is not nearly the lowest in the world—it was about $2,800 in 2000—the distribution of wealth and income is extremely unequal. The country has been ruled, in the words of the CIA, "by ruthless leaders who have badly mismanaged the economy." The rulers have siphoned off most of the country's wealth and terrorized all opposition. For the rest of the people, life is harsh and short. Infant mortality is nearly ninety-five per thousand births; only twenty-six other countries, nearly all in Africa, have a higher rate. Most people live in shacks without running water or sewage and survive by foraging or working as street vendors. One woman told journalist Ken Silverstein, "Why look for work when there isn't any?" She added, "There's only one way to find a better life, and that's to get out."

Remarkably, Equatorial Guinea's economy is projected to grow by 34 percent in 2002, the highest projected growth rate in the world. The reason is the discovery of large amounts of oil. In the past few years, oil companies, mainly from the United States, have rushed into the country after making deals with the political rulers. Small foreign enclaves are being established to house the executives who will run

workers are exploited, that is, forced to labor an amount of time in excess of the time necessary to pay for the constant and variable capital. The peculiar nature of the nonhuman means of production, their status as private property, permits the capitalists to appropriate the money that comes from the sale of the output produced during the surplus labor time. States are brought into being by these very same men of wealth to safeguard the entire enterprise. At the core of capitalist production is violence, either in the form of the slow death of unemployment or the mailed fist of the employer and the employer's state.

Capitalist economies may be engines of growth, capable of producing mountains of output, every good and service under the sun and then some, in infinite variety. But as the radical theory makes clear, the fruits of growth cannot be equitably distributed for the benefit of all. Many must be poor so that a few can be rich. Most must be insecure and afraid so that a few can face life with confidence. Nearly everyone must suffer a stunted existence so that a minority can enjoy life to the fullest. The evidence of this is so overwhelming that neoclassical economics can only survive because of its great propaganda value.

---

the oil companies and the workers who will do the relatively skilled labor. Lobbyists have been at work in Washington to make sure that the political and economic elite in the United States knows what a good deal this is going to be. The oil-dominated administration of George W. Bush has recently reopened the U.S. embassy in Equatorial Guinea, despite gross human rights abuses. Now the leaders are being presented as making improvements and the oil boom is being promoted as the key to the nation's development.

We can be certain that the production of oil, even if it is on a vast scale, will not benefit the people of this poor country. Most of the main oil company workers will be imported. A handful of jobs might go to the locals, especially jobs as servants, and these few persons will see some amelioration of their conditions. But in a country and a world of great hierarchy, money flows to the top. The oil companies will take the lion's share of the income from the oil. Some of the money will be siphoned off by the dictator and his family and friends. A few roads and even schools might be built for show with the meager tax dollars collected from the oil riches. But nothing fundamental will change. The poor rural villages, the vast majority of the country, have absolutely no way to tap into the money flow and will be left as badly off as they were before and compared to those at the top, relatively worse off.

CHAPTER SEVEN: Capitalism's Contradictions

THE RESILIENCE OF CAPITALISM

Radical critics of capitalism have a habit of speaking in terms of crises.[1] We have seen that capitalist economies are inherently unstable, subject to periodic cycles of boom and bust. Radicals have tended to see each severe crisis as a harbinger of radical change. Some have gone so far as to argue that capitalism will eventually collapse of its own weight. Crises will become so severe that production and distribution will come to a halt. Then, presumably, a new system will arise to replace capitalism. At the very least, radicals often seem to believe that each crisis will sharpen the class consciousness of workers and make them more sympathetic to radical change.

Such reasoning is misleading; it seems to make fundamental change more likely, but in fact is an obstacle to such change. An economic system is not like the leaning tower of Pisa, which, without sophisticated modern engineering, would have collapsed of its own weight. It does not mean anything to say that capitalism will self-destruct. If it is true that capitalist economies must somehow cease to function in some super crisis, it is certainly taking them a long time to do so. Furthermore, even the less preposterous view that workers' consciousness will become more radical as a result of economic crises provides a very mechanistic view of people's thoughts and actions. Unemployment is as likely to make people drink heavily or hate themselves as it is to make them revolutionaries. A crisis might make people susceptible to right-wing propaganda, more willing to bash immigrant workers than to organize with them. It is wise to remember that the 1930s gave us fascism as well as radical communism.

People who see capitalism as some sort of self-destructing mechanism, along with those who see people becoming automatically radicalized by crisis, ignore several fundamental points. First, capitalism is an extremely resilient system. Capitalist economies have survived all manner of crises, not only fending off radical challenges but emerging from crises to continue to grow very rapidly. Many of those who lived through the Great Depression probably thought that some sort of new system was going to be needed to end it and to avoid another one. Today, in the rich capitalist countries, the Great Depression is a distant memory, superseded by phenomenal growth and unprecedented improvements in working-class living standards, at least up until the mid- 1970s.

Second, capitalism is a hegemonic system, one that refuses to allow us to compartmentalize our lives and establish a kind of internal "safe haven," immune to capitalism's blandishments. Poor people in the United States dream of hitting the lottery more than they do about creating a society of equals. Go to any metropolitan grocery store with a lottery window. The line in front of it will be the longest in the store. Writers and artists dream more about "making it" than about putting their art to the service of radical change. Even those who start out as rebels too often succumb to the pull of money and power. Many of them make peace with capitalism and are content to do a little good while taking care of themselves. Some of them go all the way over and become champions of capitalism, a turn that never hurts the pocketbook.

Capitalism assaults us relentlessly. By the time children get to first grade in a rich capitalist country, they have seen tens of thousands of television commercials, each and every one of which urges them to buy or sell something.[2] Two-year-olds at a daycare center where my wife and daughter worked lit up when they heard the word, "McDonalds." They also had already learned to look under the collar of my daughter's shirt to see what the label was. By the time these kids get to regular school, they have been saturated with commercialism, and this will continue in our increasingly commodified schools. Their teachers, themselves thoroughly immersed in the market economy, will not be very likely to provide them with a critical perspective on the economic system. Much more likely, they will reinforce what has already been implanted in the children's minds. The ideology of consumerism that derives from and in turn supports capitalism is ubiquitous; it cannot be avoided or ignored. Its stunting and limiting features are everywhere apparent.

Advertisers even cleverly usurp radical slogans and images and make them their own. A cigarette ad tells women, "You've come a long way, baby." Products are routinely advertised as "revolutionary." The Italian clothing company Benetton uses radical imagery to sell expensive sweaters and jackets. The message is always that consuming things is what "liberates" us.

"Liberty," "freedom," "peace," "revolution," all of these are to be had only by buying the right product.

This hegemonic power of capitalism is not confined to the rich countries. As capitalism spread, so too did the culture of capitalism. The Nike "swoosh" is recognized in the most remote corners of the world, and Nike shoes are desired by young people everywhere. When Michael Jordan was shilling for Nike, school kids from Peru to Tibet wanted to "be like Mike."[3] I remember watching a movie about the building of a highway into the isolated Amazon river interior of Brazil. One scene showed an indigenous woman walking along a path drinking a Coke and listening to a transistor radio. In a fine cartoon movie I used to show to my students in introductory economics (titled *The History Book*), an African student comes to the United States to continue his education. He is inundated with propaganda extolling the virtues of the consumer culture. One scene shows a wealthy businessman opening up the top of the student's skull and pouring in a cornucopia of consumer goods.

Third, we must not ever forget that capitalist economies have developed the most sophisticated and menacing techniques of repression imaginable. People learn quickly that it is risky to challenge the system. You might not get a decent job if you do, and you might get fired from the job you now have. You might get your head cracked open and go to jail if you protest too much. Death often awaits the most serious challengers to the system. The death toll from strikes and other forms of labor agitation and from peasant and worker rebellions must surely number in the millions. If the United States was willing to participate in the murder of Salvador Allende in Chile, when Allende had been democratically elected president of the country, there must really be no limit to the violence capitalist governments will unleash when the accumulation of capital is threatened.[4]

Perhaps a good way to think of capitalism is that it is the perfection of class society. Class societies have existed for many centuries, but capitalism is a unique kind of class society. In a slave or feudal system, two things are apparent. First, those who do the actual work, slaves and serfs, are tied to either the slave owner or to the land. They are not "free" in the sense that a wage laborer is free. At the same time, the slave owner and the lord are not free in the same way a capitalist is free. The slave owners' and the lords' property is not the impersonal commodity property of the capitalist; it comes embedded in sets of social relationships of a more direct and personal character than is true for capitalism.

In capitalism, workers have been completely separated from the non-human means of production. These are the purchased commodities of the capitalists, who are free to do whatever they want with them. No social obligation hampers the capitalists from doing what they please with their property. This freedom allows the capitalists to devote themselves full-time to increasing their surplus. Whatever happens to the workers as a result of this—plant closings, detailed division of labor, mechanization—is not the concern of the capitalists. It is not their responsibility. In fact, when they buy into the neoclassical idea that "greed is good" they can think of themselves as high-minded citizens, serving society as they serve themselves. A lord who abandoned his serfs to the wilderness at least would have known that he had violated the will of God. And as the serfs settled on the land, the lord would be without his rents! With capitalism, the relentless pursuit of profits soon enough converts all of the land into private property, so there is nowhere for the workers to go when they are sacked, except to look for work with some other capitalist.

In capitalism, what replaces direct social relationships is the impersonal market. In this market the workers are formally free, to sell their labor to the highest bidder. Over time, the market takes on a sort of Godlike character (as in Adam Smith's famous "invisible hand"), and all social problems are laid at its doorstep. If the employer blames the sad fate of the displaced employees on the market, so too does the worker. In a large corporation, the workers have no way to personalize their employers, and this makes it easier to accept that the market is indeed to blame. But even a small employer working alongside his employees might not incur any worker wrath if he does something that harms the workers. He, too, can blame it on the market, and who is the worker to say otherwise?

It is quite possible and frequently happens that, not only will workers not blame their employers for what happens to them but they will actually identify their interests with those of the employers. This is because of the reality of competition. A group of workers' employer is in competition with other employers; if their employer does not succeed in this competition, he might be forced to close a plant and put them all out of work. Employers play upon this reality and encourage employees to connect their success with that of the boss. Once workers make this identification, it will be difficult to get them to see the necessity of solidarity with workers in other plants and in other companies.

What gives capitalism its great power, besides all of the other things I have mentioned above, is its impenetrability. It is difficult to get beyond the market, and easy for employers to hide behind it. The whole economy takes on an almost physical presence, as when a political leader talks about "growing the economy," as if it were a plant. Or when commentators speak of "market forces" pushing stock prices down or generating inflation, as if these were forces from outer space instead of socially determined phenomena. In a film I have shown to workers (*Wall Street*), the financier and Democratic Party operative Felix Rohatyn makes a comment on the wave of plant closings in the United States in the 1980s, which desolated many industrial towns and cities. Rohatyn, in his well-appointed Manhattan office, intones, "There is no substitute for being competitive." Obey the market god or perish. Each of us must face this god on our own; if we fail, we have made the wrong maximizing choices.

CHINKS IN THE GOD'S ARMOR

While capitalism is hegemonic, it is not totalitarian. We are not, or at least not all of us, absorbed into it entirely, like the characters in Aldous Huxley's *Brave New World*. One of Marx's insights into capitalism is that it is a system of contradictions. What this means is that the normal operation of the process of accumulation often has unintended results, and these results, combined with appropriate organization, can undermine capitalism and lead toward our liberation from it. Let us look at some of these.

First, capitalism always comes into direct conflict with other social formations, and these ordinarily have organizations and values antithetical to capitalism. Indigenous peoples are a good example of this contradiction. Today, there are large movements of indigenous people in many countries, for example, Mexico and Ecuador.[5] They are rebelling against the depredations of capitalism and demanding that governments and businesses stop encroaching on their land and that governments provide adequate social services and grant them greater autonomy.

All human beings have collective impulses. We are social animals, and this inherent sociability has been reflected in the way we have lived for most of our time on earth. When we look at many indigenous people, and even considering the fact that their societies have, for the most part, long been in contact with capitalism and have been influenced by it, we can see ourselves as we once were. For more than 90 percent of our existence, we lived as collective gatherers and hunters, in a mode of production marked

by egalitarian relations of production.[10] From this perspective, class society is a shocking development, and capitalist society the most shocking of
all. When someone like former British prime minister Margaret Thatcher
declares that there is no such thing as society, just a collection of competing individuals, we recoil in horror. Our entire collective history tells us
that this is not so. Even our religions, developed long before capitalism, tell
us that this is not so. Of course, religions have proved compatible with capitalism; in fact, religious institutions can become major sites of capitalist
accumulation. But many of us are still upset when religious leaders turn
out to be mere money grubbers. So far, capitalism has failed to completely
destroy our collective, and therefore, anti-capitalist, impulses. They are too
deeply rooted to be wiped out in a few hundred years.

AMERICAN INDIANS[6]

When the United States was "settled" by the Europeans, much of its land mass was
already settled by various groups of indigenous people. The Native Americans had
various forms of social organization, with some groups using agriculture and others
gathering and hunting. The European settlement spelled disaster for the American
Indians. After using the indigenous peoples to learn how to live in the new land and
after cynically allying themselves with various indigenous groups as the Europeans
fought against one another, the Europeans ruthlessly stole the indigenous people's
lands and waged wars of extermination against any who resisted. The Europeans
also spread disease, sometimes intentionally. Within a relatively short period of time,
the American Indian population had shrunk dramatically. Eventually the United
States government forced those left onto reservations, where they have been left to
survive as best they can.

   The American Indians fought valiantly against the Europeans, sometimes inflicting remarkable defeats upon the supposedly superior white men. Always they insisted that their way of life be respected and they be allowed to live as they chose. This
the Europeans could not accept; the power of capital accumulation was just too
great. The justifications the Europeans gave for what they were doing were most
remarkable. To get around their own conceptions of the sanctity of private property,
they argued that the indigenous peoples had not occupied and improved the land
and therefore could not be the land's original discoverers with legal right to it. Only
those who occupied the land and "improved" it could be the legal owners. In making

If our collective past was all we had to rely upon to confront capitalism, we would be in trouble. It would become more and more difficult to draw upon collective memory as this memory became more distant and as capitalism more deeply infiltrated our daily lives and thought processes. However, we do not have to rely only on remembering the ways of our ancestors. Capitalism itself creates new possibilities for collective thinking and acting, and this is the system's greatest contradiction. The key here is the creation of the working class, a mass of propertyless wage earners absolutely dependent on capital but far freer than slaves or serfs.

The appearance of things in capitalism, an appearance made to seem normal and proper by the neoclassical economic ideology, is one of market equality. In the labor market, labor and capital strike a bargain, one that >

such an argument, the Europeans demonstrated their woeful ignorance of indigenous peoples. Throughout the Americas, these peoples had "improved" their environments in numerous ways. Many scientists have now concluded that even regions previously thought to be "pristine" when the Europeans arrived, such as the Amazon rain forests and the dense forests of North America, were in fact "built environments," altered by their inhabitants to improve the land's productiveness.[7]

Those opposed to capitalism have not always championed the struggles of American Indians. They bought into the false notion that these were backward people doomed in any event to fall before the power of the modern world. This has been a tragic mistake. Indigenous people have an obvious right to live as they choose. But, in addition, there is much that opponents of capitalism can learn from them. Their more harmonious relationship with the natural world (American Indians speak of the needs of the "seventh future generation," quite remarkable in light of capitalism's "accumulate now whatever the cost to future health and well-being") ; their collective sense of themselves; their refusal to bow before the market god; their more humane system of justice; and their more egalitarian social structure, including the integral and equal role of women; all of these things cry out for emulation.

In the United States there is a certain infatuation with American Indians among some people. There are even whites masquerading as Indians, and there are Indians only too willing to cash in on this romanticization of indigenous peoples. What is missing here is an understanding that American Indians are real people, living in the here and now. Their circumstances are not good. Unemployment, alcoholism, and disease are epidemic in many Indian communities. In states with high American

they are not forced to make, and one that either party is free to break, the worker by quitting his or her employment and the employer by discharging the worker.

The reality of things, however, is much different. Once outside the market and inside the workplace, the worker sees just how much freedom there is. Marx describes the shift from the market to the workplace in a dramatic passage:

> When we leave this sphere of simple circulation or the exchange of commodities, which provides the 'free-trader vulgaris' with his views, and the standard by which he judges the society of capital and wage labour, a certain change takes place, or so it appears in the physiognomy of our dramatis

---

Indian populations, the prison population is disproportionately Indian.[8] Resistance, too, is alive and well. Not just in the United States but around the world, indigenous communities are struggling for the right to live as they want and to control their land and resources. It should be obvious that when they do this, they are also fighting against capitalism.

We who are not American Indians can make common cause with them only on the basis of an understanding of the contemporary conditions in which American Indians and other indigenous peoples live. My friend James Craven, a Blackfoot Indian, explains the reason:

> Under capitalism, the "For Whom" question is decided primarily on the basis of very unequal and increasingly unequal distributions of wealth, incomes, power, and "dollar votes"—and the revealed preferences of those with the most concentrated dollar votes. In traditional indigenous societies, no one ate unless all ate (among Blackfoot, the Chiefs eat last), no one had shelter unless all did, no one had clothing unless all did—communal sharing and/or divisions of the means of subsistence are based upon traditional divisions of labor and participation in providing the means of subsistence.[9]

Put simply, indigenous peoples do not believe that society gains when each person acts selfishly. This is self-evidently preposterous to them. Instead, society only survives and prospers when each person commits his or her life to the good of the whole people.

personae. He who previously was the money-owner now strides in front as a capitalist; the possessor of labor-power follows as his worker. The one smirks self-importantly and is intent on business; the other is timid and holds back; like someone who has brought his own hide to market and has nothing else to expect but—a tanning.[11]

In other words, the most fundamental contradiction of capitalism is between the freedom of the market and the unfreedom of work. Such a profound contradiction cannot escape the attention of workers for long, and when it strikes them fully, they must act upon it, at least when the opportunity arises.

The ways in which workers have responded to their realization of capitalism's primary contradiction have varied greatly. Before the advent of factory production, outworkers sometimes revolted. This was more likely to happen in urban areas, where the workers were in closer contact with one another than they were in isolated rural areas. In Philadelphia, Pennsylvania, outworkers in the early nineteenth century rioted to win higher wages. These riots were often spontaneous, but the rioters did not exercise random violence. They targeted the property of their employers, refraining from destroying either their own neighborhoods or the property of third parties. Sometimes public officials supported the strikers, and, in any event, cities did not then have the sophisticated police departments they have today, so the rioters did not have to worry about massive police repression.[12]

In early capitalism, skilled workers often labored in a guild-like arrangement. A guild was a feudal organization, a kind of feudal corporation, in which work was done in a strict but paternalistic hierarchy. Master craftsmen controlled the guild; skilled journeymen, having passed through a rigorous training, worked with the hope of becoming masters, and apprentices served as helpers to the journeymen while they learned the craft. This type of workplace carried over into capitalism. Again in Philadelphia, shoes were made in small shops, with the master-journeyman-apprentice hierarchy. For about a generation after the U.S. revolution of 1776, the antagonism that might have erupted between masters and journeymen and apprentices was muted by the paternalism of the guild structure and the hope among the journeymen that they someday could become masters. But as mass markets developed for shoes, masters more and more took on the behavior of capitalists and began treating their journeymen as wage workers. Where once the masters and journeymen marched in Independence

Day parades under the same trade banner, now the journeymen began to see their interests and those of the masters as different.

When they insisted on higher wages (or "prices" as they termed wages then, a usage that reflected their view of themselves as part of the shop), they found out how widely their interests differed. The journeymen had formed an organization of skilled shoemakers, or cordwainers as they were called because they worked on cordovan leather. Their organization established rules by which no cordwainer would work for a master who hired nonmembers and no cordwainer would work alongside of a nonmember. In modern parlance, what they strove for was a "closed shop." In 1806 the masters had the local magistrate file charges against them, claiming that

---

SKILLED WORKERS

Skilled workers are the first to form successful labor unions. They have several advantages over unskilled workers. They are often more homogeneous to begin with than are unskilled workers, of the same ethnicity and gender, and all sharing the same training to learn their craft. They are usually more literate than unskilled workers, and this helps them immeasurably to grasp the world around them and build sophisticated organizations. In England there were skilled weavers who taught themselves the differential calculus, and there were other skilled workers who had to be locked out of the Royal Society, where they went to hear talks about science. In the United States, skilled workers flocked to hear the lecturers at New York City's Cooper Union. American Federation of Labor president Samuel Gompers said that he never missed a Saturday night there, and that these lectures were the foundation of his education. In the cigar factories where Gompers learned his trade, the skilled cigar makers had one of their comrades read to them while they worked, and they paid the man's wages.[15]

At least in the beginning of capitalism, skilled workers sometimes have traditions of freedom and liberty that make them feel entitled to be treated like full citizens. Unskilled workers, often recently removed from the countryside, may not have this heritage, and this makes it more difficult for them to feel justified in confronting their employers. Skilled laborers earn higher wages than unskilled workers, and this helps them to make their unions financially stable.

Skilled workers also experienced capitalism as an attack upon their traditional culture, a destruction of their way of life, and they resented this deeply. In his magisterial The Making of the English Working Class, E. P. Thompson put this point as follows:

they were engaged in a criminal conspiracy, aimed at inflicting harm upon the masters, the nonunion workers, and the general public. The court found them guilty, thus destroying their incipient union.[13]

Labor unions (or trade unions as they are sometimes called, reflecting their origin in organizations of skilled workers, workers who followed a trade) are a universal response of workers to capitalism's primary contradiction.[14] This is true in all capitalist countries, both rich and poor. Ironically, the organization of workers into labor unions is facilitated by the accumulation process itself. Employers must control the labor process if they are to maintain the surplus time necessary for capital accumulation. To do this they employ successively more onerous control strategies, each >

The artisan felt that his status and standard-of-living were under threat or were deteriorating. . . . He was faced with: the rise of a master-class without traditional authority or obligations; the growing divide between master and man; the transparency of the exploitation as the source of the [capitalists'] wealth and power; the loss of status and above all of independence for the workers, his reduction to total dependence on the master's instruments of production; the partiality of the law; the disruption of the traditional family economy; the discipline, monotony, hours, and conditions of work; loss of leisure and amenities; the reduction of the man to the status of an "instrument."[16]

While the skilled workers have been of critical importance to the building of labor movements around the world and while there have been many radicals who came from the skilled part of the working class, it is also the case that there has always been a strong sense of looking backward among skilled workers, a belief that things should be as they once were. Of course, this is impossible once capitalism gets rolling. In addition, skilled workers usually excluded unskilled workers from their organizations, believing that their organization was not necessary for the success of the skilled workers' unions. Skilled workers also harbored racist views of the unskilled, who were usually of different ethnicity, race, and gender than the skilled workers. These attitudes and actions of skilled workers have proved to be severe impediments to the building of strong working-class organizations.[17] In contemporary capitalism skilled labor has become increasingly redundant and a weak foundation on which to build a labor movement.

of which has the possibility of enhancing the consciousness of the workers and driving them to action.

We have seen that the first control strategy was to herd workers into factories in which employers were able to study the way in which the work was done and then employ the detailed division of labor and mechanization. But when workers are forced into a central place, they come into closer contact with one another. This closeness compels them to see themselves in their workmates, and this is the start of the working-class consciousness that spells trouble for employers. A central location is also more susceptible to strikes and picketing. The discipline implicit in factory production (factory whistles, strict supervision, the need for production to be more highly coordinated than in the outworking system) shows the workers how to discipline themselves and form stable and successful organizations of their own.

The detailed division of labor has the effect of homogenizing the workers, further breaking down differences among them, a precondition for the growth of class consciousness. By making each worker an interchangeable part, the detailed division of labor also breaks down all differences among workers and makes it difficult to sustain the notion that one group of workers is superior to any other.

Mechanization reinforces the homogenizing effects of the detailed division of labor. It further leads toward an understanding of the collective nature of modern capitalist enterprise. No one worker stands out; only if all cooperate does production take place. At first, it is the machine itself that seems to dominate production, pitching people pell-mell into the reserve army of labor and dictating the pace at which the workers must labor. Some early anti-capitalist rebels, distraught at the destruction of their ways of life by factory production and machinery, formed militant armies that, under cover of night, burned down the factories and wrecked the machines. These "Luddites," as they were known in England, were not lunatics aiming at bringing progress to an end. Their machine breaking occurred only after they had failed to achieve their ends by peaceful means. Their demands included a slower introduction of machinery and a tax on machine-made cloth to provide them with economic relief, and they wanted limits placed on the labor of women and children—their own and orphans—in the factories. Most of them at the time did not enjoy the right to vote, so they could only petition the government. The British government managed to infiltrate their organization, and, once it discovered their leaders, waged violent war against them. Many of the Luddite leaders were hanged, imprisoned, or exiled to Australia. In time, workers learned to distinguish between the machines, which could conceivably be used to liberate them from the more burdensome aspects of work, and the owners of the machines, who employed technology to control and exploit them.[18]

In modern capitalism, new managerial control mechanisms have been implemented, most notably those associated with "lean production." There are various elements in lean production, but a critical one is the use of sub-contractors and what is called "just-in-time" inventory. To save costs and keep extreme pressure on the workers, companies have parts (seat cushions in automobile plants, for example) delivered by subcontractors only as they are needed, with several deliveries made everyday if necessary. Workers have learned to convert this control device into an advantage. A strike or slowdown at a relatively small parts supplier can shut down an entire company or even an entire industry. When parts are not in stock, a refusal by a group of workers to devote immediate attention to a problem and find a way to fix it can completely disrupt production.[19]

Proponents of capitalism, especially political leaders, never tire of equating capitalism and democracy. Of course, nothing could be further from the truth. In the early years of capitalism, there was often little pretense of democracy. Many countries had property qualifications for voting, so most members of the new working class had no say in who their elected officials were. In the poor countries, it was absolutely impossible for working people not to notice that the places they had inhabited for centuries had been colonized. This was a contradiction so blatant that even many of the local people who benefitted materially from capitalism understood that they were subservient to foreign interests.

As workers began to organize to improve their lives inside their workplaces, it became still more apparent that the government was not democratic, was, in fact, an instrument of class domination. Sheriffs, police, national guards, and national armies were all called upon to crush workers' resistance. Workers were beaten, shot, and killed to stop them from interfering with the accumulation of capital. Naturally, workers saw this as another contradiction of the system; they were no more free in the larger society than in the workplace, and this was true irrespective of the formal qualities of the political system. Employers were also supported by the laws and courts, uniformly hostile to the interests of working men and women. Taking the United States as an example, from the early 1800s until the middle of the Great Depression—when, due to tremendous worker agitation, things changed a bit—the courts declared unions to be criminal conspiracies, allowed employers to fire and blacklist workers for any reason, issued thousands of injunctions to force workers, on pain of going to jail, to end strikes, picketing, and boycotts, found unions guilty of violating the antitrust laws (ostensibly aimed at business monopolies), and legitimized the employers' use of forced contracts in which the workers agreed not to join unions. In England, for a while in the late 1700s and early 1800s, union membership was a crime, punishable with imprisonment.[20]

The antagonism of the state to workers and its routine support of the interests of employers forced workers to see the need for organizations in addition to their labor unions. Workers had to organize on the level of the society as a whole; they had to form political organizations.[21] Only in this way could they have any chance to both combat the employer bias of the

---

THE BRITISH LABOR PARTY

In England, the growth of a militant union movement, including the organization of unskilled workers during the late 1880s, gave rise to the formation of a working class political party. Here is how historian Wolfgang Abendroth describes this in his fine book, A Short History of the European Working Class:

> With the founding of the Independent Labor Party (ILP), 1893 saw the embryo of a mass labor party. Its ideology was derived largely from Christian socialist and democratic traditions, and it marked the beginning of the first systematic independent political activity undertaken by large sections of the working class since the defeat of Chartism. In 1894 almost a quarter of the delegates to the Trades Union Congress were members of the ILP, and the ILP began to penetrate the TUC's parliamentary committee, hitherto the lynchpin between the unions and the Liberal Party. Although this development often met with obstruction . . . a resolution in favor of supporting working-class parties was tabled successfully at the TUC in 1898. On 27 February 1900, the first conference of the Labor Representation Committee was held and called for an independent workers' party.[22]

The Labor Party immediately attracted large numbers of working-class votes, winning thirty seats in the 1906 elections. It succeeded in entering coalition governments and

state and to achieve gains not easily obtained through workplace struggle. In response to their grasp of this contradiction of capitalism, workers have signed mass petitions and delivered them to government officials; they have demonstrated directly against the government; they have formed their own political parties to try to capture control of the government; and, especially in the poor countries, they have built revolutionary organizations to fight for the end of colonialism and even for the creation of a noncapitalist, socialist mode of production. In other words, workers have made the state a site of class struggle.

The need for political organization can be understood from several practical angles. First, since employers will use their power to shape the government, workers must do the same. This is the only way that they will be able to influence the legal environment. Governments in capitalist societies will not enact laws that benefit workers unless they are pressured politically to >

forming majorities at times between 1906 and the end of the Second World War, but it never really pushed forward a strong working-class perspective. Always fearful of alienating capital and terrified of revolution, Labor's leaders actively supported Great Britain's entry into the First World War, cracked down on strikers on numerous occasions, and gave tepid support for the ill-fated General Strike of 1926. There were and are committed leftists in the Labor Party, but they have never been the dominant force within it. The labor unions are closely and until recently formally tied to the party, but the British unions, like those in the United States, have themselves been mainly conservative and content to support the only mass party they have.

The Labor Party came into its own after the Second World War. Reeling from the war's devastation and extremely unpopular for its lukewarm opposition to fascism before the war, British capital was soundly defeated by labor and the Labor Party took command of the government. As was its propensity since its inception, it shied away from a radical restructuring of the political economy. It did, however, introduce Keynesian taxing and spending programs, nationalized certain industries (typically those losing money, like coal), and created a modern welfare state, including the National Health Service. But it did not really threaten the power of capital, which in any case was not wholly averse to what Labor did, especially its socialization of the losses of the nationalized industries.

The unfortunate thing for the Labor Party is that it was presiding over an economy in long-term decline. The Second World War marked the end of Britain's world

do so. Whether it be through direct mass mobilization, as recently happened when Italian labor unions called a general strike to stop the government from making Italian labor laws more agreeable to Italian employers, or through electoral politics, political organization is necessary. Organization at individual workplaces cannot change the laws or cause governments to establish worker-friendly programs such as social security, universal health insurance, unemployment compensation, or free public schools.

Second, the workers' political organizations can be champions of broad progressive ideologies. A union is primarily a defensive organization; it can get employers to give a little and prevent them from taking a lot. So it cannot consistently be in the forefront of more radical struggles. But a political party or organization can do this. It can act in the interests of all workers, whereas a union must sometimes concern itself only with its own members. For example, the question of the nationalization of a critical

---

dominance. After the war, British capital, having lost control of Britain's empire and having lost much of its domestic physical capital, decided to pursue a strategy of deindustrialization, with the emphasis on finance and capital export. Led by the U.S. economic juggernaut, the world economy recovered and grew rapidly after the war and Great Britain shared in this growth. However, growth in the world's first capitalist economy did not nearly match that of the United States and then Germany and Japan. It became steadily more reliant on imports of goods it once produced and on exports of various types of services.

The trouble for the Labor Party was that it built up expectations among workers that could not be met without a stronger challenge to capital, one built upon a revitalized and militant labor movement. When it failed to deepen the gains it had achieved—when it failed, that is, to increase the collective power of the working class—it found itself made by the Conservatives into the scapegoat for the nation's gradual economic decline. Of course, the causes of this deterioration were structural, but labor could not attack the economy's weak structures without directly challenging capital, and this it would not do. So after periods of Labor government, the political pendulum swung in favor of the Conservatives. Labor's leaders concluded that the path to success was to imitate the Conservatives but in ways that would not completely alienate the unions and the workers. Gradually the Labor Party began to distance itself from the unions, which while themselves hardly radical, had by necessity a class perspective and tried to keep the party true to its principles.

industry might not be one that concerns a particular union, but it might be an issue to which a political party could devote an all-out effort.

A third and profound contradiction of capitalism is that between the innate ability of human beings to conceptualize their work and capitalism's necessary denial of our right to do this. Before we do our work, we have the capacity, to a degree not observable in any other species, to plan our work in advance, to think about it first. Then, on the basis of our plan, we execute the work. In a process of plan, work, rethink, re-execute, and so on, human beings have learned to make their labors increasingly productive. As Marx states it:

> A spider conducts operations which resemble those of a weaver, and a bee puts many a human architect to shame by the construction of its honeycomb cells. But what distinguishes the worst architect from the best of bees is that the architect builds the cell in his mind before he constructs it in wax. At the end of every labour process, a result emerges which had already been conceived by the worker at the beginning, hence already existed ideally. Man not only effects a change of form in the materials of nature; he also realizes his own purpose in those materials. And this is a purpose he is conscious of, it determines the mode of his activity with the rigidity of a law, and he must subordinate his will to it.[23]

As we developed our thinking-doing method of work, we also developed language, and this allowed us to transmit what we were doing across generations, to develop a cultural continuity that further sped up the technical innovations that mark human labor. In a relatively short period of time, at least by geological standards, we went from sharpened rocks to computer- controlled machines and rocket ships.

If we grant that the combination of the conceptualization and the execution of work is something that marks us as human beings, and if we accept the obvious fact that work is a necessary human activity, then it is clear that work under capitalism is profoundly anti-human. It is, again to use the language of Marx, *alienating*. Let us look at this more closely.[24]

First, we are forced to work in central spaces under the direction of others. We must be at work at a certain time, and we must stay at work, laboring with a certain mandatory degree of intensity, for a fixed amount of time (not so fixed for the tens of millions of workers forced to work overtime). The power of the employer dictates that our labor power, though embedded in us as human beings, becomes a commodity and, for the time we are at work, the property of the employer. After we become accustomed to this, habituated as it were, like a drug addict to a narcotic, we begin to think of our labor power as something divorced from ourselves. We are alienated from it.

The sale of our labor power and its centralization in factories and offices is just the beginning of our woes. The employers' engineers are forever seeking ways to divide our labor power into tiny details of unskilled and, from the human point of view, trivial actions. Combined with machinery, we get the modern assembly line, that horror chamber of alienated work. Here is how sociologist Laurie Graham describes her job on an automobile assembly line at a Subaru-Isuzu plant in the state of Indiana. I have skipped a lot of the steps, because I just want to give readers an idea of the work. Remember as you read it that the line is relentlessly moving while she is working:

1. Go to the car and take the token card off a wire on the front of the car.
2. Pick up the 2 VIN (vehicle identification number) plates from the embosser and check the plates to see
     that they have the same number.
3. Insert the token card into the token card reader.
4. While waiting for the computer output, break down the key kit for the car by pulling the 3 lock cylinders
     and the lock code from the bag.
5. Copy the vehicle control number and color number onto the appearance check sheet.

    . . .

22. Rivet the large VIN plate to the left-hand center pillar.
23. Begin with step one on the next car.

This work is so intense that it is not possible to steal a break much less learn your workmate's job so that you can double-up and rest while she does both jobs.

In the early years of the last century, the industrial engineer Frederick Taylor began to systematize managerial control of the labor process. His process of managerial control, known as "Taylorism," is now built into every workplace where it is possible to do so. Taylor claimed that there were three basic principles of "scientific management."[25] First, the management must gather up, through intense observation, which today includes sophisticated cameras and electronic devices as well as Taylor's famous stopwatch, all of the knowledge the workers possess. This is an ongoing process, because workers always find ways to ease their work burdens. They try to keep these secret from the management, but modern management finds ever more insidious ways of discovering them. Second, once the management has gained the workers' knowledge (in effect, stolen parts of his or her humanity), it puts the engineers to work to discover the fastest way to get the job done, consistent with some acceptable (to the management) degree of quality. The workers' bodies are conceptualized as machines, and rigid movements and times for these movements are prescribed for the workers. An inflexible separation is made between the conceptualization of work, which is the function of the management, and the execution of the work, which is the job of the workers.

Finally, the work subtasks are doled back to the workers, and the workers are ordered to carry them out, on penalty of some sort of discipline for failing to do so. Once a workplace is "Taylorized," and increasingly few are not, work becomes a dull and boring routine, far removed from true human labor. Workers are triply alienated. They are alienated from their labor power, which has become the property of another, the capitalist, who has his own designs for it, unconnected to any particular needs of the workers. Workers become mere costs of production to be minimized in whatever ways are possible. Workers are then alienated from their labor, which in the capitalist workplace becomes drone-like and trivial. Workers are also alienated from their products, which they make in an alienated way and then must turn over to the employer for sale in the market.

It is impossible for workers not to notice this alienation, since it is rooted in a denial of something natural to us. So it is inevitable that there will be rebellion against alienation. Workers will try to use their union and political organizations to reduce it. Their organizations may try to envision other, more humane ways to organize work and will struggle to realize them.

Capitalist workplaces are always organized as strict hierarchies, with unskilled worker at the bottom, more skilled workers a little higher up but threatened with falling lower by Taylorism, and managers above the workers. The managers themselves are also divided hierarchically; there are ascending levels of management. However, the managers are not immune to Taylorism and its resultant alienation. It is possible that alienation will reach far up the work hierarchy. Furthermore, some of those who give orders will see that their own labor is alienated in the sense that managers must engage in a host of unsavory tasks. They must constantly manipulate people. They must act like prison wardens and elementary school teachers, always watching, warning, and punishing. Even the higher managers can feel great alienation. Sometimes, this can give workers unexpected allies.

Alienation represents an intense loss of freedom. To compensate for it, people will try to find substitutes for what they lose at work. One of the major ideological underpinnings of capitalism is the notion that human happiness depends not on meaningful work but on consuming as many goods and services as possible. Every minute of every day, we are urged to buy things, and the entire premise of advertising is that this buying will make us happy, indeed, that we will be miserable if we do not buy. This pressure to buy is placed firmly in the context of extreme interpersonal competition. We must not only consume to be happy, we must keep up with the consumption of others. Just as soon as we have increased our consumption, we must increase it again or risk falling behind our neighbors.

Consumption itself, then, represents a contradiction. It can only temporarily satisfy us, for just as we consume something, we are anxious that we have not consumed enough. Consumption becomes a drug, whose potency diminishes unless we take more and more of it. It is bound to be the case that some consumers will analyze themselves and see the necessity of kicking the habit. These people may themselves be workers, and they may see the connection between their alienation at work and the alienation inherent in making consumption the center of life. If they are not workers, their insights into the emptiness of consumption may make them ripe for an understanding of capitalism's other contradictions and for cooperation with workers in their struggles. We have seen examples of this when the children of upper income parents rebel against their own privilege. This happened in the 1960s and resulted in alliances between privileged whites and poor Blacks and between students and workers. Today's student movement against sweatshops has some of this same dynamic.[26]

A final contradiction of capitalism, one that has taken on much greater importance today, is an ecological contradiction. Just as capitalism commodifies human beings, so too it commodifies the natural world. Prior to capitalism people lived in relative harmony with their natural surroundings. With capitalism, however, profound changes occur in the human-nature interaction. As peasants and gatherers and hunters are driven from their lands and agriculture is turned into a capitalist enterprise, the land loses access to human fertilizer. The cities, on the other hand, become waste dumps for human waste and centers of infectious diseases. To increase the productiveness of the land, human-made fertilizers, pesticides, and insecticides must be used and the scale of agriculture must be greatly increased. The consequences of this have been a profound and largely negative alteration of the environment. At the same time, capitalists ravage nature whenever it is profitable to do so, and the costs of this are shifted onto society as a whole and onto the poor in particular.

As working people and many others come to see what is happening to the environment, organizations and movements begin to take shape to combat the degradation of nature. Today, there are thousands of such organizations and hundreds of movements, ranging from protests against large-scale dams to the use of chemical pesticides to the clear cutting of forests to the proliferation of chemical wastes.[27]

Once people catch on to capitalism's contradictions, other insights may become possible. For example, once working people become conscious of their own exploitation, it might become easier for them to comprehend and struggle against other forms of oppression. The oppression of women by men antedates capitalism and has its roots at least partly outside of capital accumulation. The same is true for racial oppression. Yet it is difficult to maintain that although I am exploited as a worker, it is legitimate for me to exploit women and racial minorities or treat them in a discriminatory manner.

Of course, it is not impossible for us to compartmentalize our minds so that we see only one kind of inequality, just as it is not impossible for workers to become resigned to their subservience to employers, and even participate in it, as when one group of workers learns from management the techniques necessary to speed up the work and then employs these techniques on another group of workers. And anytime people begin to grasp the reality of capitalism and organize against it, employers and their allies try to crush such struggle.

THE IMPORTANCE OF DEMOCRACY AND EDUCATION

Whatever kind of organizations people construct to deal with capitalism's contradictions, it is never easy for their organizations to maintain their integrity and deepen their commitments. The history of labor unions, labor political organizations, and other institutions shows that there are strong tendencies for the culture of capitalism to insert itself into them.

Labor unions have often become businesslike in their operations, serving as sites for the personal and monetary advancement of leaders. The same can be said for political parties. "Career" labor leaders and politicians are very common. Corruption and racketeering have hardly been unknown. There are also more subtle ways in which leaders can be coopted by capital. Corporations can "promote" labor militants into the management and use labor's knowledge against the workers. More subtly still, those who lead the opposition to capital are bound to come into close contact with members of the employing class, and this contact can serve as a coopting mechanism. Union negotiators in the U.S. automobile industry sit across the bargaining table from very rich and powerful corporate executives and are far removed from rank-and-file auto workers. They may come to feel a sort of "clubbiness" with their corporate counterparts. Combined with large union salaries, this can make union leaders feel more at home with their class enemy. The result can be a loss of union militance at best and "sweetheart deals" that sell out the membership at worst.[28]

Labor organizations also have a long history of cooptation. In the United States, organized labor's political power rose substantially during the Great Depression. Franklin Roosevelt depended heavily upon organized labor for his 1936 reelection, especially the newly formed CIO (Congress of Industrial Organizations) unions led by the mineworkers' union president, John L. Lewis. To avoid labor gaining too much power, the pragmatic Roosevelt began to coopt the more pliable labor leaders, like Sidney Hillman and Philip Murray. During the Second World War, this shrewd policy paid off as "labor statesmen" like Hillman broke with the more militant Lewis to the detriment of all workers, who could not count on these leaders to support wartime labor actions aimed at raising their wages at a time when corporate profits were soaring. The war set the stage for U.S. labor's postwar junior partnership in the Democratic Party, whose conservative and generally pro-business politics organized labor has been loath to challenge.[29]

A more telling example of labor's political cooptation occurred during the First World War. In all of the advanced capitalist countries of Europe there were labor political parties, all founded on socialist principles. These parties, especially the social democratic party in Germany, had begun to win representation in national legislatures. As they grew, they began to take on the trappings of legitimacy, with staffs and offices and the like. Instead of seeing themselves as steadfast advocates of the working class, they began to see themselves as "statesmen," looking out for their nation's interest. When competition for foreign markets and colonies pushed the world's rich capitalist nations toward war, a war that workers would be expected to fight but that had nothing to do with promoting their interests, the social democratic politicians voted in favor of declaring war and financing the fighting. After the First World War, these social democratic parties never regained the fervor of their radical beginnings.[30]

It is probably not possible to completely eliminate these problems, and we must remember that the organizations of workers and their allies are always subject to business and state repression. However, two things can help to keep leadership on its toes. First, every organization must be structured in as democratic a way as possible.[31] Democratic constitutions, regular elections, membership ratification of all agreements, open meetings, grievance procedures for members, democratic procedures for recall of officers, lack of restrictions for running for office, guarantees that women and racial and ethnic minorities will always be part of the leadership and can have their own caucuses—all of these and more are needed. It is an encouraging sign that many of the contemporary movements fighting against the evils of capitalist globalization have made democratic structures and procedures central to their efforts.

Second, all working-class and allied organizations should develop permanent and democratic education programs.[32] Unions and political parties have long traditions of membership education. Some of these have aimed at empowering the membership to make decisions for themselves, but others have served primarily as leadership control devices. The questions of education and democracy go together, since objective, empowering education is very unlikely to occur in an undemocratic organization. Worker organizations should also encourage independent worker education programs, both in terms of financing and making it possible for members to attend classes, seminars, summer schools, and events. Finally, education can be an important component of an alternative culture of resistance. Culture, including art, drama, music, the media, and literature, are thoroughly embedded in commodity production, driven mainly by profits. As such, they serve as purveyors of what Marx called a "false consciousness." That is, they promote an individualistic and competitive way of thinking, detrimental to class consciousness and collective struggle.

Capitalism is a tough nut to crack. It has survived numerous recessions and depressions, including the calamitous Great Depression, world wars of unprecedented destruction and brutality, insurrections, and revolutions.

Today, capitalism dominates the world as never before, reaching into the far corners of the planet and deep within every aspect of our lives. It is difficult to think of circumstances today in which money does not pay the piper and call the tune. Resisting such a behemoth, such a hegemonic system, seems to most people to be impossible. Better to take what you can, grab what pleasure you can, and accept life fatalistically. Change is just not in the cards.

Yet capitalism has not come close to delivering the good life to all of the world's people. We have argued in this chapter that it cannot do so. It is a system rife with insurmountable contradictions. What is more, these contradictions engender resistance, at all times and in all places in one way or another. The fact that indigenous communities around the world have survived capitalism and continued to resist is, given their historical experience, proof positive that struggles against capitalism cannot be defeated and spring up again and again, sometimes in terrains where one would not think struggle was possible. Despite the power of capitalism, tiny Cuba survives and sets an example of another possible reality. Labor unions still exist. Political agitation has never died. Oppositional cultural forms continue to develop and sometimes to flourish.

Today, mass movements have sprung up around the world to challenge capitalism's hegemony. Just when capitalism seemed most triumphant, having witnessed the demise of the socialist economies, capitalism's contradictions have once again come to the fore. People have taken notice and also taken to the streets. It is to these contemporary struggles that we now turn.

CHAPTER EIGHT: Fighting for a Better World

THE END OF THE "GOLDEN AGE" OF CAPITALISM

After the Second World War, the rich capitalist economies entered a long period of economic growth. Some have referred to this period as a "golden age." The twenty-seven years between 1946 and 1973 were marked by active government interventions in the economy, using the policies laid out by Keynes: high progressive taxes and high government spending. Businesses were mainly dependent on their national economies, since most nations utilized various types of capital controls and regulations to prevent rapid capital export and currency speculation. So, as governments spent money on public investment and pursued low interest rate monetary policies, corporations did not take actions to counteract the expansionary effects of these governments actions, instead spending within national economies, and both types of spending stimulated the growth of output and employment.

At the same time, the two world wars and the Great Depression had shown the political and economic elites that capitalist societies could become extremely unstable. To avoid another depression and with it another fascist threat, to escape unflattering comparisons with the socialist economies (which now included the most populous nation on earth—China), and to preclude victories for the left wings of national labor movements (which came out of the Great Depression and the war more powerful than they had ever been), corporate and public leaders engineered a peace accord with "legitimate" labor leaders. If labor unions would cede to employers the right to run the plants, to set prices, and unilaterally introduce machinery, and if union leaders would enforce no-strike agreements and discipline unruly members, employers would guarantee steady increases in wages and the introduction and growth of fringe benefits, and they would accept the unions as legal representatives of employees. They would also not block the passage of social welfare legislation.

The long economic boom, activist governments, and the labor-management "accords" spelled significant increases in working-class living standards. These increases were more widespread and evenly divided in Western Europe than in the United States, and they were slow to reach Japan (where unions were decisively defeated by employers in the1950s, replaced by company-dominated unions and paternalistic industrial relations practices). They firmly incorporated labor into the capitalist systems of the rich nations, especially in countries like Austria and Sweden, where labor political parties dominated the government for many years.

People in the poor countries did not share much in the "golden" age, although GDP per capita growth rates were higher between 1950 and 1980 than they have been since. The use of import substitution economic policies helped to direct production inward and made some poor nations less vulnerable to fluctuating export prices. However, anytime a poor nation had the audacity to mount a serious challenge to imperialism, that is, tried to extricate itself from the international division of labor to which imperialism had condemned it, the United States and whatever allies it could muster took steps to defeat such defiance. Iran, Guatemala, Indonesia, Chile, and many other countries suffered defeat at the hand of the U.S. economic and military machine. Only where the Soviet Union offered sufficient material aid, as in Cuba and Vietnam, did anti-imperialist or anti-capitalist movements have any chance of success.

As we have seen, the long postwar expansion ended in the mid-1970s. Declining profit rates forced capitalists to recognize that modern welfare states and strong labor organizations, even those run by "responsible" leaders, were not compatible with long-term capital accumulation. The "golden age" abruptly ended, and employers and obliging governments dismantled the social welfare state, went to war against the unions, and began to implement the neoliberal program we have already examined.[1] This chapter describes and analyzes the many contemporary movements of working people to combat neoliberalism. These movements have emerged in a political and economic climate changed by the collapse of most of the world's socialist economies.

THE COLLAPSE OF THE SOCIALIST ECONOMIES

The first country in which capitalism's contradictions gave rise to a revolutionary movement successful in gaining political and economic power was

Russia. Led by the Bolshevik Party and its leader, Vladimir Ulyanov (known as V. I. Lenin), Russia's revolutionary workers took power in 1917. A long civil war followed, with the opposition to the communists supported by the rich capitalist countries, some of which sent troops to Russia. The opposition was finally defeated in the early 1920s, and the communists began to build a noncapitalist and socialist society.

It is beyond the scope of this book to provide a detailed analysis of the history of the Soviet Union and its ultimate collapse.[2] We can, however, make several relevant comments. First, the Soviet Union was greeted with extreme hostility from the major capitalist nations from its birth. The United States did not recognize the new government until the 1930s, and no nation offered a helping hand to the Soviet Union as it tried to cope with an economy devastated by the First World War and then the civil war. In addition, Lenin had believed that the revolution in Russia would spur workers in Europe to revolt too. This did not happen except in a few places, where revolts were soon crushed. Thus, the Soviet Union was forced to look inward and develop its economy without close ties to the rest of the world. This had certain advantages, because a poor nation is ordinarily sucked into the imperialist system as a distinctly junior partner. The Soviet Union was able to develop its great human and natural resource wealth without having income flee the country to the corporations and governments of the capitalist world.

Within two generations, the Soviet Union was able to build a powerful economy, one of the world's largest and one utilizing comprehensive central economic planning. The economy was not directed by the blind market forces of supply and demand but by highly skilled planners. The planners and the central government decided what outputs would be produced, with what inputs, and at what prices. By reducing the supply of consumer goods and devoting a large share of inputs to the production of capital goods, the planners were able to achieve very high rates of industrial production: steel, railroads, machinery, electric power, and the like. These then provided the basis for high rates of economic growth in a short period of time.

The strength of the Soviet economy was shown in the Second World War, when, after the German invasion had proceeded deep into the country, the Soviet armed forces were not only able to repel the invaders but to follow them back into Europe and defeat them. After the war, the Soviet Union succeeded in establishing planned economies throughout Eastern Europe: in East Germany, Poland, Rumania, Bulgaria, Hungary, and Czechoslovakia. All of these nations used central planning and inter-country trade to industrialize and provide for the basic consumption needs of their citizens.

Second, the planned economies showed what could be achieved when production was not guided by the profit motive. The planners made a conscious effort to socialize certain forms of consumption. Housing, transportation, health care, and education were all provided basically free of charge to the people. The quality of these services varied, but in general they were good and certainly far superior to what the majority of the world's poor people receive today.

Third, the Soviet Union, with its considerable military might, served as a powerful barrier to capitalist expansion and imperialism. The economic achievements of socialism served as important symbols for revolutionary movements around the world. The socialist countries also provided schooling for many aspiring radicals from the poor countries, and although there was no consistency, they also gave military and economic aid to countries fighting against colonial and imperialist oppressors. Good examples of this are Vietnam and Cuba. The Vietnamese resistance to the French and then to the United States was strengthened by its alliance with the Soviet Union. And it is difficult to imagine the problems Cuba would have faced in its confrontation with the United States had not the Soviet Union provided military and economic assistance.

Fourth, the socialist economies' achievements must be set against dismal and profound failures. As is common in countries surrounded by hostile and aggressive enemies, the least democratic forces rise to the top. The Soviet Union was on a wartime footing for most of its history, and this helped to promote the leadership of the most dictatorial people. Under Stalin's leadership the Soviet Union defeated the Nazis, but it also became an extremely repressive society. Executions, gulags, crowded prisons and psychiatric hospitals, constant fear—these were all routine features of life in socialism. The planners were tightly connected to the communist party elite, and over time a new class elite formed, with great privileges and immunities not available to ordinary persons. The planners paid little attention to the potential demands of the people for high quality goods readily available. Along with the free provision of certain basic necessities went much planning inefficiency and corruption, long lines at stores, poor quality consumer goods, and rampant black marketing. Stalin crushed the diverse and revolutionary movements in the arts that had been given birth by the Bolshevik revolution and replaced them with state-dominated "socialist realism."

Stalin's focus on rapid industrialization of the economy had many extremely harmful consequences. In order to supply food for the burgeoning industrial working class, he engineered the forced collectivization of agriculture, a process that led to the death of millions of persons and the establishment of undemocratic state farms, literally "factories in the fields." Stalin, having crushed political debate, promoted the idea that before socialist relations of production (relations of equality) could become a reality, the society's productive capacity ("the forces of production") had to fully and quickly developed. This meant in practice that workplaces in the socialist economies were organized pretty much as they were in the rich capitalist countries. Lenin himself was an admirer of Frederick Taylor, and Taylorist practices were utilized in Soviet factories. Work was as alienating in such places as it was in Detroit's automobile factories. It was good that workers could not be fired as they could be in capitalist nations, but job guarantees combined with alienating and undemocratic workplaces led to inefficiencies and widespread cynicism. What is more, the emphasis on the forces of production led to a lack of concern for the environment. Nature was seen as not integral to the building of socialism but as an instrument of large-scale production. Today the landscape is strewn with the consequences: all sorts of pollution and the dead regions around Chernobyl.

The Cold War initiated by the United States after the Second World War ultimately proved too costly for the Soviet Union and, unable or unwilling to build a revolutionary society controlled by the workers themselves, the leadership began to move the nation in a capitalist direction. It began to appear to many of them that they could gain enormous economic wealth if the old system was simply abandoned. When Gorbachev's "revolution from above" failed to win the hearts of the masses, the more reactionary elements in the leadership struck, and the great Bolshevik revolution came to an ignominious end. With important variations, the same things happened in all of the Eastern European societies. Most of these had already begun to lock their economies into the capitalist world (becoming increasingly indebted), a move inconsistent with constructing an anti-capitalist mode of production. In addition, their political subservience to the Soviet Union, marked by invasions in Hungary and Czechoslovakia, helped to debase the very notion of socialism, and this made it impossible for a progressive force to promote a new kind of noncapitalist society.

The end of the socialist economies has had both negative and positive results. Within the former socialist states, the demise of socialism and the ever-deepening encroachment of capitalism have had calamitous effects on the lives of the majority of people. While the elites in the rich nations were praising the return of democracy to the former "communist dictatorships," the societies in these countries were literally being torn apart. In all of them, there was a massive theft of what was supposed to have been the people's property. In Russia, powerful cliques of former government

THE CHINESE REVOLUTION

A socialist revolution took power in China in 1949. It was so different from the revolution in Russia that it deserves brief comment.[3] Unlike the Bolshevik revolution, the Chinese revolution succeeded after twenty-three years of civil war between the communists under Mao Tse-Tung and the pro-capitalist forces under Chiang Kai Shek. The protracted nature of the war allowed the communists to gain control of large parts of the country and win the allegiance of the majority of Chinese peasants, who comprised most of the Chinese people. The communists were also able to reorganize production and the relations of production in the areas they controlled. Then when the revolution was successful, the Chinese leadership did not have the same internal problems as did the Russians.

More so than in Russia, the Chinese revolution was a peasant revolution, and this led to an overhaul of the traditional radical theory that revolutions must be led by the working class. Once the communists took power, they took steps to solidify their support in the countryside. They immediately took the land of the large landlords and distributed it to the peasants. Even today Chinese families have land in the countryside from the original distribution after 1949. Once land was distributed, the communists began large scale political efforts to get the peasants to consolidate their small private holdings and farm the larger parcels of lands collectively. In this way, the land mass, which is not very large given China's enormous population, could be farmed more efficiently. The peasants' collective labor could dig irrigation ditches, terrace hilly farms, and work on developing complementary rural enterprises that could utilize peasant labor during the parts of the year when no farming could be done.

Mao took issue with Stalin's assertion that the forces of production had to be developed prior to generating egalitarian social relationships. Mao believed that equality would itself speed up economic development, and tried to make sure that

bureaucrats fought over who would get what. The distribution of the former state's assets was what politics was all about. The alcoholic thief Boris
Yeltsin was praised as a great democrat and statesman while he and his
cronies looted the nation.

When socialism ended, the economies of these countries disintegrated.
In almost every country, GDP fell precipitously. Unemployment and underemployment rose rapidly—a shock to workers used to full employment. To
pay their debts, including wages to public employees (who often went >

egalitarian relationships would not be sacrificed to an ideology of growth at all costs.
Great successes were achieved in collective mass education and health care, and
food self-sufficiency was achieved.

Mao also understood that an anti-capitalist revolution did not in itself insure a
good society. Class struggle would have to continue long after the revolution took
power. People's entire lives had been dominated by capitalism (and in the Chinese
case, by feudalism as well), and they would not begin to think and act in new ways
automatically. They would have to be educated to think in new ways, and they would
have to be empowered to make decisions for themselves. These ideas met with considerable resistance within the Chinese Communist Party, and many power struggles
marked the first few decades after the revolution. In his old age, Mao launched the
Great Proletarian Cultural Revolution in the late 1970s to defeat those who favored
programs and policies that, Mao believed, would restore capitalism. Unfortunately,
Chinese society, like its Soviet counterpart, lacked a rank-and-file democracy, and the
proponents of the Cultural Revolution were manipulated by powerful political
forces. Excesses occurred, but in the end these were not the main problem. Mao's
enemies had too much power within the government, and they were able to defeat
the Cultural Revolution.

Since then, conservative elements have ruled China, and although they give lip
service to Mao and the communist revolution of 1949, they have begun to move
China quickly along a capitalist path. The rural communes have been abolished and
the communal land has been divided again into small plots. Private property and
wage labor have returned in both rural and urban areas; in the latter many state
enterprises have been converted into more or less private enterprises. Profit making rules most of Chinese commerce these days; foreign investment has been
encouraged, with cheap labor acting as the main incentive; and China has sought
integration within the capitalist system.

months without getting paid), governments simply printed money, leading to runaway inflation. Millions of people lost their savings, and pensions were rendered worthless. Old people could be seen everywhere in the streets trying to sell their possession so they could eat. Diseases once thought eliminated reappeared; hunger and homelessness mounted to epidemic proportions; public services such as health and education vanished; and criminal activity became rampant. As a few people accumulated great wealth, usually through their own criminal schemes, the world witnessed the first advanced industrial countries to endure dramatic decreases in life expectancies and increases in infant mortality.

Within a dozen years of the end of socialism, many of the nations created out of the demise of the Soviet Union had to be classified as poor countries. They are saddled with foreign debts, subject to structural adjustment programs, marked by deteriorating physical environments and growing inequality, and increasingly dependent on exports and foreign investment. In the most recent years, some of these countries have begun to grow again, at least in terms of the Gross Domestic Product. There are now more open elections and greater tolerance for divergent views in some countries. But these countries have lost the achievements of socialism and have not gotten rid of some of the most pernicious aspects of the old regimes, mainly the rule of the many by the few. Civil wars have been common, and death and destruction daily facts of life.4

Despite their distance from real democratic socialism, the Soviet Union and the other socialist countries functioned as bulwarks against the spread of imperialism. Their demise has meant that there is no longer any powerful barrier to imperialism. The military might of the Soviet Union prevented the United States from acting with a completely free hand in the affairs of other nations. This is no longer the case, as is evident with the spread of the U.S. military around the globe. The United States now even has soldiers in nations that were once part of the USSR and has intervened militarily in what was once a united Yugoslavia.

The abrupt end of the socialist economies has demoralized opponents of capitalism. Even though most of us knew that these societies were class societies and not particularly democratic, still we had hope that their people would somehow transform them into the egalitarian and humane modes of production promised by the revolutions that brought them into being. Now that this cannot happen, some have concluded that socialism can never happen. All that is possible, we are told, is that we can try to make capitalism a bit more humane. Only little struggles are possible; grand struggles that seek to uproot the old and ring in the new are doomed to failure.

It is somewhat surprising that the death of what were, after all, repressive societies would be so demoralizing. I doubt that it would have been any easier to end capitalism in the United States, for example, were the Soviet Union to have continued to exist. And now that capitalism is the only game in town, so to speak, the elites in the capitalist nations no longer have a "red menace" with which to terrorize us or with which to make self-serving comparisons. Although the attacks of September 11 are being used to construct a new global villain, today capitalism stands alone and naked. And as neoliberalism has come to dominate capitalist economies, we have a capitalism unfettered by Keynesian regulation and any concern for the poor. Although it is not the capitalism of the neoclassical economists' textbooks, it is, more or less, capitalism pure and simple. As such, it is developing as Marx said it would, creating poles of wealth and misery, producing massive underemployment, encouraging growing concentration of production, generating regular economic crises, and destroying the natural environment. In a word, capitalism's contradictions are now in full view, unresolvable and becoming increasingly impossible to contain.

We argued in the last chapter that the contradictions of capitalism always spawn opposition. After a period of quiescence, when workers and their allies were so beaten down and demoralized, rebellion is once again growing. Over the past ten years, we have witnessed burgeoning movements, composed of many strands in many places, that are opposing the consequences of capitalism and, increasingly, capitalism itself, and that have grown beyond our wildest expectations. These movements are facing capitalism with its most provocative challenge in decades, perhaps since the Great Depression. In many respects, they are not traditional working-class movements. But it is their newness and their embrace of fresh tactics and ideas that is so exciting.

LABOR MOVEMENTS

We noted in the last chapter that labor unions and labor-based political parties are basic responses to capitalism's most fundamental contradictions. To classical radical analysis, these organizations are of the greatest importance because radical theory posits the collective organization and burgeoning class consciousness of workers as the most important, and essential, vehicle for struggling against and ultimately defeating capitalism. There are several reasons for this. First, the defeat of capitalism and the establishment of an alternative mode of production will require a massive transformation of both the material world and social relationships. It is precisely through work that human beings have always made such transformations, so those who do the work will have to be the leaders of any social transformation. Second, capitalism's existence depends upon the ability of capitalists to exploit wage labor. A transition from capitalism to some other system of production and distribution implies that this exploitation must end, and it is difficult to see how any group other than workers can bring about an end to exploitation. Third, work is the site of capitalism's most significant contradictions. It is at work that the freedom of the market comes into contradiction with the unfreedom of our most essential activity, namely work. And it is at work that we are most clearly denied the chance to develop our human capacities and instead confined to a narrow and stultifying division of labor.

In the rich capitalist countries, early movements of workers were inspired by a radical vision and an antipathy to the capitalist mode of production. Workers and their unions and political organizations were in the forefront of nearly all nineteenth and twentieth century mass strikes, insurrections, and revolts. A strong internationalism marked working-class organizations, as working class leaders understood that capitalism was a global system and the fate of workers in any particular place was tied to that of workers everywhere.[5]

However, despite their radical beginnings, already in the last quarter of the nineteenth century the labor movements in the rich nations began to lose their radicalism and their antipathy to capitalism. This occurred for a number of reasons. German writer Werner Sombart, in describing the U.S. labor movement, argued that the great productive capacity of the economy, along with the successful organization of the skilled workers who started the labor movement, allowed working-class living standards to rise considerably. As these rose, workers came to think that they had a stake in preserving the system that appeared to give them material prosperity. As he put it, socialism in the United States was defeated on the "shoals of roast beef."[6]

For a labor movement to succeed, either in terms of narrow economic demands or a larger anti-capitalist project, workers must be united. Unfortunately, workers in the rich capitalist countries have been divided in many ways, some extremely detrimental to radical change. Within countries, workers have been divided by race, ethnicity, and gender. These divisions have allowed employers to pit one group against another, making it impossible for workers even to form unions, much less challenge the mode of production. The American Federation of Labor (AFL) in the United States, for example, made an alliance with racist legislators from the U.S. South (lawmakers closely allied with racist southern employers) in the late 1930s in order to discredit and combat the more racially inclusive and militant Congress of Industrial Organizations (CIO).7 The antipathy of many unions toward women made it impossible to challenge the patriarchal family structure so important to the reproduction of capitalism. Men believed that wage work was the province of men and that women should tend to the home front. In doing this, they failed to see that women's home labor subsidized their employers. Nor did they see that this division of labor denied to both men and women full participation in all of life's major activities. A radical transformation of society implies a thoroughgoing egalitarianism. To the extent that men are at odds with women, Blacks with whites, and ethnic minorities with ethnic majorities, no such transformation is possible.8

Not only must workers within nations be unified, so too must workers in different nations be united. International solidarity has been an especially vexing problem. Two important problems confront the unity of the world's workers. First, capitalism has always developed in the context of a nation, with an active and complicit state. Second, capitalism has, from its beginning, developed unevenly in different parts of the world. The original capitalist nations of Europe and, later, those special cases of the United States and Japan, subjugated the rest of the world through their military and economic might, creating an imperialist system of rich and poor capitalist nations. These twin developments, nationalism and imperialism, have erected substantial barriers against the unity of the workers of the world.

Nationalism has been a powerful force allying workers with their class enemy. The establishment of official languages, the institution of a universal propaganda mechanism in the public schools, and the drafting of working people into national armies all had the effect of encouraging workers to be loyal to the nation. The converse of this loyalty has been distrust or even hatred of those who are "foreign."

This nationalism is closely connected to imperialism. The vicious exploitation of workers and peasants in Africa, Asia, and Latin America went hand in hand with the promotion of a racist ideology that taught that these peoples either deserved what they were getting or were lucky to be associated with the rich nations. Furthermore, the surplus value pumped out of the peripheral nations gave the large multinationals money that, under enough trade union pressure, they could be convinced to share with workers. This went along with successful efforts by the corporations and the government to co-opt labor leaders, through the formation of various kinds of labor- management organizations and assignment to public boards and commissions. The goal here was to convince labor's leaders, as well as union members, that imperialism was good for workers in the core capitalist nations. All of these efforts were, for the most part, successful. Labor organizations in all of the advanced capitalist countries have not only supported their own multinationals in the brutal exploitation of the economies and workers of the poor nations, they have even supported wars in which the workers of one rich nation fought against those of another.

Examples of the disuniting and conservative impact of nationalism and imperialism are numerous. In classes I taught to automobile workers in the late 1980s and early 1990s, I was taken aback by the readily expressed anti-Japanese sentiments. It was as if the Second World War had never ended; the workers seemed unable to distinguish between Japanese auto workers, who were experiencing working conditions similar to their own, and Japanese employers. Instead they joined General Motors, their employer, in Japanese bashing, a remarkable alliance given GM's joint operations with Japanese companies. In Europe, as long ago as the First World War, the workers' social democratic political parties supported their nations' entry into the war, betraying their most basic principles. In various colonial and imperialist wars, in which workers in poor nations were fighting for their independence, workers in many rich countries betrayed their poor nation brothers and sisters and backed their governments.

Two other important reasons for the failure of the workplace and political organizations to continue the radical trajectory that marked their origins are repression and co-optation. The strength of these has varied from country to country, but their impacts have been felt everywhere. The United States probably provides the best example of the effect of extreme repression. Anytime workers moved in a radical direction, they were met with state and employer violence. Shamefully, some labor leaders actively participated in state-sponsored repression of radical labor organizations. Samuel Gompers, for example, used the AFL to help the government destroy the Industrial Workers of the World.9

The carrot of co-optation is often the companion of the stick of repression. Employers may promote labor agitators into the management. The government may also bring "respectable" labor leaders into government agencies or advisory committees, as a way of forcing them into compromises that weaken union militance. Such was the case in both the First and the Second World Wars. Governments needed labor support for the wars and, at the same time, needed to curb the aggressive actions of workers who were striking to take advantage of wartime labor shortages. Labor leaders were brought into governments and governments took certain pro-worker actions as a way of both securing labor cooperation in wartime production and curbing still more militant labor actions.[10]

A kind of massive co-optation occurred in nearly all of the rich capitalist nations during the long post–Second World War economic boom. To prevent the growth of left-wing unions and political organizations and to secure worker loyalty in the Cold War, both employers and governments reached an accord with labor organizations (excluding, of course, the most progressive unions and political parties). The depth of the accord varied from nation to nation, and real gains were made by working men and women during this period, but everywhere unions and labor political parties became more bureaucratic and divorced from their members. Labor leaders became "statesmen," more comfortable with their employer counterparts and political elites than with the rank and file. As the class warfare that had marked earlier periods receded, labor's "statesmen" began to assume that the accord would last indefinitely and that working- class living standards would continue to advance. This meant, unfortunately, that labor was completely unprepared for the resumption of class warfare by employers when the economic boom ended in the middle of the 1970s.

A final set of barriers faced by labor organizations trying to live up to their radical promise is provided by the nature of capitalism itself. We have seen that capitalist accumulation creates a pool of unutilized labor—the reserve army of labor. Those in the reserve army will find it difficult to organize effectively, and if they do organize, to make common cause with those who are employed. In many poor countries, the fraction of the workforce that is unemployed, marginally employed, employed under slave-like conditions, or composed of children, is so large that to talk about traditional labor organizations as the primary weapons of the working class is naive. Although there are large and effective unions in India, most workers toil in conditions in which effective unionization is impossible. To overcome such inherent difficulties, the whole concept of a working class and working-class organization will have to be reconceptualized, with new types of organizations and new strategies and tactics developed to attack the power of capital. We will look at some case studies in the next section.[11]

To form effective working-class organizations requires that workers also build a working class culture that tries to integrate work life and community life through the creation of newspapers, theaters, sports teams, music groups, and so forth. However, it is difficult for such a culture to survive in the face of the power of capitalist culture. A community-based culture takes time to develop. I grew up in a town dominated by a large glass factory. A boy (and some girls, but not as many) could anticipate that he would work in the factory just as had his parents and grandparents and that he would participate in the same sports and fraternal clubs as they had. Life was not especially easy, especially for women, but it was at least coherent and gave the appearance of going on indefinitely. Continuities of time and space are necessary for the formation not just of working-class organizations but of that sense of community memory that gives life meaning and purpose. As you might guess, the factory is no longer in my home town; the company shut it down when it was no longer profitable enough and when new plants were easier to open in nonunion areas in the United States or in poor foreign countries. When the plant closed, more than jobs were lost. A way of life became just a fading memory.

Finally, and perhaps of the greatest importance, capitalism works relentlessly to destroy our full human capacities. As Leo Panitch and Sam Gindin put it, "Every progressive social movement must, sooner or later, confront the inescapable fact that capitalism cripples our capacities, stunts our dreams, and incorporates our politics."[12] For example, at work we are usually confined to the performance of routine work that utilizes only a fraction of our human capacity to conceptualize and execute work. Years of such labor habituates us to behavior not conducive to independent thought and action. It is probably the case that most workers do not see themselves as capable of running their own workplaces, much less the whole of society's productive mechanisms. In his fine book *Rivethead*, automobile worker Ben Hamper describes the hell of laboring in an auto factory. All that he can think about is getting through each day. Creativity is expressed in finding ways to get a few minutes of rest by learning to do two jobs on the assembly line. By doubling up on the two jobs, he could give his workmate a rest, and then he rested while his buddy did his job. Or he took to fantasizing or playing imaginary games to kill the time and to keep from thinking about what the meaninglessness of his work said about his life. After work, he had little energy for anything but drinking or watching television. Hamper was exceptional in that he began to write about his experiences, sometimes while resting on the job. But eventually the job drove him crazy and he had to be hospitalized.[13]

Life in capitalism seems to have no end but to continue trivial work and to consume as much as possible. Nothing else seems possible. Yet even given the seemingly insurmountable difficulties facing the organizations of the working class, fundamental social change can only be brought about with the participation and leadership of those who make this system tick and comprise the overwhelming majority within it.

CONTEMPORARY SOCIAL CHANGE MOVEMENTS

The growing inequality and the accompanying misery caused by a generation of neoliberalism began, in the early 1990s, to stimulate reactions by those adversely affected. French public sector workers struck in 1995 to protest budget and benefit cuts, leading to massive demonstrations and sympathy strikes.[14] South Korean workers began to revitalize their labor movement and directly challenged government policies throughout the decade.[15] The Zapatistas rebelled on January 1, 1995, the day the North American Free Trade Agreement went into effect. Environmentalists, peasants, and workers began to challenge the World Bank, the International Monetary Fund, and the World Trade Organization. A worldwide anti-globalization movement began to develop and flex its muscles wherever these organizations and others like them met: in Seattle in 1999, in Washington in 2000, in Genoa in 2001, in New York City in 2002, and in many other places over the past several years.

The anti-globalization movement is made up of disparate groups, sometimes at odds with one another over both strategy and tactics. There are those who want a return to the social democratic Keynesianism of the post–World War Two prosperity; they believe that what are needed are global institutions that seek to stabilize the world economy and redistribute income and wealth more equitably. There are those who have focused their attention upon specific problems, such as the catastrophic social and environmental consequences of large-scale dams, the plight of sweatshop laborers, the evils of the prison-industrial complex, the horrors of child labor, the anti-labor nature of "free trade" agreements, the liberation of women doubly exploited by capitalism as wage and as household workers, the cancellation of the debts of poor nations, reparations for those damaged by colonialism and racism, the harm done by privatization of public services, and a host of others.[16]

Among this second group of activists, there are growing numbers who have begun to see that all of these problems are systemic in nature, that is, they have their roots in capitalism itself. In this more radical group, there are sharp disagreements concerning what kind of society should replace capitalism and the best tactics to be used to effectuate a transition. Should there be an emphasis on local autonomy and economic self-sufficiency? Should society continue to rely on markets, or should there be central planning? Should there be the kind of direct, consensus- based democracy favored by the anarchists in the various movements, or is there a need for a more traditional radial political party? Is there any role for violent revolution or is this an outmoded form of struggle? This diversity and flux will be apparent in examining some specific struggles connected, either directly or indirectly, to the anti-globalization movements.

The Teamsters for a Democratic Union

There are strong tendencies for unions to become overly bureaucratic organizations, removed from the day-to-day lives of the members. The exigencies of class struggle have served all too often as an excuse for the absence of democracy. In Western Europe, for example, labor unions have been much more successful than they have been in the United States. With the exception of France, union density (the ratio of union membership to total nonsupervisory employment) is much higher in Western Europe than in the United States. Yet unions, which are often part of highly centralized national labor federations bargaining with large groups of employers, are generally far removed from their memberships. After the Second World War, a type of labor-management co-governance was established in many countries, notably Germany and Austria, while in other countries such as Sweden, labor political parties, closely allied with the unions, have actually controlled the national government.

These various arrangements represented a labor-management "accord," forced upon employers by strong unions and by the exigencies of the Cold War. However as top union leaders shared workplace governance and became part of national governments, they drifted away from their base in the actual workforce. Decisions came to be made in a thoroughly top- down manner. This has made it very difficult for the unions to both recognize that the "accord" has been vanquished by neoliberalism and to rally the rank and file against it. As a consequence, the European labor movements are adrift, looking for ways to rejuvenate themselves and pose a credible threat to employers and neoliberal governments, the latter of which have often been run by the social democratic parties presumably supportive of labor.[17]

In the United States, unions are, almost uniformly, run by bureaucrats, who are only minimally responsible to the membership. The reasons for this are not the same as in Europe, but the results have been the same. And in the United States not only are unions undemocratic, they have also been known to operate as criminal rackets. There are many examples of this, none more blatant than the International Brotherhood of Teamsters.[18] By the 1980s, it had become a commonplace for the union's national officers to be indicted for criminal activities and sentenced to prison terms.

The Central States Pension Fund of the Teamsters Union, upon which some 400,000 members and beneficiaries depend for retirement income, loaned billions of dollars to captains of organized crime to build casinos and hotels in Las Vegas and to finance various and sundry other criminal schemes. A large loan in Las Vegas was actually secured by $5 million in gamblers' IOUs! It is estimated that the fund lost some $385 million in loans never repaid or made at below-market interest rates. Local 560 in Union City, New Jersey, was the personal fiefdom of the Provenzano family, itself associated with the Genovese organized crime family. The national officers of the union were elected by delegates to the national convention, but these delegates were, for the most part, appointed by the official they were supposed to nominate and elect. Most officers of the union made exorbitant salaries, often drawing money from several union offices held simultaneously. The reform group Teamsters for a Democratic Union (TDU) uncovered the salaries of Teamster officers and discovered scores of them making in excess of $100,000 per year. When Jackie Presser was appointed union president in 1983, his annual salary was $565,000. The party held at the national convention to celebrate his ascension to the throne cost $647,960.

Dissident groups had formed among the members to fight against corruption, but until the early 1970s, none had survived. It was dangerous to be a dissident in the Teamsters. Union thugs routinely beat up "troublemakers," and murder was not unknown. However, a group of dedicated reformers, many of them forged in the radical political movements of the 1960s, came together to form the Teamsters for a Democratic Union. Not only did the TDU want to reform the Teamsters, they also wanted to rebuild the larger labor movement and renew its commitment to the creation of a more equitable and just society. Slowly, through face-to-face meetings with members, patient research, the creation of a dissident newspaper (the *Convoy*), running TDU candidates for local union office, skillful public relations, building alliances with other reform groups (for example, the Association for Union Democracy), and demonstrations at national conventions, the TDU began to win the respect of the rank and file and to increase its membership.

There are a number of labor laws that might have been used against the Teamsters, but these had proven ineffective. Finally, in the early 1980s the federal government, prodded by the TDU and the Association for Union Democracy, used a criminal statute, the Racketeering Influenced and Corrupt Organizations Act (RICO), to finally bring the union to justice. To avoid massive prosecutions, the union reached a "consent agreement" that put the union in the hands of federally appointed trustees and guaranteed open and fair elections to union office. Buoyed by this victory, reformers began to run for office. The TDU threw its support behind Ron Carey, leader of the large New York City local of United Parcel Service (UPS) workers. Carey and the TDU built a grassroots campaign, and the Carey slate was swept into office.

Carey began to root out the crooks, democratize the union, fund and encourage member education programs, and organize sophisticated rank-and-file-based contract campaigns to win better contracts in collective bargaining. Building on these successes, Carey was reelected national union president in 1996, defeating the son and namesake of legendary former president Jimmy Hoffa. Led by the TDU, debates raged within the union over its future course, but this time, the future looked brighter than ever.

The high point of Carey's administration came in 1997 when it waged a historic and successful strike against UPS. The TDU had been organizing within UPS for years against the labor-management cooperation scheme promoted by the company and convinced the workers that this was nothing more than a way to co-opt them into believing that they were an equal partner with the management, while at the same time the company was making them work harder and longer. The rank and file organized this strike, with the full cooperation and support of the union leadership, and the results of this work showed. The union reached out to the public, which gave the strike very strong support. The defeat of a very powerful, transnational corporation appeared to give the entire labor movement a badly needed boost and seemed to be the harbinger of a new day for organized labor.

Unfortunately, Carey's 1996 election victory over Hoffa was tainted. Instead of relying entirely on the membership for reelection, Carey hooked up with operatives from the national Democratic Party who, perhaps unknown to him, organized an elaborate and illegal kickback scheme to help fund Carey's campaign. Once this became known, Hoffa Jr. and his many right-wing allies started howling for Carey's head. In the end, the election was overturned by the government overseers and Carey was denied the right to participate in the rerun election. The TDU did put forward a candidate, and he did relatively well considering the circumstances. But Hoffa Jr. prevailed. Since then, Hoffa himself has won reelection, and the union has lost much of its fighting spirit. Fortunately, the TDU is alive and well, and this has kept Hoffa on his toes and prevented the union from sinking back into a sea of corruption. Hopefully, the reformists will be able to regain power in the not too distant future.[19]

Reform movements exist in a number of other U.S. unions, and a few of those in which there are not such rank-and-file groups have still managed to do good work, organized immigrant workers, and are pushing for a more independent labor politics. There are also signs of labor union reawakening in many other parts of the world. The left wing is on the move in some British unions, and the ranks are getting restive in the rest of Europe as well.[20] As we noted above, in 1995 French workers, led by public employees, brought the economy to a standstill through strikes and mass demonstrations, widely supported by the public, and succeeded in preventing neoliberal cutbacks in public services and wage and benefit reductions for public workers. Just recently, Italian workers took to the streets in the hundreds of thousands to protest proposed neoliberal changes in the country's pro-worker labor laws.[21] Canadian workers, led by the Canadian Auto Workers, have participated in struggles against privatization, cuts in social welfare, and the right turn of the political parties traditionally allied with labor.[22] In the poor countries, progressive and radical unions have formed in Mexico and South Korea, and there are democratic forces at work in most of the poor world's labor movements.

Traditional labor organizations are a permanent part of capitalist societies, and given that they often represent a large fraction of a country's workers, they must of necessity be a major part of all broader movements to challenge capitalism. Yet the defensive nature of unions and the hegemonic power of capitalism have made many labor organizations conservative and unwilling to address and attack the fundamental problems facing most of the world's people. In many places, the unemployed form such a large part of the workforce that traditional union struggles cannot do them much good. In addition, there are pressing problems of daily community life that unions are ill-equipped to tackle. As a consequence labor unions and labor political parties are today not generally in the forefront of global struggle. Other kinds of organizations have formed to fill the void left by organized labor. In my view, the future trajectory of social struggle will depend upon the extent to which organized labor movements reconstitute themselves to become integral parts of a larger movement.

The Landless Workers Movement and the Workers Party in Brazil

Brazil is the largest country in Latin America and one of the largest in the world. Its economy generates the world's ninth largest Gross Domestic Product; its land mass contains several of the world's largest and most industrialized cities and many rich agricultural and bio- diverse regions. At the same time, however, Brazil is a poor country, with all of the indices that typify poor countries: mass poverty, appalling inequality, high infant mortality among the poor, and authoritarian rule by the wealthy.23

Like many poor nations, Brazil has a turbulent political history. From time to time, what have been called "populist" political movements have arisen, largely as a result of various kinds of revolts among the peasants and workers. Populist movements usually have a strong nationalistic component, an ideology that encourages people to struggle for the good of the nation. Populist leaders show a considerable sympathy for the oppressed poor and a disdain for those rich persons who act merely out of selfishness, with no concern for the poor or for the nation. But they also embrace those businesspersons who want to invest domestically. Populists are not fundamentally radical; they are nearly always anti-communist and opposed to those working-class movements oriented toward socialism.

Once in power, populist leaders face serious dilemmas. They have to make concessions to the poor or face the wrath of their most ardent supporters. Once concessions are made, however, the poor demand more and business leaders get increasingly nervous. In addition, the rich capitalist countries, most notably the United States, begin to fence in the new government, opposing any nationalizations of foreign capital and large-scale land redistributions. These are also opposed vehemently by the more conservative domestic elements, including large landholders, many local capitalists, and in Latin America, the Catholic Church. What transpires in most cases is either a move to the right by the populist government or its overthrow, often with foreign (U.S.) support and, if necessary, direct intervention.

In 1964, the United States helped to overthrow the populist government of João Goulart, which was replaced by a brutal military dictatorship. The generals ran the country for the next twenty-one years. They engineered what today would be called neoliberal economic changes, which after a few years of high GDP growth gave way to a severe economic crisis in the 1970s and early 1980s. To obtain needed foreign exchange, the government agreed to IMF structural adjustments and World Bank–financed dam projects, and these had disastrous consequences for the already poor majority of Brazilians. All of this generated opposition, and despite years of violent oppression, Brazil's workers and peasants succeeded in forming lasting organizations, most notably the Workers Party and the Landless Workers' Movement.

The Workers Party (PT are the Portuguese initials) was "founded in 1980 by unionists, leftist Christians, and Marxist militants, all convinced that the emancipation of the workers will be the task of the workers themselves and stirred by a desire to invent a different, radical, democratic, libertarian socialism that breaks with the old model of Stalinism and social democracy."[24] Since its founding, the Workers Party has developed a large mass following and has won several important elections. Its leading figure, "Lula" da Silva, was elected president of Brazil in 2002 on a platform of resisting neoliberalism.

The Workers Party controls several large Brazilian cities, including the government of Porto Alegre, the capital of the state of Rio Grande do Sol. This is a large and important industrial city and the site of the recent "Social Forum," a yearly meeting of progressive and radical activists and NGOs. The Party also now controls the state government as well.

Among the most important initiatives of the Workers Party has been the enactment of the "participatory budget." In mass public meetings, open to everyone, the people themselves determine how the money allocated to their locality should be spent. As Michael Löwy explains:

> In other words, it is the population itself which determines, in an original demonstration of direct democracy, if the budget's funds should be used to build a road, a school, or a medical center. Subsequent assemblies let the population monitor the implementation of the chosen projects, while a City

Council of the Participatory Budget, made up of delegates elected by the
assemblies, manages the distribution of the budget to the different neighborhoods, following criteria decided on in common.[25]

As a result of neoliberal policies implemented by the national government,
each locality is saddled with part of the debt the nation owes to the International Monetary Fund. This limits the power of the people to make budget decisions, but it has also led to widespread and militant political
organization, which should rebound to the party's benefit in the long run.
The Workers Party state government in Rio Grande do Sol has also organized the people in opposition to the importation of genetically modified
organisms, which the large agribusiness multinationals are trying to introduce. These would not only damage the environment and the health of the
people, but they would threaten the livelihoods of thousands of peasants.

Today the Workers Party faces a serious split between its radical and
reformist wings. In his quest for the presidency, Lula da Silva chose a conservative running mate, in an attempt to gain wider legitimacy and to make
his candidacy acceptable to the United States. It will be interesting to see if
the radicals in the party can prevent it from becoming like all too many of
the formerly radical and progressive political formations in Latin America.

Of perhaps even greater importance than the Workers Party is the Landless Workers Movement (its Portuguese initials are MST). In response to deteriorating economic conditions and rooted in the liberation
theology of some sectors of the Catholic Church, the MST began its struggle
in 1985 by occupying an unoccupied plantation in southern Brazil. The MST
is somewhat millenarian in its outlook, and this reflects its religious origins.
But the desire to create a better world on this earth, a "kingdom of God," has
strong anti-capitalist overtones. In a remarkable 1973 document, certain
Brazilian church leaders stated: "Capitalism must be defeated: it is the greatest evil, the accumulated sin, the rotten root, the tree that produces all these
fruits which we know so well: poverty, hunger, disease, death. . . . For this reason, we must pass beyond private ownership of the means of production (factories, land, commerce, banks)."[26]

Unlike the traditional church teachings, the liberation church preached
that the poor should become actors in the world and not just passive recipients of unjust treatment who would be rewarded in the hereafter. The MST,
today a secular organization though one in which most members have
strong religious beliefs, has taken strong actions to liberate the idle land of

the rich and put it to the use of poor communities. MST national board member Joao Pedro Stedile describes the group's achievements as follows:

> Our most important success of all has been to build an organization and a social movement. We've won back the worth and dignity of the peasant. That has immeasurable value. It doesn't show up in statistics. But when a person stops being humiliated, stops being a slave, and they can walk with their head up, master of their own future, that's the most important we're building.
>
> Beyond that, over the last 18 years, we've gotten land for 300,000 families, and though many of them remain poor, nobody in our settlements goes hungry. Everybody has work all year around. There are schools in all the settlements. All the children go to school. Everyone can build their own home. The houses may be humble, but nobody has to pay rent to anyone. At the very least, the people enjoy the basic rights of all people. That's what taking the land means.
>
> We're not satisfied with these modest achievements. Because in Brazil there are four million landless families. Our struggle is to broaden the movement, open up more battles, mobilize more people, because it's not just a matter of allowing a few people to solve their problems. This is important, of course. It offers an example. It's a form of mass education. But the fundamental thing is to change society, and solve the problems of all Brazilians, of all the poor.[27]

Although the land seizures have a legal basis in the Brazilian constitution, which demands that land be utilized for social purposes, the MST's militant actions (including occupations of government buildings) have met with violent repression from both landlords and the government. Hundreds of poor people have been murdered, and very few perpetrators have been brought to trial. But still the MST has persevered and grown. It has a strong ally in the Workers Party, and together these two organizations offer not just hope to the poor majority of Brazilians but an alternative way to organize society.

Throughout Latin America, radical movements are proliferating. Some, like the MST in Brazil and the Indian movement in Ecuador, are based in rural areas and center around control of land and resources. Others, like the unemployed workers' movement in Argentina, which has pioneered a tactic of blockading highways and bringing economic activity to a standstill, are based in urban barrios and focus on demands for jobs and better community services.[28] If ways could be found to unite these organizations democratically with more traditional labor unions, an extremely powerful anti-capitalist movement could be forged.

The "Poors" of South Africa

The valiant struggle of the black people of South Africa—African, colored, and Indian—to end the system of racial oppression known as apartheid galvanized progressives around the world. Through a combination of armed struggle, nonviolent confrontation, strikes, boycotts, and international solidarity, apartheid was defeated in 1994 and one of its most prominent victims, Nelson Mandela, was elected president of the nation. Mandela's party, the African National Congress (ANC), allied with the South African Communist Party (SACP) and the largest labor union confederation (the Congress of South African Trade Unions, or COSATU), promised a new day for the poor and dispossessed majority of this rich African nation.[29]

That free elections were held and that Mandela was elected president was a remarkable achievement. Widespread violence and destruction were avoided, and from this point forward South Africa's black majority were now a political majority as well. Given the seeming impregnability of apartheid, its collapse and the ANC victory were astounding. As John Saul put it:

> South Africa has been able to realize and to stabilize the shift to a constitutionally premised and safely institutionalized democratic order—making peace without suffering the crippling backlash from the right wing, both black and white, that many had predicted and without suffering the collapse into chaos or dictatorship that some had seen to be threatened by the establishment of majority rule. Moreover, this political stability was sustained through the five years of Mandela's presidency, reconfirmed by the very mundaneness of the 1999 election, and has been carried unscathed into the Thabo Mbeki presidency. A cause for celebration, surely, on a continent where apparently lesser contradictions have proven far more difficult to resolve.[30]

The ANC had used a revolutionary and socialist rhetoric in its struggle against white rule. As late as 1989, Mandela spoke of "the need for some sort of socialism to enable our people to catch up with the advanced countries of the world and to overcome their legacy of poverty."[31] The new government promised:

> The engine of growth in the economy of a developing, nonracial and nonsexist South Africa should be the growing satisfaction of the basic needs of the impoverished and deprived majority of our people. We thus call for a program of

Growth through Redistribution in which redistribution acts as a spur to growth and in which the fruits of growth are redistributed to satisfy basic needs.[32]

Furthermore, "In our growth path, accumulation depends on the prior redistribution of resources. Major changes will have to take place in existing power relations as a necessary condition for this new growth path."[33]

This economic program resonated strongly with the dispossessed masses of the country. Millions of people in South Africa were unemployed, living on extraordinarily low incomes, subject to a host of illnesses and diseases, going hungry, and living in segregated and substandard housing. The majority of people were denied all basic human rights and were routinely the victims of police and military violence.

The ANC has been slow to fulfill the promises it made to the people. Indeed, as is the case for most poor countries, political independence was not accompanied by economic independence. Most of the nation's nonhuman means of production remained in the hands of their previous owners. Some property has been shared with a new class of rich black South Africans, many of them stalwarts of the ANC. Soon after being elected, Mandela embraced neoliberalism and his government began to enact neoliberal policies: cuts in government spending, concessions to foreign investment, a high interest rate monetary policy, and the privatization of essential public services. In his moving book *We Are the Poors*, Ashwin Desai, put the matter bluntly:

Before long, democracy was more or less stifled within the ANC and its Communist and trade union allies. People who couldn't be bought were marginalized. It soon got to the point where you could get expelled from the South African Communist Party for advocating Communism. Once the conservative nationalists had cemented their hegemony within the party, self-serving deals were done with local white elites and international capital. By 1996 Thabo Mbeki—then deputy president of South Africa, later successor to Nelson Mandela as leader of the ANC and president of South Africa—was calling himself a Thatcherite and the ANC had voluntarily imposed its own structural adjustment program on South Africa. Taxes on the rich were cut, exchange controls dropped, and tariffs protecting unionized South African workers from imports from sweat shops were abandoned. Around a hundred thousand jobs were lost each year and a million in all by 2001. Water, electricity, housing and health care were taken from those who couldn't pay.[34]

It has taken the poor majority some time to understand that its former standard bearer had more or less joined hands with its apartheid enemy. But recently the poor have begun to revolt, especially against the government's policy of evictions from public housing of those who cannot pay their rent and the cutoff or denial of essential services such as water, electricity, and health care for the same reason. The consequences of the government's "austerity" have been deadly. Again, Desai states the matter starkly:

> By 2002 over 6 million South Africans were HIV positive and without any access to the lifesaving medication that, even a not completely rabid neoliberal budget, could safely satisfy. People were aghast at a comment made by the president's spokesperson that medicines that prevented mother-to-child transmission of the virus were undesirable because of the healthy orphans it left the state to deal with. The majority of the population are living on less than R 140 (about $15) per month. One in four black children do not have enough to eat every day. Only 3 percent of arable land had been redistributed and much of that had been given to black commercial farmers and not to landless peasants. Over a million people had been disconnected from water because they couldn't pay; 40,000 children were dying from diarrhea caused by dirty water each year. Cholera returned with a vengeance, infecting over 100,000 people in Kwa-Zulu Natal alone. People starved in rural areas, throngs of street-kids descended on every town to beg and prostitute themselves, petty-crime soared, and the jails reached 170 percent capacity.[35]

By the end of the 1990s, the "poors" of South Africa were in revolt. This revolt was largely spontaneous and it was to a considerable extent nonracial. One of the most important local revolts took place in the township of Chatsworth in Durban, the biggest city on South Africa's east coast. The residents of this largely Indian area began to confront the government concerning evictions. Mass meetings, marches, demonstrations, legal maneuvering, people's music, and the occupation of houses all put public officials on the defensive. A defining moment came when an African official berated the crowd and declaimed that Indians were privileged and had no right to complain. An elderly woman protester said, "We are not Indians, we are the poors."A new class struggle was beginning in South Africa.

It is difficult in a short space to give readers the flavor of the "poors" movement. Out of their desperate need for water, electricity, schools, housing, and health care, ordinary people mobilized, spontaneously at first and with deeper organization afterward, to literally take what they felt they had a human right to. People marched on the offices and homes of public officials, often dodging police bullets and clubs, to loudly demand that the government serve their needs as it had once promised and for which they had suffered so much and fought so bravely. Ordinary people, aptly named "struggle electricians" and "struggle plumbers," began to reconnect electricity and water supplies for those who could not, because of government austerity policies, pay their bills. They also began to disconnect the power and water of public officials! Militant organized groups blocked evictions of those who could not pay their rents. Ordinary people began to break down the insidious barriers of race that the apartheid state had so ruthlessly and cynically established. Ordinary people took on large corporations when the official unions would not. Ordinary people occupied the land that was rightfully theirs but that the government had declared could only be had for market value. Traditional religious events were put to new use, as when a festival of lights was named the festival of no lights to protest electricity cutoffs. Youth put hip-hop music at the service of the struggle, and when people had no food, they could use the community cooking pot.

The "poors" movement is still in its infancy. Many victories have been achieved, but only a small fraction of the population has been mobilized. Yet even at this stage, it is possible to identify several important aspects of the "poors" movement in South Africa. First, as is true of many social movements in poor countries, the revolt of the "poors" is not led by what we might call traditional members of the working class. While COSATU has engaged in various protests against government policies, the labor unions have not been central to the new mass movements. Instead, the unemployed, the underemployed, and disaffected youth have formed the core constituency. Second, the "poors" have been largely led by women. Poor women in poor countries are at the bottom of the social hierarchy. Often brutalized by men, who themselves have suffered extreme hardship, poor women are left to hold families together, finding whatever work they can to keep food on their tables and roofs over their heads. Absolute desperation, combined with bitter anger, has compelled women not only to participate in radical activities but to lead them. This is of the greatest importance, because it puts the issue of gender oppression at the forefront of the larger class struggle. Social progress cannot be made if those most oppressed are shunted aside in favor of a male definition of class struggle.

Finally, the "poors" have focused their fight on local concerns, but these issues of evictions and utility shutoffs are intimately tied to global capitalism and the neoliberal assault on working-class living standards. In our daily lives, it is usually impossible to directly confront much less defeat the World Bank or the World Trade Organization. But it is possible to win concrete local victories, such as the return of an evicted family to its house or a moratorium on utility disconnections. It is possible to confront local officials and force them to back down, and it is possible to change the contours of local power. These local struggles allow people to empower themselves and, with support from sympathetic intellectuals and activists operating on a more global level, to raise their consciousness of what ultimately causes their misery and to link up with fellow sufferers around the world. Global movements must originate at the local level, the level at which people actually experience life.

If local actions are critical, at the same time it is necessary to link these up to larger struggles. The many local South African movements began to do this in 2001 in conjunction with the United Nations World Conference Against Racism, held in Durban, South Africa. Groups began to meet and make plans for mass demonstrations and cultural events at the conference and for making common cause with a wide variety of protest organizations. Groups involved in protesting evictions, in fighting against privatization, various socialist formations, activist student and faculty groups, independent union activists, certain progressive NGOs, and the Landless People's Movement (which had recently engaged in an unsuccessful land occupation) all decided to make common cause at the conference, both to show solidarity with similar groups around the world and to show the world the true nature of the South African government. In describing a powerful speech made at one of the preparatory meetings by poet, international activist, and former prisoner with Mandela on Robben Island, Dennis Brutus (who walked out into the audience to explain "global apartheid," a phrase that might resonate more powerfully than the word "imperialism"), journalist Tracey Fared tells us:

> By the time we left the meeting, there was a buzz amongst all of us like I have never felt before. People were talking to each other. Suddenly so many things made sense. Why our water was getting cut off and our people thrown onto the street. Why our children had to pay school fees or else. Why the local clinics had been closed down. Why Engen [the local affiliate of Exxon Mobil] had retrenched workers to increase its share price. Why foreign companies are happy to give Yengeni's [4 by 4 cars] to local elites. Why our president doesn't

support the intifadah. Why the youth of the North are also out on the streets
and why our Minister of Finance hates them so . . .

One did not have to jet all over the world like Dennis to fight global
apartheid effectively. One simply has to start building organizations, building
power in the communities where one lives—confronting, militantly, the most
terrible aspects of your oppression. And after that—one must link up with
others around you, all over the world.[36]

The World Summit on Sustainable Development, held in Johannesburg in
August 2002, provided another occasion for bringing masses of oppressed
South Africans into a global context of struggle. The South African struggles
are important for the questions they raise. Like much of the globalization
movement, the organizations around which these struggles have developed
are highly decentralized, make decisions by consensus, and ebb and flow
with specific crises and meetings of global elites. How can such organizations be held together over long periods of time? Will it be necessary for
them to forge a common ideology and a common strategy for putting this
ideology into practice? It is one thing to force a local government to back
down over issues of life and death such as housing and water. It is another
to stop the national government from pursuing the policies that lead to the
shutoffs in the first place, much less to replace the government with people's power. To do these things, will a political party be needed? If so, how
will it avoid the problems associated with such parties in the past, problems
that have given the whole idea of party formation such a bad odor?

The Student Anti-Sweatshop Movement

The anti-globalization movement burst upon the international scene in
Seattle, Washington, in 1999 when massive protests stopped the World
Trade Organization in its tracks. The movement is an extremely disparate
one, made up of people and groups of various political stripes, from anarchists to disillusioned social democrats to radical environmentalists to
advocates of the abrogation of third world debt to conventional trade
unionists. As noted above, all of these groups and persons have been meeting in Porto Alegre, Brazil, in a series of "Social Forums" to try to build an
alternative politics capable of challenging global capitalism.

It is too early to ascertain the general thrust of the movement. Some envision a new kind of capitalist globalization, which puts into place interna-

tional institutions and policies aimed at a substantial and progressive redistribution of the world's resources and income. Perhaps the IMF, the World
Bank, and the WTO can be reformed by, for example, the insertion of labor-
and environment-friendly clauses placed in their bylaws and constitutions.
Or Keynes and Tobin taxes could be levied on financial transactions, the proceeds then used for development projects aimed at the world's poor. Others
envision a more strictly localized political economy that deemphasizes international trade and concentrates on local self-sufficiency. Some environmentalists and anarchists fall into this camp, with the anarchists more likely to
take an anti-capitalist stance. A third grouping opposes the term "anti-globalization movement," instead insisting, as we have in this book, that the root
cause of inequality, underemployment, low wages, overwork, child labor,
and all of the other evils we have documented is capitalism. It is true that the
movement of capital around the world has sped up over the past thirty years,
but this should not be called globalization. It is simply what is inevitable in a
capitalist world. As we have seen, capitalist economies have been global from
their beginning. Therefore, being anti- globalization does not make any
sense unless this also means that you are anti-capitalist.

There are some signs that the misnamed anti-globalization movement
is becoming increasingly anti-capitalist, if not directly then at least in
terms of its actions. A look at one of the participant groups, the student
anti-sweatshop movement, will help to clarify what I mean by this.[37]

In Chapter Seven, we saw that capitalist economies are riddled with
contradictions, and these contradictions often generate opposition. For
example, the gap between capitalism's hype and its reality is so great that
some people are bound to notice and be moved to do something about it.
Sometimes even those who live fairly comfortable lives notice and take
action. Some college students in the United States, for example, became
revolutionaries in the 1960s, and thousands more participated in the civil
rights and antiwar movements. In France, in 1968, students closed many of
the universities and almost succeeded in forming a student-worker
alliance that might have toppled the government. In the world's poor
countries, universities have often been centers of radical ferment.

There are many events that might wake people up and make them
think and act. For college students, it might be a war that threatens their
lives and those of their contemporaries in other countries. It might be a
part-time job, a trip abroad, an internship with a labor union or a social
service organization, church activity, a teacher's lectures, discussion with

classmates, a speaker on campus, a film, or labor struggles on their own campuses. A number of circumstances conspired in the 1990s to create a new student movement, one with great promise for promoting radical change. A significant manifestation of this movement is the student-led struggle against sweatshops.

Several factors help to explain the origins and development of the anti-sweatshop movement. First, there were a series of exposures of working conditions in the subcontracted plants of high profile companies like Nike and media personalities like Kathie Lee Gifford. Independent labor groups, like the National Labor Committee and the Chinese Staff and Workers Association, and the anti-Nike "Press for Change"group begun by former AFL-CIO official Jeff Ballinger organized campaigns to publicize the conditions of garment and other low-wage workers in both the rich and poor countries. The disparity between the lifestyle of people like Gifford and Nike CEO Phil Knight and the poverty of the workers, as well as the chasm between the price of the shoes and garments and the wages paid to the workers, resonated among many youth who began to see how crassly they were being manipulated by the slick advertisements for the products they had been encouraged to buy.

Second, the sweatshop workers themselves had begun to organize. One of the important insights gained by the student activists is that poor workers are not just victims of corporate abuse; they are active agents trying to find ways to improve their own circumstances. *Fuerza Unida*, for example, was a boycott organization formed by laid-off Levi Strauss workers in San Antonio, Texas. Workers in the maquiladora plants in Mexico have formed independent unions and conducted strikes and factory occupations in the face of brutal repression. Some students actually went to Mexico to see for themselves what was happening to workers. By observing first-hand the rebellion of workers, the students began to see that they were not just helping poor people but engaging in a collective struggle with them, a struggle transforming their own as well as the workers' lives.

Third, significant changes were occurring in the house of labor in the United States. The AFL-CIO, under the leadership of John Sweeney and his New Voice team, began to promote the organization of new members as necessary for labor's survival. A large number of potential new members were immigrants, and many of them worked in sweatshops. And some unions, often influenced by the anti-sweatshop students they took on as interns and summer employees in the AFL-CIO's Union Summer program, began to see that the conditions of sweatshop workers overseas would have to improve dramatically if the capital flight that characterized the garment and other labor-intensive industries was to be halted. The AFL-CIO also dropped its virulent anti-communism, and this made it easier for unions both to hire progressive organizers and staff and to cooperate with more radical labor unions in other countries.

Finally, the colleges and universities to which the young future activists came to study had become thoroughly corporatized. They had become, in David Noble's words, "sites of capital accumulation."[38] Universities were busy selling patent rights to large corporations and making deals with sports equipment companies like Nike. They were financing their corporate activities on the backs of the students, who saw more and more money spent on capital equipment (research facilities, for example) and administrative staff and less and less spent on teachers and classrooms. Furthermore, they were contracting out food and other services to vendors like Sodexho-Marriott that exploited low-wage and often immigrant labor and were engaged in such dubious ventures as the private prison business. And the universities themselves were using sweatshop labor in the form of underpaid and overworked graduate students, who taught most of the undergraduate classes in many departments. Students could see right in front of their eyes an obvious contradiction between capitalism's promise and its reality. The colleges preached the purity of their academic mission but practiced something different—an unabashed pursuit of money and power.

In response to all of this, the students began to organize themselves into groups, on individual campuses and eventually in national organizations, to force their schools to stop buying sweatshop-produced clothing, to stop selling themselves to the corporations, to recognize the unions of their graduate students, to stop contracting with union-busting campus purveyors or force these purveyors to recognize unions, and to stop their own union busting when janitors, cafeteria workers, and other staff formed unions.

Out of all of this ferment came the United Students Against Sweatshops (USAS), which was formally established in 1998 and which serves as a model for the new student movement.. In its four years of existence, the USAS has had great initial successes. It has developed a growing understanding of the corporate university and the global economy, and it has already faced a strong backlash from corporations and their academic apologists, including, of course, the neoclassical economists. This backlash gives proof that the group is having a real impact on the way corporate America does business.

The history of the USAS exhibits many interesting developments: the attempt by the schools and the federal government to co-opt the movement through the formation of the Fair Labor Association (FLA) and the students' response in creating the more aggressive Workers Rights Consortium (WRC); the students' realization that their war against sweatshops in other countries had to be seen in light of the existence of sweatshops on their own campuses and throughout the United States; and the lead role played by neoclassical economists in the corporate-led backlash against the USAS. As an economist, I found this last point familiar. I always say that whatever the average person thinks is socially desirable, the neoclassical economist is ready to argue is not and vice versa. Following in the footsteps of economists like Walt Rostow (of Vietnam War infamy), they hold that sweatshops are good, a necessary stage on the road toward development, introducing backward peasants to work discipline and the wonders of the market economy. Thankfully, some progressive economists, like Robert Pollin and Stephanie Luce, have taken sharp issue with their mainstream brethren, taking the trouble to actually do some empirical work that nicely refuted the ideologically blinded neoclassical economists, who would rather take the high road of abstract theorizing than the tougher job of empirical investigation.[39]

The internal dimensions of the USAS are also important and reflect problems common throughout the anti-globalization movement. The question of democracy has been particularly vexing as the organization has struggled with the conflict between the desire for consensus and universal participation and the need for leadership and responsibility for day-to-day decisions. As one activist framed the difficulty, "What is a leader? How should we be treating each other? If we don't ask those questions, we create organizations that no one wants to be part of."

Important problems have also arisen concerning race and gender. Racial tensions have appeared within the new student movement, not surprising given the fact that Black and white students often come to college from different social circumstances and for somewhat different reasons. Black students have pointed out that the focus on sweatshop workers in other countries allows white students a way to feel righteous without acknowledging racially charged domestic issues such as the racist destruction of public assistance and the racist criminal injustice system. USAS members have been acutely aware of this issue and have engaged and cooperated with minority students on a number of campaigns, but there is a long way to go before a radical and multiracial movement becomes a reality.

Gender has been a less divisive issue. So many of the sweatshop workers, as well as the student activists, are women that it would be impossible to maintain patriarchal relationships within USAS and have any success. This is not to say that patriarchy does not exist within USAS, but it appears to be much less harmful to the movement than it was in the 1960s. One of the outcomes of USAS struggles has been a recognition of the women who do the work as more than just victims. Women workers in both poor and rich countries have often taken the lead in fighting against both their employers and the governments that fully sanction their employers' repressive actions.

The anti-sweatshop movement has made common cause with the U.S. labor movement, and this may prove to be of crucial importance. Multiple alliances have been built between the AFL-CIO, both at the federation and individual levels, and the student group. In fact, in the summer of 2001 the USAS declared itself a "student/labor solidarity organization." This is a hopeful development, as it guarantees labor a committed cadre of student supporters and a pool of talented future organizers and staff persons. Still, the student-labor alliance is not without its pitfalls. The students must be careful to maintain their independence and not get co-opted by the more conservative labor movement. This is critical because the students are more likely to take a radical perspective on political and economic matters, and their independence might allow them to help move organized labor in a radical direction. USAS seems to be developing a more anti- capitalist, as opposed to a merely anti-corporate, analysis, in line with a significant segment of the large anti-globalization movement worldwide.

The FARC in Colombia and the Maoists in Nepal

If capitalism is to be replaced with a democratic and egalitarian mode of production, a fundamental question is how the transition from capitalism to the new system of production and distribution is to take place. Is it possible to build up alternative economic mechanisms within capitalist economies and, through the increasing weight of these mechanisms undermine and ultimately replace capitalism? Or could radical, worker-based political parties win elections and then use the state to engineer a peaceful transition? Or will capitalism only yield to violent force, that is, revolutionary armed struggle?

The first successful socialist transformations took place as a consequence of revolutions, first in the Soviet Union, then in China, Cuba, Vietnam, and a few other places. The means of production were socialized through the forcible expropriation of private property after, in some cases, many years of military struggle. In every case, the economy transformed was formerly in a poor nation; no socialist revolution has ever occurred in a rich country.

The Cuban revolution was the last successful revolution built on armed struggle. After the death of Che Guevara in Bolivia, where he was trying to foment a Cuban-style revolution, and the failure of Cuban-inspired revolutions in Nicaragua and El Salvador, the idea that capitalism could and should be defeated by military means lost favor. The collapse of the Soviet Union and its satellite allies further distanced radicals from an embrace of revolutionary war.

Indeed, the demise of the formerly socialist economies and the shift of China toward capitalism has called into question the possibility of creating any alternative to capitalism. Furthermore, the possibility of transcending capitalism through peaceful political means was dealt a lethal blow by the violent overthrow of the democratically elected socialist president of Chile, Salvador Allende. Allende used completely legal methods to begin the socialization of the Chilean economy, but he and his party were defeated, and Allende himself was murdered, by the Chilean military, itself fully (and illegally) aided and abetted by the United States. The fascist violence unleashed by General Pinochet even reached the streets of Washington, where one of Allende's ministers, Orlando Letelier, was murdered in a car bombing. Looking at Chile in historical perspective, it is difficult not to reach the conclusion that the rich nations, led by the United States, will never tolerate an attempted peaceful transition.[40] The entire history of imperialism shows that even reformist politics can expect a negative reaction, backed ultimately by military force and undercover operations, from the United States and its allies.

In reaction to the failures of all attempts at peaceful transition and in defiance of the hopelessness felt by large segments of the left after the fall of the Soviet Union, two remarkable efforts to defeat capitalism militarily are taking place in the South American country of Colombia and in the Asian nation of Nepal. Both revolutions have been so thoroughly vilified by the mainstream media that it is worth trying to gain a more objective picture of both of them.[41]

Colombia achieved political independence from Spain in 1810, but like most of the nations in Latin America, political independence brought neither peace nor economic independence. Conflicts soon erupted over control of the land. By the middle of the nineteenth century, most of the land and all of the domestic political power was concentrated in a few rich families. Wealth was generated mainly by the production of coffee for export. Also by mid-century, the two dominant contemporary political parties, the Liberals and the Conservatives had been formed. Although both are bourgeois parties, the Liberal Party has often been associated with various kinds of rebellious movements, especially in the countryside where peasants were often in revolt against landowners.

By the second decade of the twentieth century, a working class had begun to form and organize, both in the cities and in the rural plantations. Radical political parties, including a Communist Party, were formed. Strikes and peasant rebellions were met with brutal and deadly violence, as in 1928 when striking United Fruit Company workers were slaughtered by government forces.

Between 1930 and 1946, the Liberal Party ruled and introduced land reforms that angered the Conservatives. The Conservatives regained power in 1946 and began to undo the Liberal reforms, with the liberal use of violence. In 1948, Liberal leader Jorge Gaitán was assassinated by Conservative agents, and this unleashed a ten-year civil war known as "La Violencia," in which 300,000 Colombians died. During this period, armed guerilla groups formed among the peasantry, and these were the precursors to the FARC. One of the rebel leaders of that period, Manuel Marulanda Velez, is today chief commander of the FARC.

The internal class struggle in Colombia cannot be understood without also understanding that the United States has been deeply involved in Colombian affairs for a century. In 1903, the United States orchestrated the separation of Panama from Colombia so that the Panama Canal could be built under U.S. control. In the 1950s, the United States began to provide the government with counterinsurgency training, and in 1955 the United States aided Colombian military dictator Gustavo Rojas Pinilla (who came to power in a 1953 coup) wage war against guerillas with a $170 million loan. While Rojas Pinilla was eventually replaced and "La Violencia" brought to an end by a Liberal-Conservative agreement to rotate power, the guerillas began to consolidate their strength, establishing "independent republics" based on economic self-rule. In 1964, these rebel areas were attacked by massive military force, compelling the guerillas to flee to the southwestern mountains. In this same year, the FARC was formed, and soon afterward it declared an armed revolt.

Both Liberal and Conservative governments pursued policies aimed at destroying the FARC and the several other armed groups that formed in the 1960s and 1970s. At the same time, they initiated programs aimed at making the countryside completely capitalist. This meant that peasants had to be dispossessed. Peasants fought back but eventually were forced to move to the cities to become wage workers or migrate to more remote regions of the country. In these areas, they came into contact with the FARC and provided thousands of new recruits to the rebel army.

In their new homes, many peasants turned naturally to the cultivation of coca, the only crop that provided them with a means to survive. The growing of coca provided the United States with good cover for its escalating aid to the Colombian government. The United States could say that it was merely trying to stop the flow of a dangerous drug into the United States. Its position was strengthened when the FARC began to tax coca production. Given that there was no way for the FARC to stop coca production unless it controlled the entire economy and could implement its program and give peasants an alternative way to live, it was natural that it would levy a tax on the major cash crop in FARC-held territories. However, the United States could then argue that FARC was profiting from the drug trade and was no different than the big Colombian drug cartels. Of course, what the United States really fears is the establishment of a socialist society in Colombia. The hypocrisy of the United States becomes apparent when it is understood that the right-wing paramilitary groups that have been formed to fight the FARC are closely allied with, and indeed probably intertwined with, the Colombian military, with which the United States has very cordial relations.

Since the 1980s, the government has been forced to recognize the growing power of the FARC, which has won actual or de facto control of large parts of the country. The FARC has proved a formidable foe, with a large army and sophisticated weaponry, which it has captured from the Colombian military or bought on the black market. It has used a wide range of tactics, including destruction of infrastructure and oil pipelines, kidnaping of politicians and business leaders, and assassination of suspected government collaborators. It has also participated in numerous negotiations with the government and has tried to present a peaceful image abroad.

The remarkable growth of the FARC can be explained by two factors. First, despite such superficial signs of development as a relatively high life expectancy (slightly over seventy years) and literacy rate (91.3 percent), the fact is that most Colombians live in abject misery. Open unemployment is in excess of 20 percent, and well over half of the population lives below the poverty level. Government repression of opposition groups is vicious. Today, more union leaders are murdered in Colombia than anywhere else in the world. Environmental degradation is everywhere. In response to charges that the FARC recruits children (it accepts those at least fifteen years of age), FARC commander Simon Trinidad said,

> It sounds beautiful when you say that children shouldn't be guerillas, but children are in the streets of the cities doing drugs, inhaling gasoline and glue. According to the United Nations: 41% of Colombians are children, 6.5 million children live in conditions of poverty, another 1.2 million living in absolute poverty, 30,000 live in the streets, 47% are abused by their parents, and 2.5 million work in high risk jobs. These children meet the guerillas and they don't have parents because the military or the paramilitaries killed them, and they ask the guerillas to let them join. We are carrying out our rule that no children younger than 15 years of age join.42

Second, as Trinidad suggests, the FARC gives poor people hope that their lives might improve. In FARC-controlled territories, for example, farmers are not exploited. The coca buyers and the larger coca farmers are taxed, and the proceeds are used not only to finance the FARC's revolutionary war but to pay for the development of the region's infrastructure and government. The military successes of the FARC also give courage to the poor, as they see that their oppressors are not invulnerable. As the FARC encourages self-discipline and people's democracy, poor workers and peasants begin to gain the knowledge and experience to take charge of their own lives. Schooling, housing, more equal justice, an enhanced role for women, all of these are powerful and positive features of the FARC.

Given the FARC's roots in the Colombian Communist Party and given that party's adherence to the Soviet line for many years, and given especially the harsh reality of constant warfare and the authoritarian structures war necessitates, it is not possible to know what the FARC would do if it won power in Colombia (either alone or in alliance with other revolutionary groups). However, the magnitude of the U.S. government's support for the Colombian government and military, known officially as "Plan Colombia" and embracing an expensive low intensity and very dirty and ugly war against the guerillas, tells us that the FARC is a genuine threat to capitalism in an important country in South America. If the FARC were just a front for the production and distribution of drugs, the U.S. response would not be of the same magnitude. The war against drugs in Colombia is really just a cover for something far more significant. Latin America is in turmoil and anti-capitalist sentiments are rapidly gaining adherents—in Venezuela, Ecuador, Argentina, Brazil, and most other nations. A victory for revolutionary forces is Colombia is viewed as a disaster for corporate capitalism. Such a victory might well occur if the FARC were facing only the Colombian government. But the involvement of the world's hegemonic power makes this less likely or at least very much more difficult.

The situation in Nepal is quite different from that in Colombia. While Nepal became a sovereign nation in 1816, it was dependent for well over a century on Great Britain and, since Indian independence, on its large bordering neighbor. In 1846, the Kot massacre, in which many feudal nobles were murdered, established a single family, the Ranas, as the nation's de facto rulers. The official head of state was the king. Because the British were unable to subdue the Nepalese militarily, they settled for behind the scenes influence through the Ranas. The Ranas supplied the British with its famous Gurkha fighters, and the British allowed the country to exist in relative isolation from big power politics. After the Indians won independence, the Nepalese king reasserted royal authority. The Nepalese kings were then able to maintain the nation's independence by playing China and India off against one another. India, however, has never been satisfied with this independence and has used its greater wealth and military power to continuously exert influence in Nepal. India's aim is to annex Nepal as it did Sikkim, or at least make it accept Indian troops as is the case in neighboring Bhutan.

Nepal is one of the world's poorest nations, with massive poverty (about half the population living in poverty), low GDP per capita (a little over $1,000), very low life expectancy (58 years of age), extensive illiteracy (overall literacy is 58 percent, while that for women is 14 percent), widespread underemployment, and an extremely unequal distribution of wealth and income. People live mainly in isolated rural areas; more than 80 percent of the population works in agriculture and only 3 percent in industry. There are few good roads, and the vast majority of the people are without modern amenities, including televisions, radios, and telephones. The physical terrain itself is daunting and includes the majestic Himalayan mountains. The relations of production in the countryside can best be described as feudal, with little wage labor, direct appropriation of the surplus produced by the workers, long-term debt peonage, and child labor. On top of extreme economic exploitation, there is also the caste oppression inherent in the state religion of Hinduism, oppression of ethnic minorities, and maltreatment of women. Industry is controlled by the local elites and foreigners, mainly Indians.

Given the right catalysts, objective conditions such as exist in Nepal can lead to political turmoil and even revolution. When so many people live without hope, events that make them understand that their circumstances are not inevitable and can be changed through their own actions can create revolutionary conditions. The winds of change began to blow after the Second World War. Radical movements arose in India after independence and, more importantly, the peasant masses of China, under the leadership of the Chinese Communist Party, overthrew the feudal lords and capitalist business leaders, both domestic and foreign, and established an egalitarian socialist society. The Chinese revolution had a profound effect on radical intellectuals in Nepal, and in the same year as the Chinese revolution (1949) the Nepalese Communist Party was formed.

Radical forces in Nepal, especially among the young, were also deeply influenced by China's Cultural Revolution. Communist influence gradually began to permeate rural areas, and the Communists increased their agitation for fundamental social reforms. In 1990 the Communists allied themselves with anti-monarchy forces among reformers in a popular uprising, the result of which was an end to the monarch's absolute rule and the establishment of the semblance of a representative government. The king, however, still retained control over the royal army.

The government soon fell into the hands of pro-Indian property owners, who were the strongest opponents of the king and in league with Indian capital and supported by Indian secret police. This led the Communists to give some support to the king, who responded by keeping the army neutral when a faction of the Communist Party, reorganized as Nepal Communist Party (Maoist), declared an armed revolt in 1996.

The Nepal Communist Party (Maoist) had made a detailed analysis of Nepalese society and had concluded that a peasant-based armed struggle, patterned after that led by Mao Tse-tung in China, could succeed in defeating the forces of Nepalese feudalism and their foreign allies and liberate the country and its poor peasant majority. The often rugged and remote landscape would be a great advantage, providing cover for the radical army and making government counterattacks difficult.

Remarkably, the careful planning and organizing of the Maoists has paid off. The revolt has taken hold and captured the imagination of the rural masses. Within a relatively short period of time, large swaths of the countryside came under revolutionary control. Arms were captured from fleeing police and soldiers, and these were used to widen the war. Today, even the cities have proved vulnerable to attacks by the revolutionary army, which is now capable of liberating political prisoners in towns and cities and destroying urban infrastructure. In areas that the rebels have been unable to completely capture, they have been able to take stored grain from large landowners and distribute it to the poor who actually produced it.

In areas under revolutionary control, life has changed radically. Peasants have obtained true possession of their plots of land and no longer owe obligations to landlords. They have been encouraged to engage in various forms of collective farming on lands expropriated from large land holders and on lands formerly owned by the state itself. Local people's justice has replaced the justice of police and feudal nobility. Peasants have been afforded the opportunity to go to school, and have also built new schools and houses. Women have been encouraged to take on new roles and men to respect these new roles. Many new revolutionaries, including soldiers, are women. Health education, including birth control education, has begun. Caste and ethnic oppression are no longer tolerated.

Needless to say, the Maoists have faced growing animosity and organization from their class enemies. Royal neutrality was ended in June 2001 when pro-Indian members of the royal family assassinated the king and his entire immediate family. The king's younger brother took power and appointed a new successor to the throne, his much-reviled son, and a new prime minister. After a brief period in which the new government made peace overtures to the Maoists and promised to implement land and other reforms, these overtures were accepted by the Maoists who put forward a plan for the creation of a Nepalese republic. Unfortunately, events have shown that the government was insincere, and the Maoists reinstituted their liberation war in late November 2001. However, as has happened in Colombia, the government is now more openly supported by greater powers: India, as has been historically the case, and now by the United States as well. Even China, which has moved decisively back toward capitalism and does not want to antagonize the United States, has openly condemned the Maoists. As with the FARC in Colombia, the revolutionary war has entered a new and dangerous phase, with possible successes likely to be violently contested by the United States.

A NEW SOCIETY

Critics of capitalism are always asked what is their alternative to capitalism. In one sense this is an unfair question, because it implies that if critics do not have a full-blown alternative system of production and distribution ready at hand then their criticisms of capitalism are somehow not justified. Of course, this is ridiculous. Lung cancer is still bad even if we cannot cure it.

Furthermore, the notion that people will only struggle to make fundamental change if they have in mind a clear plan for a new society flies in the face of historical experience. As eminent radical scholar Harry Magdoff puts it, "If and where socialism next comes, it will be the outcome of a struggle by workers and their allies. Their defeats and victories, the experience gained in the struggles are bound to influence the nature of the Socialism that will evolve. Democratic socialism will, and should, be designed and adapted in response the aims of the people and their available resources, not by designs created by intellectuals for all times and for all peoples."

There are any number of blueprints for an alternative system of production and distribution. All of them are interesting and provide food for thought.[43] But they cannot serve as substitutes for the long-term struggles that will ultimately bring forth a new society. What is more, these blueprints are usually based upon their authors' experience in the rich countries. Magdoff goes on to say, "I haven't read all the publications in this vein. In those I have read, however, there is a common thread. Explicitly or implicitly, the authors' field of vision is the 'good life' of the middle or upper working class. Homage may be paid to the billions of wretched of the earth, including bones thrown to them, but the focus of their models are the countries they live in. And those are countries of the West. Generally overlooked is that post-revolutionary societies will have to overcome the baggage of the old, including the transformation of human consciousness from a competitive to a collective way of life. Is it reasonable to assume that this complex history can be foretold and a social transformation designed by the wisest of women and men? Does one design a new society the way engineers draw plans for a bridge?"[44]

There are many examples of production and distribution already occurring in a noncapitalist manner. We have the tens of thousands of years of experience of indigenous peoples, some of whom are still practicing a relatively egalitarian and collective economics. We can and should learn as much as we can from these peoples. In addition, there are many examples of noncapitalist production taking place within capitalist societies, from the worker cooperatives in the Basque region of Spain to the remarkable cooperative community of Gaviotas in war-ravaged Colombia.[45] All of these production and distribution systems are worthy of close study. It is doubtful, given the hegemonic power of capitalism, that these enterprises will undermine capitalism from within, but they do give evidence of what is possible.

If it is not appropriate to lay out a blueprint for a new society, we can at least delineate some important principles that should guide us in our struggle for an alternative to capitalism. Various authors have put forward principles that, in the words of Leo Panitch and Sam Gindin, will provide a "motivating vision."[46] As we struggle, we should push our movements toward an embrace of equality, democracy, the reintegration of work, and ecological balance.

It should be clear from this book that most of the world's people will have little or no chance to develop their full human capacities as long as there exists such significant wealth and income inequalities. A market system simply reinforces the inequalities that already exist, and the neoliberalism of the past thirty years has made inequality much worse. Therefore, if we want to build a society in which people are free and able to develop their capacities, we must unashamedly and forthrightly insist on equality. There is no convincing reason why each of us should not receive an aliquot part of the world's resources. Of course, there may be reasons why a particular person might deserve a bit more at a particular point in time (a sick person requires more health care than a healthy one), but in general, equality should be our goal.

Once we make equality a primary goal, many things become clear. First, there can be no justification for all of the many kinds of not directly economic inequality that exist. Equality means that women must be the equals of men, ethnic and racial minorities the equals of majorities, gays the equals of straights, and so forth. We do not mean that a new society cannot tolerate differences; indeed, differences ought to be celebrated. But inequality is not the same as difference; the former is pernicious, the latter is not.

Second, equality implies that many people in the rich countries will no longer be able to pursue unbridled consumption. Individual consumption in the rich countries and among the elites in the poor countries will have to be reduced. Neoclassical economists like Brad DeLong of the University of California at Berkeley have suggested that the world is already "slouching toward utopia."47 He argues that nearly a billion people in the world are approaching the standard of living of the U.S. middle class, and by implication, slowly but surely, over the fabled "long run," the rest of the world will get to this standard of living as well.

Such a view is untenable. It misses three key points. First, the well-being of a minority of persons (even a billion people is well under 20 percent of the world's population) is fundamentally dependent on the lack of well-being of everyone else. That is, I enjoy a decent standard of living because at the base of the world's economies are large layers of terribly poor and exploited workers. This is simply the way capitalism works. Second, the world could not stand the resource and environmental strain of a U.S. middle class lifestyle. For example, there are way too many cars in the rich countries. Can we imagine what the environmental cost would be if every Chinese and Indian household had as many cars as the average U.S. household? Third, DeLong suggests that it is technological change that accounts for the rise of a large worldwide middle class. However, there is little direct

---

A PARTICULARLY PERNICIOUS ARGUMENT

Neoclassical economists like Brad DeLong and Paul Krugman never tire of singing the praises of capitalism. According to them, at some point in the future we will all be middle class. And to take some of the wind from the sails of those of us who point out that gross wealth and income inequality show no sign of disappearing, they state that the circumstances of the poor, at least in the rich countries (and, according to Krugman and DeLong,, the same is true for "lower middle-class households in relatively poor countries") is not so bad after all.48 Most poor people today in a country such as the United States have access to consumer goods that even well-off persons could only have dreamt of one hundred years ago.

I doubt that Krugman and DeLong know much about the lives of poor people even in rich countries. If they did, they would know that the television set owned by the poor family from Pittsburgh referred to in Chapter Two does not make them better off than an upper middle-class family in late nineteenth century England, a family which did not have a television or many other modern conveniences but did have house servants to do the most onerous work. And Krugman gives the game away when he says, "On sheer material grounds one would almost surely prefer to be poor today than upper middle class a century ago [a contention for which he provides no evidence, surely because there is none]. Social status is another matter—but let's

correlation between the advance of technology and living standards. What is necessary for people's living standards to improve is that they organize collectively to appropriate part of the growing surplus technological change makes possible to themselves. Surely the plight of working people around the world today, who often labor in relatively high-tech workplaces but remain destitute, puts the lie to DeLong's arguments.

A third consequence of the demand for equality is that a lot of consumption will have to be satisfied collectively. Transportation, child care, housing, and much more will have to be collectively provided, so that all can have equal amounts of it or whatever special amounts they need in excess of the average. An egalitarian world will not be able to tolerate a proliferation of so many privately owned goods and services.

The third point implies that we will not be able to rely on markets and competitive behavior if we want to create a just and equitable society. Markets and acquisitive behavior simply re-create what we already have. And when they are applied to what is a relatively egalitarian society, as is the >

---

reserve that topic for another day."[49] Yes, indeed, it is another matter, but neither Krugman nor DeLong will ever talk about it. What is more, how can it plausibly be argued that the upper middle classes of rich countries did not confer benefits upon their children that made these children and their children the main beneficiaries of modern technological change? Today's poor are not going to be able to do this.

A much better question to ask is whether or not the poor, especially the billions in today's poor countries, were better off a hundred years ago, before capitalism invaded their lives. Here the answer is unequivocally "no." Centuries of capitalist conquest and imperialism rendered most of the world's people incapable even of feeding themselves, something they could do in, say, 1491, the year before Columbus' infamous voyage. Given what we now know about the technological achievements of so-called primitive peoples, it is clear that had the Europeans not come along, most of the world's people might very probably have experienced steadily rising standards of living.[50] So, in effect, what the DeLong/Krugman argument really amounts to is this: first, capitalism brings economic and social ruin and death to hundreds of millions of persons; then after a long downward spiral, struggle among some of capitalism's victims brings a modicum of material comfort to a minority of the world's people; and this proves that we are awash in progress in this best of all possible worlds.

case today in China, what we see is the return of capitalism and its attendant inequality and unfairness.

In our struggles, we must strive for maximum democracy. Of course, we will need to debate what democracy means, but the top-down revolutionary parties of the past provide no blueprint for the future. As Panitch and Gindin put it, "The whole point of a socialist project conceived in terms of developing individual and collective capacities is to make the deepening and extension of democracy viable. This entails the most serious commitment to conceiving and trying to establish the types of representation and administration that contribute to breaking down the organizationally reinforced distinctions between managers and workers, politicians and citizens, leaders and led, and to overcoming the barriers that separate what we are from what we might become."[51]

An important principle that should underlie any revolutionary movement is the reintegration of human labor. As long as most people perform work unworthy of what human beings can do, it is foolish to talk about human liberation. It must be recognized that the detailed division of labor is not a technological necessity and must be eliminated as rapidly as humanly possible. This means that burdensome work will have to be mechanized, or if that isn't possible, shared out on an equitable basis. This will not be easy for many people to accept, including leftist intellectuals, but it must be done.

Last but hardly least, we must dedicate ourselves to reintegrating ourselves with our natural environment. The evidence grows more glaring every day that capitalism is condemning us to an unsustainable natural world. If we condemn capitalism for nothing else, we can damn it for its creation of hundreds of ghastly and polluted megalopolises, for its defilement of our rivers, seas, and forests, for the rampant destruction of species, and for its corruption of our food supply.

Capitalism is probably the most resilient and hegemonic system of production and distribution ever devised, and its supersession by an egalitarian mode of production is going to take a long time and will involve a variety or tactics. We have to be willing to organize patiently, educate patiently, suffer setbacks patiently, and accept that we may be long dead before capitalism is transcended. Our example here will show future generations that we practiced the selflessness that will be the foundation of the new society.

Suggested Further Reading & Notes

CHAPTER ONE

A good place to get an understanding of the mainstream economists' methods and to learn a great deal about capitalism, is Paul Sweezy's *The Theory of Capitalist Development* (New York: Monthly Review Press, 1970). On the "new" economy, see the April 2001 issue of *Monthly Review* magazine. For good material on the pretensions and weaknesses of mainstream economics, see the regular articles of Edward S. Herman in *Z Magazine.*

1 A World Wide Web search (using the "Google" search engine) for "China's economic miracle" yielded 9,640 references.
2 Keith Hammond, "The Optimists Had It Right," Business Week (August 31, 1998): 146.
3 John K. Glassman and Kevin A. Hassett, Dow 36,000: The New Strategy for Profiting from the Coming Rise in Stock Prices (New York: Three Rivers Press, 2000). For a good antidote to this book and others like it, see Robert J. Shiller, Irrational Exuberance (Princeton, NJ: Princeton University Press, 2000).
4 The next five paragraphs draw heavily on Michael D. Yates, "The 'New' Economy and the Labor Movement," Monthly Review 52 (April 2001): 28–42. See also Jeff Madrick, "Is the New Economy New?," WorkingUSA (Nov.-Dec. 1999): 43–44.
5 Robert Reich, The Work of Nations: Preparing Ourselves for 21st Century Capitalism (New York: A. A. Knopf, 1991).
6 Jeff Madrick, "Is the New Economy New?," WorkingUSA 5 (Nov.-Dec. 1999): 43–44.
7 See Business Week Online at http://www.businessweek.com/ for April 9, 2001.
8 See The Editors, "The New Face of Capitalism:

Slow Growth, Excess Capacity, and a Mountain of Debt," Monthly Review 53 (April 2002): 1–14.
9 Ibid.: 11–2.
10 John Maynard Keynes, The General Theory of Employment, Interest and Money (Amherst, NY: Prometheus Books, 1997), originally published in 1936. The quote is from Keynes' A Tract on Monetary Reform (London: Macmillan, 1924).
11 Paul Burkett and Martin Hart-Landsberg, "The Use and Abuse of Japan as a Progressive Model," in Leo Panitch (Ed.), Socialist Register 1996 (London: Merlin Press, 1996).
12 David Card and Alan Krueger, Myth and Measurement: The New Economics of the Minimum Wage (Princeton, NJ: Princeton University Press, 1995).
13 See John Schmitt, "Cooked to Order," The American Prospect 7 (May-June 1996), available at http://www.prospect.org/print/V7/26/schmitt-j.html.
14 See " 'Superstar' Feldstein and His Little Mistake," Dollars & Sense (Dec. 1980): 1–2. A "Google" web search on "Feldstein and Social Security" will yield many hundreds of hits.
15 Francis Fukuyama, The End of History and the Last Man (New York: Free Press, 1992).

CHAPTER TWO

On the origins of capitalism, see Ellen Meiksins Wood, *The Origin of Capitalism* (New York: Monthly Review Press, 1999). A contrary view is Andre Gunder Frank, *Reorient: Global Economy in the Asian Age* (Berkeley, CA: University of California Press, 1998). For a good discussion and plenty of data on inequality and poverty in the United States, see the excellent book by Lawrence Mishel, Jared Bernstein, and John Schmitt, *The State of Working America, 2000–2001* (Ithaca, NY: Cornell University Press, 2001). Another good book is James Galbraith and Maureen Berner (Eds.), *Inequality and Industrial Change: A Global View* (Cambridge: Cambridge University Press, 2001). Also, Frank Ackerman et al. (Eds.), *The Political Economy of Inequality* (Washington, DC: Island Press, 2000). There are plenty of good websites for tracking down data. Try www.inequality.org; www.census.gov (for the United States); and www.worldbank.org. Both *Z Magazine* and *Dollars & Sense* frequently have good articles on the issues discussed in this chapter. An interesting web article on the impact of inequality on the spread of infectious diseases is Paul Farmer, "Social Inequalities and Emerging Infectious Diseases," at http://www.cdc.gov/ncidod/EID/vol2no4/farmer.htm.

1   See E. K. Hunt and Howard J. Sherman, *Economics: An Introduction to Traditional and Radical Views* (New York: Harper & Row, 1972); Marc Bloch, *Feudal Society: Social Classes and Political Organization* (Chicago: University of Chicago Press, 1982).

2   On the origins of capitalism, see Ellen Meiksins Wood, *The Origin of Capitalism* (New York: Monthly Review Press, 1999); Maurice Dobb, *Transition from Feudalism to Capitalism* (London: Verso, 1978); and Michel Beaud, *A History of Capitalism* (New York: Monthly Review Press, 2001).

3   See Harry Magdoff, *The Age of Imperialism: The Economics of U.S. Foreign Policy* (New York: Monthly Review Press, 1969); Eduardo Galeano, *Open Veins of Latin America: Five Centuries of the Pillage of a Continent* (New York: Monthly Review Press, 1973); Beaud, *A History of Capitalism.*

4   See the relevant chapters in Howard Sherman and Andrew Zimbalist, *Comparing Economic Systems: A Political-Economic Approach*

(San Diego, CA: Academic Press, 1984). Also, John G. Gurley, *China's Economy and the Maoist Strategy* (New York: Monthly Review Press, 1976) and Karen Wald, *Children of Che: Childcare and Education in Cuba* (Palo Alto, CA: Ramparts Press, 1978).

5   See the chart at http://www.cnn.com/WORLD/global.rankings/

6   For a good introduction to the economic history of Latin America, see Celso Furtado, *Economic Development of Latin America* (Cambridge: Cambridge University Press, 1977).

7   On Mexico, see James D. Cockcroft, *Mexico: Class Formation, Capital Accumulation, and the State* (New York: Monthly Review Press, 1983) and Donald Clark Hodges and Daniel Ross Gandy, *Mexico: The End of the Revolution* (New York: Praeger, 2001).

8   For a good introduction to these institutions, written for the general reader, see Sarah Anderson et al., *Field Guide to the Global Economy* (New York: The New Press, 2000). Also, see Robin Hahnel, *Panic Rules!: Everything*

You Need to Know about the Global Economy (Cambridge, MA: South End Press, 1999).

9   United Nations Department of Economic and Social Affairs, World Statistics Yearbook (New York: United Nations, 2001), 125.

10 See Jerry W. Sanders, "Two Mexicos and Fox's Quandary," The Nation, 272 (Feb. 26, 2001): 18.

11 Pritchett's article, "Forget Convergence: Divergence Past, Present, and Future," is on the World Bank's website at http://www.worldbank.org/fandd/englidh/0696/articles/090696.htm

12 Ibid.: 4.

13 Mark Weisbrot, Dean Baker, Egor Kraev, and Judy Chen, "The Scorecard on Globalization 1980–2000: Twenty Years of Diminished Progress," at http://cepr.net/globalization/scorecard_on_globalization.htm.

14 See Leo Huberman and Paul M. Sweezy, Cuba: Anatomy of a Revolution (New York: Monthly Review Press, 1961) for this background history.

15 United Nations Department of Economic and Social Affairs, World Statistics Yearbook, op. cit., 51, 36, 200.

16 See Joy Gordon, "Cuba's Entrepreneurial Socialism," The Atlantic Monthly 279 (January 1997): 18–30.

17 Most of the data on inequality in the United States is taken from Lawrence Mishel, Jared Bernstein, and John Schmitt, The State of Working America 2000/2001 (Ithaca, NY: Cornell University Press, 2001). The upper limit for the fourth quintile for 2000 can be found in the appropriate table (Table A-2) at the United States Census Bureau website, which is http://www.census.gov.

18 Paul Krugman, "The Rich, the Right, and the Facts," The American Prospect 11 (Fall 1992): 19–31.

19 For detailed explanations of Gini coefficients, see Howard Wachtel, Labor and the Economy (San Diego, CA: Harcourt Brace Jovanovich, 1988) and Ronald G. Ehrenberg and Robert S. Smith, Modern Labor Economics (Reading, MA: Addison-Wesley, 1997).

20 Ibid.

21 For all the U.S. data on poverty you will ever need, including the poverty level of income, see http://www.census.gov and click on "poverty."

22 See Doug Henwood, "Distributing the Booty," at http://www.panix.com/~dhenwood/Wealth_distrib.html.

23 These astonishing facts can be found in an article by Barbara Crossette in the New York Times Online for September 28, 1998 at http://www.nytimes.com/learning/teachers/featured_articles/19980928monday.html.

24 Branko Milanovic, "True World Income Distribution, 1988 and 1993: First Calculations Based on Household Surveys Alone," The Economic Journal 112 (January 2002): 51–92.

25 Peter Montague, "Economic Inequality and Health," at http://www.korpios.org/resurgent/Inequality&Health.htm.

26 See the source listed in note 19 above.

CHAPTER THREE

Much useful data on unemployment and underemployment in the United States (as well as lots of data on employment), and to a lesser extent in the other rich capitalist countries can be found in the Mishel, Bernstein, and Schmitt book, *The State of Working America, 2000–2001* suggested above. An introductory summary can be found in my *Longer Hours, Fewer Jobs: Employment and Unemployment in the United States* (Monthly Review Press, 1994). Philip Harvey's fine book, *Securing the Right to Employment* (Princeton, N.J.: Princeton University Press, 1989), is a neglected classic that shows that full employment is very feasible. The International Labor Organization publishes many studies of both unemployment and employment. See its website at http://www.ilo.org. The U.S. Bureau of Labor Statistics also contains lots of good data as well as links to foreign labor statistics and articles from its publication, *The Monthly Labor Review*. The BLS website is http://www.bls.gov.

1   Jonathan Silvers, "Child Labor in Pakistan," The Atlantic Monthly 277 (February 1996): 79– 92.

2   Ibid.: 7. The page number here is from the online edition of The Atlantic Monthly, found at http://www.theatlanti...issues/96feb/pakistan/pakistan.htm

3   I use an example like this in my book, Longer Hours, Fewer Jobs (New York: Monthly Review Press, 1994), 65.

4   Philip Harvey, Securing the Right to Employment (Princeton, NJ: Princeton University Press, 1989). I summarize Harvey's results in Chapter Four of Longer Hours, Fewer Jobs.

5   Some of Brenner's research is reviewed in Chapter Four of Longer Hours, Fewer Jobs. See especially the table on page 67.

6   Reported in Marcel Bédard, "The Economic and Social Costs of Unemployment" (Quebec: Applied Research Branch, Strategic Policy, Human Resource Development, 1996): 14.

7   Ibid.: 20.

8   See Chapter Four of Longer Hours, Fewer Jobs, op. cit. Also, see the Bureau of Labor Statistics website at http://www.bls.gov.

9   Unemployment rates for any recent month or year can be found at the BLS website cited in note 8 above. They can also be found in the BLS's publication, Monthly Labor Review.

10 Ibid.

11 Tim Weiner, "In Corn's Cradle, U.S. Imports Bury Family Farms," New York Times, Feb. 26, 2002.

12 New York Times, March 3, 2002.

13 Harry Brill, "The Bureau of Labor Statistics (BLS) and the Census Bureau: Partners in Deceit," Z Magazine 12 (September 1999): 39–44.

14 Doug Henwood, editor of the Left Business Observer, calculates that if all of the black men in prison were added to the black labor force and counted as unemployed, the black male unemployment would rise to over 20 percent. See his note on "unemployment" at http://www.leftbusinessobserver.com/Stats_unempl.html.

15 See Chapter Four in Longer Hours, Fewer Jobs, as well as the BLS website at http://www.bls.gov.

16 Dominique Vidal, "Miracle or Mirage in the Netherlands?," Le Monde Diplomatique, July 1997, online at http://www.en.monde-diplomatique.fr/1997/07/netherlan.

17 See Steven Erlanger, "German Unemployment Is Growing Problem for Schröder," New York Times, February 7, 2002, and "Japan's Jobless Highest Ever," at wysiwyg://69/http://www.guardian.c...ession/story/0,7369,609854,00.html

18 See International Labor Organization, Key Indicators of the Labour Market 2001-2002 (Geneva, Switzerland: International Labour Organization, 2002), 262–267. This is a monumental statistical source, with data on numerous labor market variables for nearly every country in the world.

19 See the Indigenous Law Resources at http://www.austlii.edu.au/au/other/IndigLRes/1991/6/6.htmlww.austlii.edu.au/au/other/IndigLRe s/1991/6/6.html14.

20 See "Immigrant and Ethnic Minority Communities in the UK," at http://www.socstats.soton.ac.uk/courses/st218318/11_Ethnic_minorities_UK_handout.PDF.

21 This appeared originally in Kenning, Winter 2000. It can be found online at http://www.durationpress.com/kenning/list.html. For background on the U.S. prison system, see the Summer 2000 issue (July/August) of Monthly Review magazine.

22. Gary Martin, "Employment and Unemployment in Mexico in the 1990s," Monthly Labor Review 123 (November 2000): 3–18.

22 Ibid.: 7.

23 Ibid.: 9.

24 Ibid.: 9.

25 See Sophie Beach, "China's Unseen Unemployed," The Nation 268 (February 15, 1999): 20.

26 International Labour Organization, Report on Worldwide Employment 2001 (Geneva, Switzerland, 2001).

CHAPTER FOUR

Once again, I strongly recommend *The State of Working America*. The ILO, BLS, and World Bank websites already cited are also useful resources for employment statistics. Karl Marx's *Capital*, Vol. I, is as relevant today in its discussion of work as it was when published in 1867. There are many websites available for gathering information about informal and sweatshop employment. Two useful ones are http://www.sweatshopwatch.org and http://www.wiego.org. The best book ever written on the implications of capitalism for the nature of work is Harry Braverman, *Labor and Monopoly Capital: The Degradation of Work in the Twentieth Century* (New York: Monthly Review Press, 1974). A good analysis of the most modern managerial techniques aimed at controlling workers is Mike Parker and Jane Slaughter, *Working Smart: A Union Guide to Participation Programs and Reengineering* (Detroit: Labor Notes, 1995). An excellent article on child labor is Jonathan Silvers, "Child Labor in Pakistan," *The Atlantic Monthly* 277 (February 1996), 79–92. For a fine book on work in advanced capitalism, see Studs Terkel, *Working* (New York: Avon, 1974). To find out about Bolivian tin miners and their wives and widows (and by extension millions of workers in the third world), see Domitila Barrios de Chungara, *Let Me Speak* (New York: Monthly Review Press, 1978). On the condition of overwork in the rich nations, see Juliet Schor, *The Overworked American* (New York: Basic Books, 1991).

1 This and the next four paragraphs rely on Harry Braverman, *Labor and Monopoly Capital: The Degradation of Work in the Twentieth Century* (New York: Monthly Review Press, 1974). See also Mike Parker and Jane Slaughter, *Working Smart: A Union Guide to Participation Programs and Reengineering* (Detroit: Labor Notes, 1995).

2 See the International Labour Organization (ILO) report "Agriculture; Plantations; other Rural Sectors," available at http://www.ilo.org/public/english/dialogue/sector/sectors/agri.htm

3 Ibid., 6 (in the web article cited in note 2).

4 See the remarkable article by Jeremy Seabrook, "The Soul of Man under Globalism," *Race & Class* 43 (April-June 2002): 1–25. This article is must reading for anyone who still believes that there is anything progressive about peasants being forced into the market economy.

5 Taken from David Gonzalez, "Central America's Cities Grow Bigger and Poorer," *The New York Times*, March 17, 2002.

6 These numbers were culled from United Nations Department of Economic and Social Affairs, *World Statistics Pocketbook* (New York: United Nations, 2001).

7 International Labour Organization, *Key Indicators of the Labour Market 2001-2002* (Geneva, Switzerland, 2002), 23–25.

8 Seabrook, "The Soul of Man under Globalism," op. cit.

9 "Women Workers in Indonesia," available at http://www.marxist.com/women/indonesian_wom_workers301.html.

10 See Pedro Conceição, Pedro Ferreira, and James K. Galbraith, "Inequality and Unemployment in Europe: The American Cure," in James K. Galbraith and Maureen Berner (Eds.), *Inequality and Industrial Change* (New York: Cambridge University Press, 2001), 124.

11 The ten jobs with the largest projected growth

between 2000 and 2010 can be found at http://stats.bls.gov/news.release/ecopro.to7.htm

12 Tony Horwitz, "9 to Nowhere: The Grim Side of 90s Growth Jobs," The Wall Street Journal, December 1, 1994.

13 Ben Hamper, Rivethead: Tales from the Assembly Line (New York: Warner Books, 1994).

14 Horwitz, "9 to Nowhere," op. cit.

15 See the BLS website at http://www.bls.gov/ news.release/ocwage.nro.htm.

16 Karl Marx, Capital, vol. 1 (London: Penguin Books, 1976, originally published in 1867), 364–365.

17 See Kebebew Ashagrie, "Statistics on Working Children and Hazardous Child Labour in Brief," at http://www.ilo.org/public/english/ comp/child/stats.htm.

18 See http://www.antislavery.org/homepage/ news/cameljocks300102.htm

19 See http://www.catwinternational.org/fb/india. html This case is also reported in Robert I.. Friedman, "India's Shame: Sexual Slavery and Political Corruption Are Leading to An AIDS Catastrophe," The Nation 268 (April 8, 1996).

20 See Jonathan Silvers, "Child Labor in Pak- istan," The Atlantic Monthly 277 (February 1996). The quote is on page 5 of the online version at http://wysiwyg://38/http://www.theatlanti... issues/96feb/pakistan/pakistan.htm.

21 See http://www.wiego.org/main/fact1.html.

22 See wysiwyg://76http://www.onevillage.co.uk/ unemployment.htm.

23 Jacques Charmes, "Informal Sector, Poverty and Gender: A Review of Empirical Evidence," available at http://www.wiego.org/textonly/ publi1.shtml.

24 Information on India is taken from Barbara Harriss-White and Nandini Gooptu, "Mapping India's World of Unorganized Labour," in Leo Panitch and Colin Leys (Eds.), Socialist Register 2001 (New York: Monthly Review Press, 2000), 89–118.

25 Robert Weil, "The Chinese Revolution at Fifty," unpublished manuscript, 2001. Also see Sophie Beach, "China's Unseen Unemployed," The Nation 268 (February 15, 1999): 20, and Jiang Xueqin, "Letter from China," The Nation 271 (March 4, 2002): 23–25.

26 See http://www.sweatshopwatch.org/swatch/ industry/ This is an excellent website for information on sweatshops.

27 Lawrence Mishel, Jared Bernstein, and John Schmitt, The State of Working America 2000/2001 (Ithaca, NY: Cornell University Press, 2001), 120, 119.

28 Ibid., 399.

29 Ibid., 128.

30 Harriss-White and Gooptu, "Mapping India's World of Unorganized Labour," 91.

31 David Gonzalez, "Central America's Cities Grow Bigger and Poorer," op. cit.

32 See Domitila Barrios de Chungara, Let Me Speak (New York: Monthly Review Press, 1978).

33 Tamaki Kazunari, "Karoshi—Recently Certified Suicides from Overwork," at http://www.jca. apc.org/joshrc/english/15-1.html.

34 Juliet Schor, The Overworked American (New York: Basic Books, 1991).

35 A good website for exploring the issue of overtime and unemployment is www.vcn.bc.ca/timework/worksite.htm.

CHAPTER FIVE

A good overview of the history of economic thinking is still Robert Heil-broner's The Worldly Philosophers, 7th revised edition (New York: Touchstone Books, 1999). The basic neoclassical model of labor markets is presented, along with summaries of empirical research, in Ronald Ehrenberg and Robert Smith, Modern Labor Economics: Theory and Public Policy, 7th edition (New York: Addison-Wesley Publishing, 2000). A classic popularly written defense of libertarian neoclassical economics is Milton and Rose Friedman, Free to Choose: A Personal Statement (New York: Harcourt Brace

Jovanovich, 1980). A positive account of neoliberalism is Thomas Friedman, *The Lexus and the Olive Tree* (New York: Farrar, Straus & Giroux, 1999). A good rejoinder is Noam Chomsky, *Profit Over People: Neoliberalism and Global Order* (New York: Seven Stories Press, 1999).

1   A best-selling textbook today, for which the author was paid the largest advance ever paid for a textbook, is N. Gregory Mankiw's Principles of Economics (Fort Worth, TX: South-Western College Publishing, 1998).

2   For a good introduction to the history of economic theory, see Mark Blaug, Economic Theory in Retrospect (Homewood, IL: Richard D. Irwin, 1968).

3   Adam Smith, An Inquiry into the Nature and Causes of the Wealth of Nations (New York: Modern Library, 1937), 14. One of the most important advocates of Smith's view and a relentless critic of Keynes and of socialism is Friedrich Hayek. See his Individualism and Economic Order (Chicago: University of Chicago Press, 1948) and The Road to Serfdom (London: Routledge and Kegan Paul, 1962).

4   For a good introduction to living wage politics and economics, see Robert Pollin and Stephanie Luce, The Living Wage: Building a Fair Economy (New York: New Press, 1998).

5   On this, see any mainstream labor economics textbook. A standard text is Ronald G. Ehrenberg and Robert S. Smith, Modern Labor Economics: Theory and Public Policy (Reading, MA: Addison-Wesley, 1997).

6   Ibid. A good neoclassical book on the economics of unions is Albert Rees, The Economics of Trade Unions (Chicago: University of Chicago Press, 1989).

7   The standard neoclassical arguments for privatization of public services, as well as powerful criticisms of them, can be found in Elliot D. Sclar, You Don't Always Get What You Pay For: The Economics of Privatization (Ithaca, NY: Cornell University Press, 2000).

8   See Peter Temin, Did Monetary Forces Cause the Great Depression? (New York: Norton, 1976).

9   One of the better contemporary liberal neoclassical economists is Paul Krugman, who writes a regular syndicated newspaper column. See his book The Return of Depression

Economics (New York: W.W. Norton, 1999).

10 See John K. Galbraith, American Capitalism: The Concept of Countervailing Power (Boston: Houghton Mifflin, 1956).

11 John Maynard Keynes, The General Theory of Employment, Interest and Money (New York: Harcourt, Brace, 1936). Also see D. E. Moggridge, Keynes (Toronto: University of Toronto Press, 1993).

12 Keynes, The General Theory of Employment, Interest and Money, op. cit.

13 See Paul Baran and Paul M. Sweezy, Monopoly Capital: An Essay on the American Economic and Social Order (New York: Monthly Review Press, 1966).

14 For details, see Lynn Turgeon, Bastard Keynesianism (Westport, CT: Greenwood Publishing Group, 1996).

15 On these policies, see any standard economics textbook, such as Mankiw, Principles of Economics, op. cit.

16 For a discussion of the basic neoclassical arguments and a strong counter argument, see Jim Crotty and Gerald Epstein, "In Defense of Capital Controls," in Leo Panitch (Ed.), Socialist Register 1996 (New York: Monthly Review Press, 1996), 118–149.

17 Thomas L. Friedman, The Lexus and the Olive Tree (New York: Farrar, Straus & Giroux, 1999), 86–87.

18 See Barbara Ward, The Rich Nations and the Poor Nations (New York: Norton, 1962); W.W. Rostow, The Stages of Economic Growth: A non-Communist Manifesto (Cambridge: Cambridge University Press, 1964).

19 See Gary Becker, Human Capital: A Theoretical and Empirical Analysis with Special Reference to Education (Chicago: University of Chicago Press, 1975). Becker, a winner of the Nobel Prize in Economics (which, unlike the other prizes, is not paid out of Alfred Nobel's legacy but by the Swedish Central Bank), is a very important neoclassical economist because

he has argued that the assumption of economic self-interest can be used to examine all sorts of human activities, such as marriage, divorce, and criminal behavior.

20 The World Bank website contains a great number of reports espousing this sort of thinking. Go to http://www.worldbank.org.

21 See Lance Pritchett's article, "Forget Convergence: Divergence Past, Present, and Future," which can be found on the World Bank's website at http://www.worldbank.org/fandd/englidh/0696/articles/090696.htm. See also Robert Barro and Xavier Sala-i-Martin, Economic Growth (New York: McGraw-Hill, 1995).

22 See David M. Gordon, Theories of Poverty and Underemployment: Orthodox, Radical, and Dual Labor Market Views (Lexington, MA: Lexington Books, 1972).

23 Pritchett, "Forget Convergence: Divergence Past, Present, and Future," op. cit.

24 Ibid.

25 See the list of references at http://www.nuff.ox.ac.uk/Economics/Growth/refs/augsol.htm.

26 See the scathing criticism of Summers by Michael Albert, "Markets _ber Alles," at http://www.lol.shareworld.com/zmag/articles/oldalbert8.htm.

27 Ilene Grabel, "Neoliberal Finance in the Developing World," Monthly Review 53 (April 2002): 34–46.

28 See Robert E. Scott, NAFTA at Seven: Its Impact on Workers in All Three Nations (Washington, DC: Economic Policy Institute, 2001).

29 Tim Weiner, "In Corn's Cradle, U.S. Imports Bury Family Farms," New York Times, February 26, 2002.

30 See Geoffrey Harcourt, Some Cambridge Controversies in the Theory of Capital (Cambridge: Cambridge University Press, 1972).

31 Howard Botwinick, Persistent Inequalities: Wage Disparity under Capitalist Competition (Princeton, NJ: Princeton University Press, 1993).

32 See Gary S. Becker, The Economics of Discrimination (Chicago: University of Chicago Press, 1971). For some excellent articles on discrimination, see the following website, which contains articles by economist Patrick Mason and others: http://http://garnet.acns.fsu.edu/~pmason/research.html.

33 Lawrence Mishel, Jared Bernstein, and John Schmitt, The State of Working America 2000/2001 (Ithaca, NY: Cornell University Press, 2001), 151.

34 David Card and Alan Krueger, Myth and Measurement: The New Economics of the Minimum Wage (Princeton, NJ: Princeton University Press, 1995); Pollin and Luce, The Living Wage: Building a Fair Economy, op. cit.

35 David J. Blanchflower and Andrew J. Oswald, The Wage Curve (Cambridge, MA: MIT Press, 1994).

36 Albert Rees, "An Overview of the Labor-Supply Results," The Journal of Human Resources IX (Spring 1974): 158–180.

CHAPTER SIX

Paul Sweezy's *Theory of Capitalist Development* (New York: Monthly Review Press, 1970) is still an excellent introduction to radical economics. Every reader should study Marx's classic, *Capital*, Vol. 1 (London: Penguin Books, 1976). It is one of the greatest books ever written. Almost every page has some remarkable insight. Don't miss the chapters on "The Working Day" and on "Machinery." Paul Baran and Paul Sweezy's *Monopoly Capital* (New York: Monthly Review Press, 1966) is a modern radical classic. So too is Harry Braverman's *Labor and Monopoly Capital* (New York: Monthly Review Press, 1974). On imperialism see Harry Magdoff's *The Age of Imperialism* (New York: Monthly Review Press, 1969). A lively and moving account of the impact of imperialism on Latin America is Eduardo Galeano's *Open Veins of Latin America* (Monthly Review Press, 1973). Modern radical analyses can be found in the pages of the journals *Monthly Review, Review of Radical Political Economics, Science & Society*, and many others. An excellent website for radical discussion and information is that of my friend Louis Proyect at http://www.marxmail.org. Also see the Progressive Economists Network (PEN-L) at http://csf.colorado.edu/mail/pen-l/. A strong reaction against neoclassical economics is building among students and teachers around the world, most strongly in Europe. See the Post-Autistic Economics Network at http//www.paecon.net.

1 Edmund Wilson, To the Finland Station: A Study in the Writing and Acting of History (Garden City, NY: Doubleday, 1953).

2 See Andre Gunder Frank, "Open Letter about Chile to Arnold Harberger and Milton Friedman," Review of Radical Political Economics 7 (Summer 1975), 61–76. Frank's interesting essay "The Cold War and Me," can be found at http://csf.colorado.edu/bcas/sympos/syfrank.htm. It shows clearly the ideological nature of neoclassical economics.

3 R. Frank, T. Gilovich, and D. Regan, "Does Studying Economics Inhibit Cooperation?," Journal of Economic Perspectives 10 (1993), 45–64.

4 See Karl Marx and Frederick Engels, The Communist Manifesto (London: Penguin Books, 1967) and Karl Marx, Capital, vol. 1 (London: Penguin Books, 1976).

5 Ellen W. Schrecker, McCarthyism and the Universities (New York: Oxford University Press, 1986).

6 Ann Fagen Ginger and David Christiano, The Cold War Against Labor, 2 vols. (Berkeley, CA: Meiklejohn Civil Liberties Institute, 1987).

7 A perusal of the early volumes of the radical magazine Monthly Review indicates that a number of articles about economic matters had to be written under pseudonyms.

8 Marx and Engels, The Communist Manifesto, op. cit., 83.

9 E. K. Hunt and Howard S. Sherman, Economics: An Introduction to Traditional and Radical Views (New York: Harper & Row, 1972), chapter five.

10 An exceptional account of this can be found in E. P. Thompson, The Making of the English Working Class (New York: Pantheon Books, 1964).

11 The following account is based on that of Karl Marx in Capital, vol. 1, op. cit. The contemporary Marxist economist Anwar Shaikh has written a number of introductory essays (and many advanced articles as well) on Marxian economics, which can be found on his website at http://homepage.newschool.edu/~AShaikh/.

12 "NewsWatch," Labor Notes, #277 (April 2002): 4.

13 Harry Braverman, Labor and Monopoly Capital: The Degradation of Work in the Twentieth Century (New York: Monthly Review Press, 1974).

14 Marc Linder and Ingrid Nygaard, Void Where Prohibited: Rest Breaks and the Right to Urinate on Company Time (Ithaca, NY: Cornell University Press, 1998).

15 See Laurie Graham, On the Line at Subaru-Isuzu (Ithaca, NY: Cornell University Press, 1995); Mike Parker and Jane Slaughter, Working Smart: A Union Guide to Participation Programs and Reengineering (Detroit: Labor Notes, 1995); and Christian Berggren, Alternatives to Lean Production (Ithaca, NY: Cornell University Press, 1992).

16 See the essays in Cyrus Bina, Laurie Clement, and Chuck Davis (Eds.), Beyond Survival: Wage Labor in the Late Twentieth Century (Armonk, NY: M. E. Sharpe, 1996). Also see Eric Helleiner, States and the Reemergence of Global Finance: From Bretton Woods to the 1990s (Ithaca, NY: Cornell University Press, 1994).

17 See the brief summary of theories of the state (and the sources cited) in Melvyn Dubofsky, The State and Labor in Modern America (Chapel Hill, NC: North Carolina University Press, 1994), xv–xviii.

18 For the United States, see Franklin Folsom, *Impatient Armies of the Unemployed* (Niwot, CO: University Press of Colorado, 1991).

19 James Petras, "The Unemployment Workers Movement in Argentina," *Monthly Review* 53 (January 2002): 32–45.

20 See Jeremy Brecher, *Strike* (Boston: South End Press, 1972).

21 Stephen Slesinger and Stephen Kinzer, *Bitter Fruit: The Untold Story of the American Coup in Guatemala* (Garden City, NY: Doubleday, 1982); Edward S. Herman and Noam Chomsky, *The Political Economy of Human Rights*, 2 vols. (Boston: South End Press, 1979).

22 Paul Baran and Paul Sweezy, *Monopoly Capital* (New York: Monthly Review Press, 1966). *Monthly Review* magazine, of which Paul Sweezy is a founder and editor, regularly features articles utilizing the theoretical framework laid out in *Monopoly Capital*.

23 Simon Clarke, *Marx's Theory of Crisis* (New York: St. Martin's Press, 1994); Fred Moseley, *The Falling Rate of Profit in the Postwar United States Economy* (New York: St. Martin's Press, 1991).

24 See The Editors, "Slow Growth, Excess Capital, and a Mountain of Debt," *Monthly Review* 53:11 (April 2002): 1–14.

25 For details on radical crisis theories, see James O'Connor, *The Meaning of Crisis* (Oxford: Basil Blackwell, 1987); Anwar Shaikh, "Marxist Theories of Crisis," in Tom Bottomore (Ed.), *A Dictionary of Marxist Thought* (Oxford: Basil Blackwell, 1983); Robert Brenner, *The Economics of Global Turbulence* (London: Verso, 2002). Baran and Sweezy's book is cited in note 22.

26 Sam Gindin, "Social Justice and Globalization: Are They Compatible?," *Monthly Review* 54 (June 2002): 2.

27 This insert is based on Ken Silverstein, "U.S. Oil Politics in the 'Kuwait of Africa'," *The Nation* 274 (April 22, 2002), 11–18.

28 Gindin, "Social Justice and Globalization," op. cit.: 4.

CHAPTER SEVEN

For an interesting account of how advertising affects children, go to the website: <http://www.rprogress.org/pubs/gpi1999/consuming_kids.hyml>. How schooling reinforces capitalist values is well documented in Samuel Bowles and Herbert Gintis, *Schooling in Capitalist America* (New York: Basic Books, 1976). Naomi Klein takes aim at advertisers in *No Logo* (New York: Picador USA, 2000). Although his politics are weak, Walter LaFeber gives us a fascinating account of Nike's use of Michael Jordan and Jordan's worldwide impact in *Michael Jordan and the New Global Capitalism* (New York: W.W. Norton & Co., 1999). The use of state repression of anti-capitalist groups is documented in Robert Justin Goldstein, *Political Repression in Modern America* (New York: Schenkman Publishing Co., 1978). Rebellions among indigenous peoples are explored in Robert Biel, *The New Imperialism* (London: Zed Books, 2000). The classic account of early labor protest in England is E. P. Thompson's *The Making of the English Working Class* (New York: Random House, 1966). A history of mass strikes in the United States is Jeremy Brecher, *Strike* (Boston: South End Press, 1972). On the Luddites, see the gruesome account in Glyn Hughes's novel, *The Rape of the Rose* (New York: Simon and Schuster, 1993). On Taylorism in its most modern guises, see Mike Parker and Jane Slaughter, *Working Smart: A Union Guide to Participation Programs and Reengineering* (Detroit: Labor Education and Research Project, 1994). An introduction to labor unions can be found in Michael D. Yates, *Why Unions Matter* (New York: Monthly Review Press, 1998).

1   A perusal of any radical journal will show an inordinately high incidence of the word crisis.

2   See the article, "Consuming Kids," at http://www.rprogress.org/pubs/gpi1999/consuming_kids.html. Also, Brian Swimme, "How Do Our Kids Get So Caught Up in Consumerism?," at http://www.newdream.org/newsletter/swimme.html.

3   See Walter LaFeber, Michael Jordan and the New Global Capitalism (New York: W.W. Norton & Co., 1999).

4   Seymour M. Hersh, The Price of Power: Kissinger in the Nixon White House (New York: Summit Books, 1983).

5   See James Petras, "U.S. Offensive in Latin America: Coups, Retreats, and Radicalization," Monthly Review 54 (May 2002): 15–31.

6   I want to thank Jim Craven for his help with this insert. There are many books and articles about American Indians and other indigenous peoples. Two good ones are Peter Matthieson, In the Spirit of Crazy Horse (New York: Penguin Books, 1992) and Ward Churchill, A Little Matter of Genocide: Holocaust Denial in the Americas, 1492 to the Present (San Francisco: City Lights Books, 1997).

7   See the remarkable article by Charles C. Mann, titled "1491," in The Atlantic, available at http://www.theatlantic.com/issues/2002/03/mann.htm.

8   Tom Howard, "Prison Racial Disparity: Native Americans Make Up Disproportionate Percentage of Inmates," Billings Gazette, January 14, 2002.

9   Letter to the author, April 13, 2002.

10 Marshall Sahlins, Stone Age Economics (Chicago: Aldine-Atherton, 1972).

11 Karl Marx, Capital, vol. 1 (London: Penguin Books, 1976), 280.

12 See Herbert G. Gutman, Work, Culture, and Society in Industrializing America: Essays in Working-Class and Social History (New York: Knopf, 1976).

13 An excellent book on the nature of U.S. labor law and related subjects is William E. Forbath,

Law and the Shaping of the American Labor Movement (Cambridge, MA: Harvard University Press, 1991).

14 See Michael D. Yates, Why Unions Matter (New York: Monthly Review Press, 1998).

15 Samuel Gompers, Seventy Years of Life and Labor: An Autobiography (New York: E. P. Dutton & Company, Inc., 1943).

16 E. P. Thompson, The Making of the English Working Class (New York: Vintage Books, 1966), 202–203.

17 See Paul Buhle, Taking Care of Business: Samuel Gompers, George Meany, Lane Kirkland and the Tragedy of American Labor (New York: Monthly Review Press, 1999).

18 Thompson, The Making of the English Working Class, 547–602.

19 See Mike Parker and Jane Slaughter, Working Smart: A Union Guide to Participation Programs and Reengineering (Detroit: Labor Education and Research Project, 1994).

20 There are many examples in Forbath, Law and the Shaping of the American Labor Movement.

21 Yates, Why Unions Matter, 81–103.

22 Wolfgang Abendroth, A Short History of the European Working Class (New York: Monthly Review Press, 1972), 63. This insert relies heavily on Abendroth.

23 Marx, Capital, vol. 1, 284.

24 On alienation in Marx, see Bertell Ollman, Alienation: Marx's Concept of Man in Capitalist Society (Cambridge: Cambridge University Press, 1971); István Mészáros, Marx's Theory of Alienation (London: Merlin Press, 1970).

25 Harry Braverman, Labor and Monopoly Capital: The Degradation of Work in the Twentieth Century (New York: Monthly Review Press, 1974), 85–123.

26 Liza Featherstone and the United Students Against Sweatshops, Students Against Sweatshops: The Making of a Movement (New York: Verso, 2002).

27 There is an extraordinarily large literature on environmental concerns and struggles. For a

good introduction to the connection between capitalism and ecological disaster, see John Bellamy Foster, Marx's Ecology (New York: Monthly Review Press, 2000).

28 See Yates, Why Unions Matter, 39–52.

29 See David Milton, The Politics of U.S. Labor: From the Great Depression to the New Deal (New York: Monthly Review Press, 1982).

30 For Europe, see Abendroth, A Short History of the European Working Class, 69–100.

31 An excellent book on union democracy, of special use to rank-and-file activists, is Mike Parker and Martha Gruelle, Democracy is Power: Rebuilding Unions from the Bottom Up (Detroit: Labor Notes, 1999).

32 On labor education, see Michael Yates, "An Essay on Radical Labor Education," Cultural Logic, 2 (1999) at http:/eserver.org/clogic/.

CHAPTER EIGHT

A good book dealing with many of the issues raised in this chapter is Daniel Singer, *Whose Millennium? Theirs or Ours?* (New York: Monthly Review Press, 1999). Another good book is Leo Panitch and Colin Leys (Eds.), *Socialist Register 2000* (Monthly Review Press, 1999). In this chapter I have also drawn on my article, "Workers of All Countries Unite: Will This Include the U.S. Labor Movement?," *Monthly Review* 52:3 (July/August 2000), 46–59.

1 On the many changes undergone by capitalist economies since the end of the post-Second World War boom, see the many articles on the subject during this period in Monthly Review magazine. A good example is Harry Magdoff, "International Economic Distress and the Third World," Monthly Review 33 (April 1982): 3–5. Also see the essays in Samuel Bowles, David M. Gordon, and Thomas E. Weiskopf (Eds.), The Capitalist System, 3rd Ed. (Englewood Cliffs, NJ: Prentice-Hall, 1986).

2 See Daniel Singer, Whose Millennium? Theirs or Ours? (New York: Monthly Review Press, 1999), 12–13. Also, see Paul M. Sweezy and Charles Bettelheim, On the Transition to Socialism (New York: Monthly Review Press, 1971).

3 See John G. Gurley, China's Economy and the Maoist Strategy (New York: Monthly Review Press, 1976); William Hinton, Fanshen: A Documentary of Revolution in a Chinese Village (New York: Vintage Books, 1968); Edgar Snow, Red Star Over China (New York: Grove Press, 1968); and Jonathan D. Spence, Gate of Heavenly Peace: The Chinese and Their Revolution, 1895–1980 (New York: Penguin Books, 1982).

4 See David M. Kotz and Fred Weir, Revolution from Above: The Demise of the Soviet System

(New York: Routledge, 1997).

5 See John Bellamy Foster, "Marx and Internationalism," Monthly Review 52:3 (July/August 2000): 11–22.

6 Werner Sombart, Why Is There No Socialism in the United States? (White Plains, NY: International Arts and Sciences Press, 1976).

7 See Paul Buhle, Taking Care of Business: Samuel Gompers, George Meany, Lane Kirkland, and the Tragedy of American Labor (New York: Monthly Review Press, 1999), and Melvyn Dubofsky, The State and Labor in Modern America (Chapel Hill, NC: University of North Carolina Press, 1994).

8 See Michael D. Yates, Why Unions Matter (New York: Monthly Review Press, 1998), 104–29.

9 See Robert Justin Goldstein, Political Repression in Modern America (New York: Schenkman, 1978), and William Forbath, "The Shaping of the American Labor Movement," Harvard Law Review 102 (January 1987): especially Appendix B.

10 See David Milton, The Politics of U.S. Labor: From the Great Depression to the New Deal (New York: Monthly Review Press, 1982).

11 See Barbara Harriss-White and Nandini Gooptu, "Mapping India's World of Unorganized Labor," in Leo Panitch and Colin Leys (Eds.), Socialist Register 2001 (New York:

Monthly Review Press, 2000).

12 Leo Panitch and Sam Gindin, "Transcending Pessimism: Rekindling Socialist Imagination," in Leo Panitch and Colin Leys, Socialist Register 2000 (New York: Monthly Review Press 1999).

13 Ben Hamper, Rivethead (New York: Warner Books, 1991).

14 Singer, Whose Millennium, Theirs or Ours?, 129–151.

15 James Crotty and Gary Dymski, "Can the Korean Labor Movement Defeat the IMF?," Dollars & Sense, No. 220 (Nov.–Dec. 1998): 16.

16 For a good discussion of many movements, see Mike Prokosch and Laura Raymond, The Global Activist's Manual: Local Ways to Change the World (New York: Thunder's Mouth Press/Nation Books, 2002).

17 See Asbjørn Wahl, "Labor's Demand for a Social Europe," Monthly Review 54 (June 2002): 45–55.

18 This section relies on Michael Yates, Power on the Job: The Legal Rights of Working People (Boston, MA: South End Press, 1994), 177–181, and sources cited therein. See also Dan LaBotz, Rank-and-File: Teamsters for a Democratic Union (London: Verso, 1997).

19 A good source on the Carey debacle is the magazine, Labor Notes. Its website is http:///www.labornotes.org.

20 Warren Hoge, "Radical Union Leaders Are Threatening a Hot British Summer," The New York Times, July 23, 2002.

21 See the article "More Than Two Million at Rome Demo: Organizers," at http://www.commondreams.org/headlines02/0323-01.htm.

22 See Sam Gindin, "Notes on Labor at the End of the Century: Starting Over?," in Ellen Meiksins Wood, Peter Meiksins, and Michael Yates (Eds.), Rising from the Ashes: Labor in the Age of "Global" Capitalism (New York: Monthly Review Press, 1998).

23 This section relies on Michael Löwy, "The Socio-Religious Origins of Brazil's Landless Rural Workers Movement," Monthly Review 53 (June 2001): 32–40; Michael Löwy, "A 'Red' Government in the South of Brazil," Monthly Review 52 (November 2000): 16–20; Larry Rohter, "Brazil's Prized Exports Rely on Slaves and Scorched Land," The New York Times, March 25, 2002; and Cynthia Peters and Justin

Podur, "They Can Walk with Their Heads Up," Dollars & Sense, No. 241 (May/June 2002).

24 Löwy, "A 'Red' Government in the South of Brazil": 16.

25 Ibid.: 16–17.

26 Löwy, "The Socio-Religious Origins of Brazil's Landless Rural Workers Movement": 34.

27 Cynthia Peters and Justin Podur, "They Can Walk with Their Heads Up," op. cit.

28 James Petras, "The Unemployed Workers Movement in Argentina," Monthly Review 53 (January 2002): 32–45.

29 This section relies upon Ashwin Desai, We Are the Poors: Community Struggles in Post- Apartheid South Africa (New York: Monthly Review Press, 2002); John S. Saul, "Cry for the Beloved Country," Monthly Review 52:8 (January 2001): 1–51; Patrick Bond, "Defunding the Fund, Running the Bank," Monthly Review 52:3 (July/August 2000): 127–140); and Andrew Nash, "Mandela's Democracy," Monthly Review 50:11 (April 1999): 18–28.

30 Saul, "Cry for the Beloved Country": 4–5.

31 Nash, "Mandela's Democracy": 26.

32 Saul, "Cry for the Beloved Country": 16.

33 Ibid.

34 Desai, We Are the Poors, 10.

35 Ibid., 11.

36 Ibid., 127–128.

37 This section relies heavily on Liza Featherstone and United Students Against Sweatshops, Students Against Sweatshops (London and New York: Verso, 2002) and on a review of this book by Michael Yates in a forthcoming issue of Monthly Review.

38 See David Noble, Digital Diploma Mills (New York: Monthly Review Press, 2002).

39 See Doug Henwood and Liza Featherstone, "Clothes Encounters," Lingua Franca 11 (March 2001), available at http://www.sasua.org/experts.html.

40 On Chile, see Donald Freed, Death in Washington: The Murder of Orlando Letelier (Westport, CT: Lawrence Hill & Co., 1981).

41 This section relies on data from the CIA website: http://www.cia.gov/cia/publications/factbook/index.html, and also Alfredo Molano, "The Evolution of the FARC," NACLA Report on the Americas 34 (September 2000): 23; Garry M. Leech, "An Interview with FARC

Commander Simon Trinidad," NACLA Report on the Americas 34 (September 2000): 24; "An Overview of Recent Colombian History," available at http://www.igc.org/colhrnet/time-line.htm; Louis Proyect, "Revolution in Colombia, Part Two: Origins of the Guerilla Groups," available at http://www.columbia. edu/~lnp3/mydocs; "The Letter of Dr. Baburam Bhattarai on Palace Massacre in Nepal," available at http://www.monthlyreview.org/0601etter.htm; "Birth Pangs of Democracy: Commentary from Dr. Baburam Bhattarai in Nepal," ibid.; and Li Onesto, "Red Flag Flying on the Roof of the World," available at http://www.rwor.org/a/v21/1040-049/1043/interv.htm.

42 Leech, "An Interview with FARC Commander Simon Trinidad."

43 An interesting schema is provided by Michael Albert and Robin Hahnel, Looking Forward: Participatory Economics for the Twenty-First Century (Boston: South End Press, 1991).

44 Both quotes are from a letter to the author from Harry Magdoff, July 1, 2002.

45 On the Basque cooperatives, see Sharryn Kasmir, The Myth of Mondragón: Cooperatives, Politics, and Working-Class Life in a Basque Town (Albany, NY: State University of New York Press, 1996), and Alan Weisman, Gaviotas: A Village to Reinvent the World (White River Junction, VT: Chelsea Green Pub., 1998).

46 Leo Panitch and Sam Gindin, "Transcending Pessimism: Rekindling Socialist Imagination," in Leo Panitch and Colin Leys (Eds.), Socialist Register 2000 (New York: Monthly Review Press, 1999).

47 This is the title of DeLong's forthcoming book. See Paul Krugman's "Reckonings" column in The New York Times of June 18, 2000.

48 Ibid.

49 Ibid.

50 See Charles C. Mann, "1491," The Atlantic (March 2002), available at http://www.theatlantic.com/issues/2002/03/mann.htm.

51 Panitch and Gindin, "Transcending Pessimism: Rekindling Socialist Imagination," 24.

Index